A COLLECTION

OF

PSALM AND HYMN TUNES, CHANTS, ANTHEMS, AND SENTENCES,

ORIGINAL AND SELECTED,

FROM THE BEST STANDARD COMPOSERS:

ADAPTED

FOR THE USE OF THE PROTESTANT EPISCOPAL CHURCH IN AMERICA,

AND FOR CONGREGATIONS OF OTHER DENOMINATIONS,

AS WELL AS FOR SOCIETIES AND SCHOOLS.

BY H. W. GREATOREX,

ORGANIST AND DIRECTOR OF THE MUSIC IN CALVARY CHURCH, NEW YORK.

HARTFORD:
A. C. GOODMAN & CO.
NEW YORK:—STANFORD & SWORDS, AND D. APPLETON & CO.
PHILADELPHIA:—THOMAS, COWPERTHWAIT & CO.
BOSTON:—PHILLIPS, SAMPSON & CO.

STEREOTYPED BY
THOMAS B. SMITH,
216 William Street.

PRINTED BY
W. S. WILLIAMS.
Hartford, Conn.

PREFACE.

The Editor of this work trusts that the following pages will be found generally useful in the service of the church. His aim has been to furnish good music, rather than light, frivolous melody—to restore, as nearly as practicable, the old standard tunes and chants to their original harmonies, while, in the selection of the new, he has endeavored to avoid vulgarity, or straining after effect.

He flatters himself that the large number of chants will be found acceptable, for even where chanting is not practiced, hymns in metre, of four lines in each stanza, may be sung to almost all of the double chants, thus giving nearly one hundred new tunes if required.

He would recommend to those in favor of congregational singing, to use the same words to the same tunes, invariably, and in a short time the association between the words and the music will enable the congregation to sing most of the tunes.

It will be observed that the time marks are omitted throughout the whole work, as the space they usually occupy more than compensates for their loss. Marks of expression are also avoided—the character of the words sufficiently indicating the sentiment of the music to which they are attached.

A SHORT CATECHISM
ON THE ELEMENTS OF MUSIC.

PART I.

RHYTHM.

CHAPTER I.

Question. What is a musical sound or tone?

Answer. A sound produced by the vibration of any sonorous substance,—as, a bell, an organ pipe, a string, wire, or reed; or by the human voice, &c.

Q. What distinct properties has every pure musical tone?

A. It may be long or short, high or low, loud or soft.

Q. Into how many departments, then, may the elementary principles be divided?

A. Three.

Q. What is the first?

A. *Rhythm*—treating of the length of tones.

Q. What the second?

A. *Melody*—relating to the pitch of tones.

Q. What the third?

A. *Expression*—determined by the loudness of tones.

CHAPTER II.

Q. Does not the performance of a piece of music occupy a certain portion of *time?*

A. Yes.

Q. Must that time be divided?

A. Yes, into equal parts, called *Measures.*

Q. By what character are the measures separated?

A. By a *Bar.*

Q. Are measures divided?

A. Yes, into parts of measures.

Q. When a measure is divided into two parts, what is it called?

A. *Double Measure.*

Q. How is it accented?

A. On the first part.

Q. Can you illustrate it by an example in words?

A. Ho-ly, | Fa-ther, | Mighty, | Spirit. |

Q. What is a measure of three parts called?

A. *Triple Measure.*

Q. How accented?

A. On the first part,—as, Trinity, | Unity. |

Q. What is a measure of four parts called?

A. *Quadruple Measure.*

Q. How accented?

A. Strongly on the first, and slightly on the third,—as, Whensoever, | Powerfully. |

Q. What is a measure of six parts called?

A. *Sextuple Measure.*

Q. How accented?

A. On the first and fourth parts,—as, Infallibility, | Infinitessimal. |

Q. How must we mark the parts of measures in order to insure their equality?

A. By a motion of the hand, usually called *Beating time.*

Q. What motions or beats has Double time?

A. Two—Downward beat, and Upward beat.

Q. What Triple?

A. Three—Downward beat, Inward beat, and Upward beat.

Q. What Quadruple?

A. Four—Downward beat, Inward beat, Outward beat, Upward beat.

Q. What Sextuple?

A. Six—Downward beat, Downward beat, Inward beat, Outward beat, Upward beat, Upward beat.

CHAPTER III.

Q. How are the various lengths of sounds represented?

A. By differently shaped characters.

Q. Will you now beat Quadruple time?

(While the teacher sings *la* to each beat, at a convenient pitch, say F in the first space in the treble, the pupils count,)

A. Downward beat, inward beat, outward beat, upward beat.

Q. The sound I have just sung is therefore one beat long. How is it represented?

A. By a character made thus, ♩ called a *Quarter Note.*

Q. I will now sing a note as long as two beats. Will you beat time as before?

A. (Teacher singing *la.*) Downward beat, upward beat.

Q. How is this represented?

A. By a character shaped thus, 𝅗𝅥 called a *Half Note.*

Q. How is a sound as long as three quarters represented?

A. By placing a dot after the half note, thus, 𝅗𝅥. A dot after a note adds one half to its length.

Q. How is a sound as long as four quarters represented?

A. Thus, 𝅝 called a *Whole Note.*

Q. Are there any other notes in common use?

A. Yes. *Eighth Notes,* made thus, ♪ ♪ or tied together, ♫

Sixteenth Notes, made thus, 𝅘𝅥𝅯 𝅘𝅥𝅯 or tied together,

Thirty-second Notes, made thus, 𝅘𝅥𝅰 𝅘𝅥𝅰 or tied together,

Q. When three notes are sung to one part of a measure, what are they called?

A. *Triplets,*—and are marked thus, ♪ ♪ ♪ (3) or ♫ (3)

Q. We are often required in music to beat a part, or parts, of a measure,—or a whole measure, or a number of measures,—in silence. What characters are used to denote this?

A. Certain characters, called *Rests,* which correspond in length to the notes from which they receive their names.

Q. How many are in common use?

A. The *Whole Rest,* made thus 𝄻. *Half Rest,* 𝄼. *Quarter Rest,* 𝄽. *Eighth Rest,* 𝄾. *Sixteenth Rest,* 𝄿.

CHAPTER IV.

Q. Are there any varieties of measure?

A. Yes.

Q. How obtained?

A. By the use of different notes on each part of the measure.

Q. If the parts of Fourfold measure are quarter notes, what is it called?

A. *Four-four Measure*, and is marked thus, $\frac{4}{4}$ or C It is also called *Common Time.*

Q. What do the figures at the commencement of a piece of music indicate?

A. The upper figure shows the number of parts in each measure, the lower indicates the kind of note used to fill each of those parts. Thus $\frac{4}{2}$ means four half notes in each measure. $\frac{3}{4}$ means three quarters in each measure. $\frac{3}{2}$ three halves. $\frac{6}{8}$ six eighths, &c.

Q. What varieties of time are in common use?

A. In Double Measure.

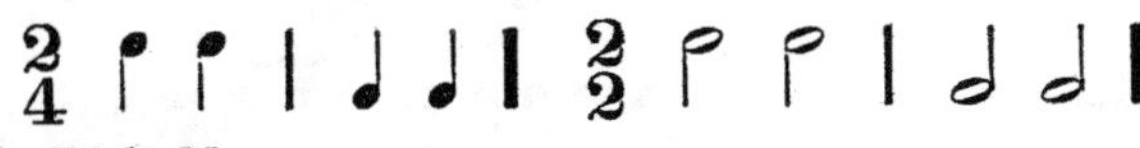

In Triple Measure.

In Sextuple Measure.

Q. Is it necessary that the same kind of notes should be used in each measure?

A. No. Different notes may be used, but the value must not exceed the primitive notes, as,—

PART II.

MELODY.

CHAPTER V.

Q. Of what does *Melody* treat?

A. Of the pitch of sounds.

Q. What is that series of sounds, called the *Scale?*

A. A succession of eight sounds, which may be represented as follows:

Q. How do we designate the sounds of the scale?

A. By numerals.

Q. How is the scale written?

A. On five horizontal lines, called a *Staff.*

5th line.	
4th line.	4th space.
3d line.	3d space.
2d line.	2d space.
1st line.	1st space.

and on the spaces between those lines.

Q. What is each line and space called?

A. A degree. A staff contains nine degrees,—five lines and four spaces.

Q. If more than nine degrees are wanted, what is used?

A. The spaces above and below the lines, also additional lines, called *Leger,* or *added lines.*

Q. We will place *one* on the first leger line below,—how are the rest placed?

A.

Q. When the scale is thus written, what name do we give *one?*

A. *Do.* (Pronounced Doe.)

Q. What, *two?*

A. *Re.* (Ray.)

Q. What, *three?*

A. *Mi.* (Mee.)

Q. *Four?*

A. *Fa.* (As fa, in father.)

Q. *Five?*

A. *Sol.* (Sole.)

Q. *Six?*

A. *La.* (A, as in father.)

Q. *Seven?*

A. *Si.* (See.)

Q. *Eight?*

A. *Do,* again.

Q. Have they any other names?

A. They are also named from the first seven letters of the alphabet; but, as *one* is placed on the first added line below, we must commence with C.

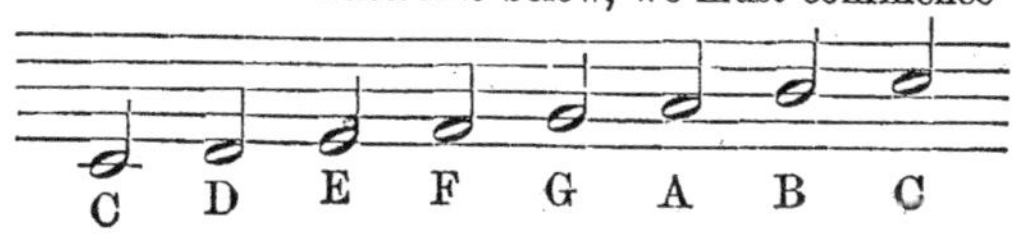

CHAPTER VI.

Q. What characters are used to determine the names of the degrees of the staff?

A. *Clefs,*—the *Treble,* or *G Clef,* G and the *Bass,* or *F Clef,* F the Treble Clef fixes G upon the second line of the staff; the Bass Clef fixes F on the fourth line of the staff.

Q. Is then the F on the fourth line on the bass staff only one note below the pitch of the G on the second line of the treble staff?

A. No. It is nine tones lower in pitch,—for example:—

C D E F G A B C

C D E F G A B C

The male voices generally sing in the bass clef, and the female in the treble. The treble clef is also used for the tenor,—the voices singing eight tones, or an octave below the real pitch.

CHAPTER VII.

Q. Is there any term for expressing the distance of one tone to another?

A. The distance or step from one tone in the scale to another is called an *Interval.*

Q. Of what intervals is the scale composed?

A. Of whole tones and half tones.

Q. In what order?

A. From one to two, and from two to three, are whole tones; from three to four a half tone; from four to five, from five to six, and from six to seven, are whole tones; and from seven to eight a half tone.

Q. When we have learned to sing the scale in regular progression, what should we do next?

A. We should learn to strike each sound separately, or in connection with any other sound.

Q. How ought we to commence?

A. By learning the perfect intervals,—as the third, fifth, and eighth, and determining the imperfect intervals,—as the second, fourth, sixth, and seventh, from them.

Q. How can we fix in our minds the interval of the third?

A. By singing 1, 2, 3,—1, 3,—1, 3,—1, &c.

Q. How the fifth?

A. By singing 1. 2, 3, 4, 5,—1, 5,—1, 5,—1, &c.

Q. How the eighth?

A. Sing 1, 2, 3, 4, 5, 6, 7, 8,—1, 8,—1, 8,—1, &c.

Q. What is the best method to fix these intervals in the memory?

A. Sing in the following order:—

1 3 5 8	3 1 5 8	5 1 3 8	8 1 3 5
1 3 8 5	3 1 8 5	5 1 8 3	8 1 5 3
1 5 3 8	3 5 1 8	5 3 1 8	8 3 1 5
1 5 8 3	3 5 8 1	5 3 8 1	8 3 5 1
1 8 3 5	3 8 1 5	5 8 1 3	8 5 1 3
1 8 5 3	3 8 5 1	5 8 3 1	8 5 3 1

Q. How can we strike seven correctly?

A. Sing one, then think of eight, and sing the next sound of the scale below it. Seven naturally leads to eight.

Q. How can we strike four?

A. Sing 1, then think of 3, and sing the next sound above it. Four naturally falls to three.

Q. How can we strike two?

A. 1 or 3 will serve as a guide to 2; as 5 will to 6.

CHAPTER VIII.

Q. As the human voice is capable of producing sounds higher and lower than the eight sounds of the scale, how can we represent those tones?

A. When we sing above eight, we consider eight as one of a scale above, and when we sing below one, we think of one as eight of a new scale below.

Q. How can we write this?

A. Thus:

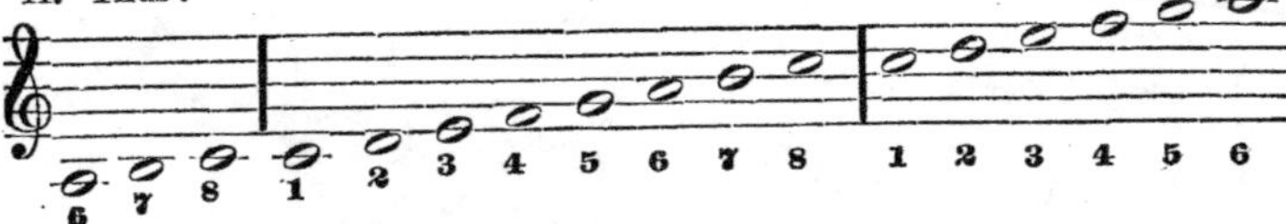

Q. Into how many classes is the human voice generally divided?

A. Into four,—*Treble* or *Soprano*, *Alto*, *Tenor*, and *Bass*.

Q. What is the usual compass of each class?

A. The Bass from F to C, the Tenor from C to G, or the Alto from G to C, or and the Treble from C to A,

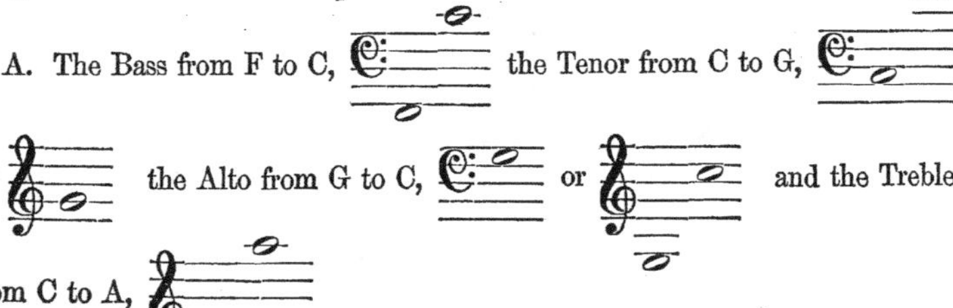

CHAPTER IX.

Q. The *Natural* (or *Diatonic*) *Scale* consists of five tones and two semitones. Can the tones be divided?

A. Between any two sounds a tone distant from each other,—as from one to two, another sound may be sung.

Q. What is that scale termed which consists of semitones only?

A. The *Chromatic Scale.*

Q. How are these semitones obtained?

A. Either by elevating the lower, or depressing the upper, of the two sounds.

Q. What is the sign of elevation?

A. A ♯ (*Sharp*) placed before the note.

Q. What is the character used to depress a note?

A. A ♭ (*Flat*) placed before the note intended to be lowered.

Q. What character is usually employed in ascending?

A. The sharp,—thus,

Q. Which is used mostly in descending?

A. The flat,—thus,

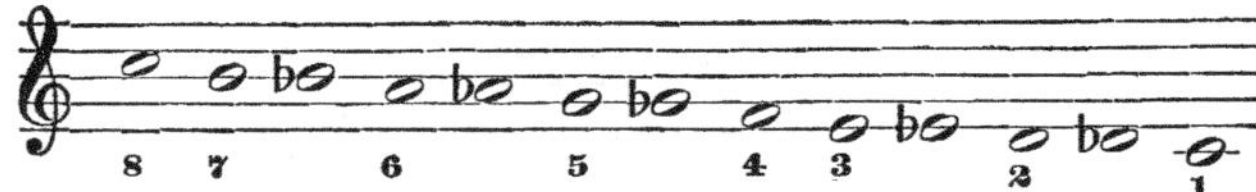

Q. How do we name these chromatic tones?

A. In speaking of them by numerals we say, sharp one, sharp two, flat four, &c.; by letters, C sharp, D flat, &c. By syllables, the termination of the syllable appropriated to the natural note is changed,—for the sharps to *i* (pronounced ee,) as, *do, di,—re, ri,—fa, fi,—sol, si,—la, li.* For the flats to *e.* (pronounced as a, in late,) as *si, se,—la, le,—sol, se,—mi, me,* &c.

Q. If a note has been sharped or flatted, how is it restored?

A. By a ♮ (*Natural*) placed before it.

Q. What are these characters called when they occur in a piece of music?

A. *Accidentals.*

Q. Does an accidental affect a note throughout the whole piece?

A. No,—only throughout the measure in which they occur. A bar destroys their effect.

CHAPTER X.

Q. Is there any other scale besides the Diatonic and Chromatic?

A. Yes,—there is the *Minor Scale.*

Q. How is that formed?

A. From one to two a whole tone, from two to three a half tone, from three to four a whole tone, from four to five a whole tone, from five to six a half tone, from six to seven a whole tone and a half, from seven to eight a semitone:—

CHAPTER XI.

Q. We have hitherto taken C as *one* of the scale, or as the *key note.* As the scale is then said to be in its natural position: can any other note be taken as the key note, or tonic?

A. Any other note may be taken as one of the scale, from which note the scale derives its name,—as, the scale or key of G, the key of D, &c.

Q. When any other letter than C is taken as the tonic, what is said of the scale?

A. It is transposed.

Q. In transposing a scale, what is of the utmost importance?

A. To preserve the order of the intervals.

Q. If we take G (the fifth of the scale) as the tonic, how can we preserve the order of the intervals?

A. The intervals will be all correct till we come to F, the fourth of the old, and the seventh of the new scale, when, as there must be a whole tone between 6 and 7, and a semitone between 7 and 8, we must make F sharp by placing a # before it.

Q. Is this character to be placed before every F?

A. No. It is placed at the commencement of the line, and affects all the Fs in the piece. It is then called the *Signature.* The signature of the key of G is therefore one sharp.

Q. How much higher than the key of C is that of G?

A. A fifth higher, or a fourth lower,—as a fifth above, and a fourth below, is the same thing.

Q. What is the next regular transposition by sharps?

A. The fifth of the scale of G:—D. But as, if we continued the scale upwards, it would take it out of the range of the voice, we will write D on the space below the lines.

Q. What note must we sharp in order to preserve the order of intervals?

A. The fourth of the old scale, C, which becomes the seventh of the new key.

Q. What is the signature of the key of D?

A. Two sharps.

Q. What is the next regular transposition by sharps?

A. A—being the fifth of the key of D.

Q. Is the same rule followed as in the previous transpositions?

A. Yes. The fourth of D is made sharp, and becomes the seventh of A,—the signature of A being three sharps.

Q. What is the next regular transposition by sharps?

A. E—the fifth of the scale of A. And by following the same rule, and sharping D, (the fourth of the key of A,) which becomes the seventh of the new scale, we make the signature of the key of E to be four sharps.

Q. What keys are the next in order?

A. B:—five sharps. F♯:—six sharps. C♯:—seven sharps, &c. But as these are seldom used, and follow the same rule, there is no necessity to proceed further.

CHAPTER XII.

Q. We will now take F (the fourth of the natural scale) as the key note. What note must we alter to preserve the proper order of intervals?

A. We must flatten the seventh of the scale of C—which becomes the fourth of the key of F—in order to make the intervals correct: as there must be a semitone between three and four, and a whole tone between four and five.

Q. What will be the signature of the key of F?

A. One flat.

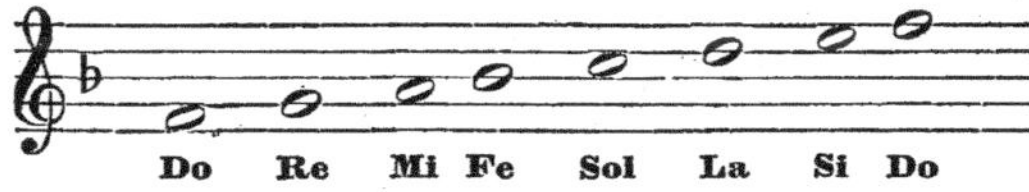

Q. What is the next regular transposition by flats?

A. The fourth of the scale of F, which will be B flat.

Q. How do we transpose the scale into the key of B flat?

A. We must flatten E, the seventh of the key of F, the fourth of the new scale of B flat,—which therefore will have as its signature two flats.

Q. What is the next regular transposition by flats?

A. E flat, the fourth of the key of B flat.

Q. How is the scale transposed into E flat?

A. According to the same rules as before. Flatten the seventh of the old key, which becomes the fourth of the new, and the signature will be three flats.

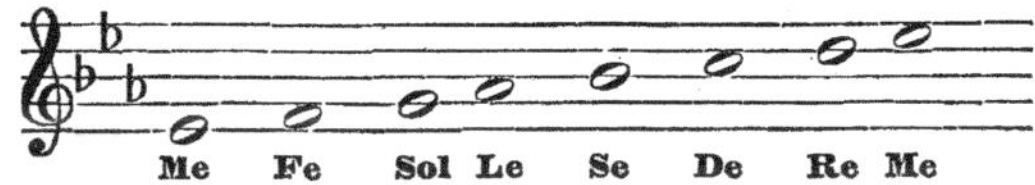

Q. What are the next keys in succession?

A. A♭:—four flats. D♭:—five flats. G♭:—six flats, &c., which all follow the same rules for transposition.

CHAPTER XIII.

Q. The key is frequently changed, (transposed,) during the performance of a piece of music. What is that change called?

A. *Modulation.*

Q. What are the most common modulations?

A. From one to five, and from one to four.

Q. How is the modulation from one to five effected?

A. By sharping the fourth of the key, which immediately becomes the seventh of a new key. A sharp seventh is called the leading note, as it leads to eight.

Q. Which is the note of modulation from any key to its fifth?

A. The sharp fourth.

EXAMPLE.

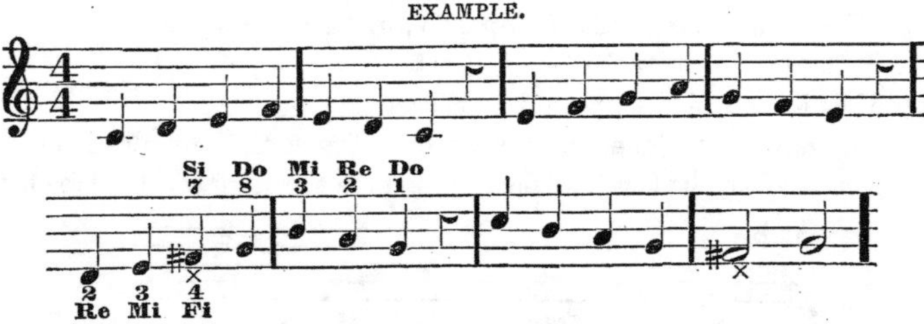

Q. When a modulation occurs, do we make any change?

A. The melodic relations of sounds, and often the syllables applied in solmization, must be changed according to the new key.

Q. How is the modulation from one to four effected?

A. By flatting the seventh of the key, which becomes the fourth of the new key.

Q. What is the note of modulation by fourths?

A. The flat seventh.

EXAMPLE.

Q. The examples have been given in the natural key of C. Are the same rules followed in other keys?

A. The same rule is applied in all the keys.

CHAPTER XIV.

Q. We have hitherto spoken of tones and semitones as intervals. Are there any others?

A. Yes. *Unisons*, *Seconds*, *Thirds*, *Fourths*, *Fifths*, *Sixths*, *Sevenths*, *Eighths*, or *Octaves*, besides others, which are now immaterial to our purpose.

Q. What is an unison?

A. The unison, (though not strictly an interval, is treated as such in the theory of music,) is from one to one. In counting intervals, the note from which you begin to count is always reckoned as one.

Au Unison.

Q. What is a second?

A. A second is an interval from one letter to the next. If it includes a semitone, it is called a minor second; if a tone, a major second.

Major Seconds.

Minor Seconds.

Q. What is a third?

A. An interval from one letter to the next but one. If it includes a tone and a semitone, it is called a minor third; if two tones, a major third.

Minor Third. **Major Third.**

Q. What is a fourth?

A. From any one letter to the next but two. Including two tones and a semitone, it is a perfect fourth; if it includes three tones, a sharp fourth.

Q. What is a fifth?

A. An interval containing two tones and two semitones is a flat fifth; one including three tones and a semitone a perfect fifth.

Q. What is a sixth?

A. An interval of three tones and two semitones is a minor sixth; one of four tones and a semitone a major sixth.

Q. What is a seventh?

A. An interval of four tones and two semitones is a minor, or flat seventh; of five tones and one semitone, a major, or sharp seventh.

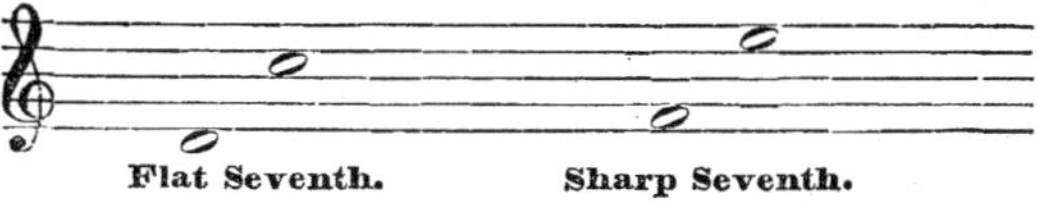

Q. What is an octave?

A. All octaves are equal, including five tones and two semitones.

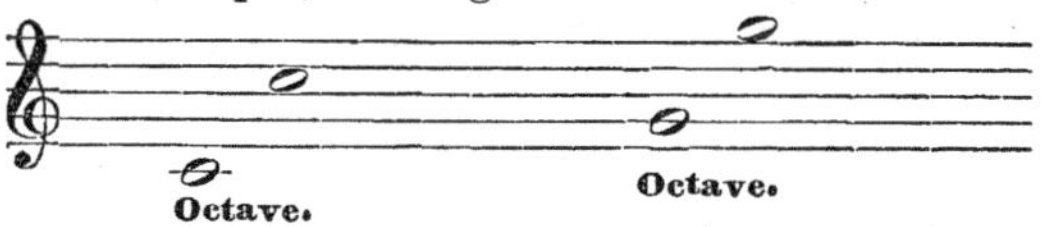

CHAPTER XV.

Q. What are *Passing Notes?*

A. When notes not properly belonging to the harmony are introduced, they are called Passing Notes.

Q. What is an *Appogiatura?*

A. When a passing note precedes the principal note, it is called an Appogiatura.

EXAMPLE.

Q. What is a *Syncope?*

A. When a note commences on an unaccented, and is continued on the accented part of a measure, it is said to be syncopated.

EXAMPLE OF SYNCOPATION.

Q. What is a *Tie?*

A. A Tie ⁀ is used to connect two notes together so that they become but one,—as in the above example. It is also used to show how many notes are to be sung to one syllable. It is used also to denote a Legato style of performance.

Q. What is the meaning of *Legato?*

A. When music is to be performed in a smooth, gliding manner, it is marked Legato.

Q. What is *Staccato?*

A. When the notes are to be performed in a short, pointed, detached manner, it is said to be Staccato, and is generally marked thus,—

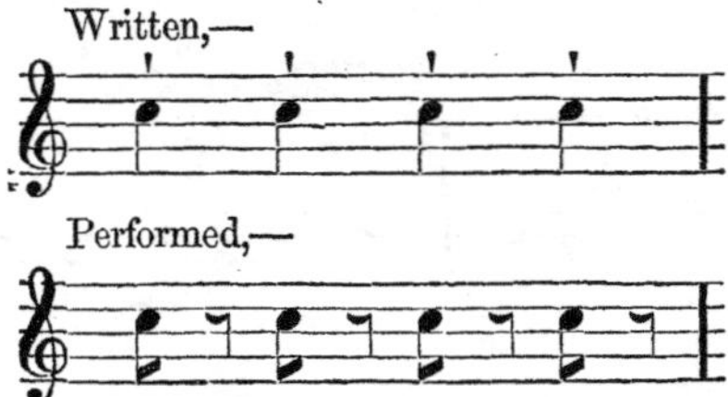

Q. What is a *Pause?*

A. A Pause 𝄐 indicates that a note or rest is to be prolonged beyond its usual length.

Q. What is a *Repeat?*

A. Dots across the staff require the repetition of certain parts of the piece.

Q. What is the use of a *Double Bar?*

A. To indicate a division of the phrases of the piece.

Q. What is a *Close?*

A. A Close denotes the termination or end of a piece of music.

EXAMPLES.

Repeat. **Double Bar.** **Close.**

PART III.

EXPRESSION.

CHAPTER XVI.

Q. What are the principal means of giving Expression to a piece of music?

A. The *Dynamic* degrees of force, and the appropriate delivery of the words.

Q. How many degrees of force are in common use?

A. Six:—*Pianissimo,* (*pp*) Very Soft; *Piano,* (*p*) Soft; *Mezzo Soprano,* (*mp*) Rather Soft; *Mezzo Forte,* (*mf*) Rather Loud; *Forte,* (*f*) Loud; *Fortissimo,* (*ff*) Very Loud.

Q. What is an "*organ tone*"?

A. A tone commenced, continued, and ended, with an equal degree of force.

Q. What is a *Crescendo?*

A. A tone commencing soft, and increasing in force to the end, is Crescendo, and is marked *Cres.*, or <

Q. What is *Diminuendo?*

A. A tone commenced loud, and diminishing to soft. It is marked *Dim.*, or >

Q. What is a *Swell?*

A. A tone partaking of the Crescendo and Diminuendo. It is designated thus,— <>

Q. What is *Sforzando?*

A. A single sound, struck suddenly and with force. It is marked *sf.* or *fz.* or >, or ∧.

Q. What is most essential in order to give expression?

A. To study attentively the character of the words; to deliver them with a distinct and clear articulation, duly emphasizing those words which require it; to preserve the vowel sounds in all their purity; to take breath at those places only in which you can pause while reading the words, and avoid equally the extremes of a tame, lifeless delivery, and ranting.

INDEX TO THE PSALMS.

INDEX TO THE HYMNS.

GREATOREX'S

COLLECTION OF CHURCH MUSIC.

ST. ANN'S. C. M.

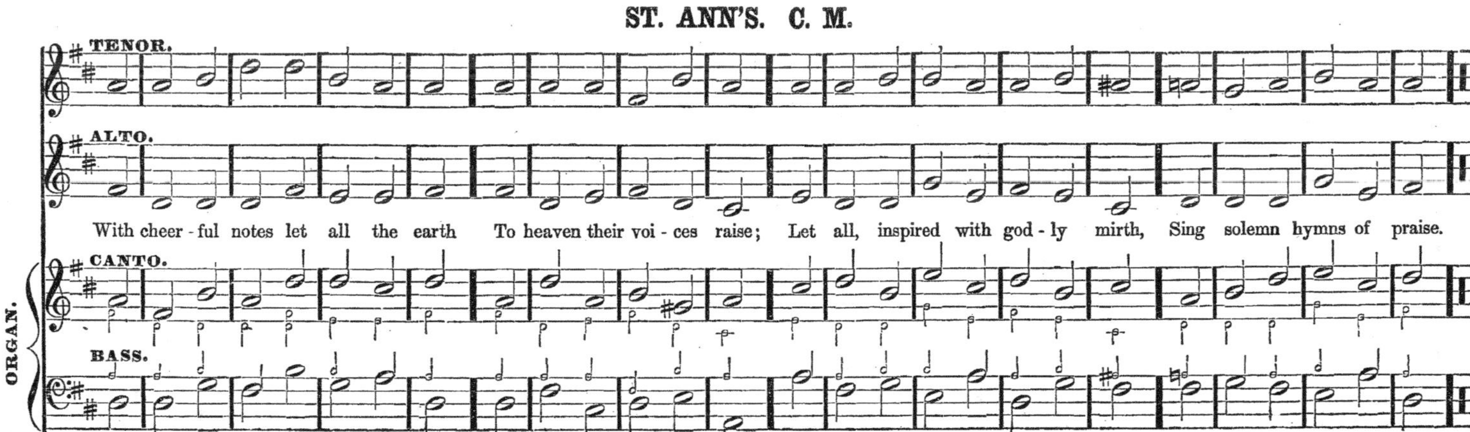

IRISH. C. M.
O ren - der thanks, and bless the Lord; In - voke his sa - cred name; Ac - quaint the na - tions with his deeds,—His match - less deeds pro - claim.
COMPTON. C. M.
Lord, in thy sight, O let my prayer, Like morn - ing in - cense rise; My lift - ed hands ac - cept - ed be, As evening sac - ri - fice.

ST. MARTIN'S. C. M.
The spa - cious earth is all the Lord's, The Lord her full - ness is; The world, and they that dwell there - in, By sovereign right are his.
WHITEHOUSE. C. M.
Blest is the man, whose softening heart Feels all an - oth - er's pain; To whom the sup - pli - ca - ting eye Is nev - er raised in vain.

FARRANT. C. M.

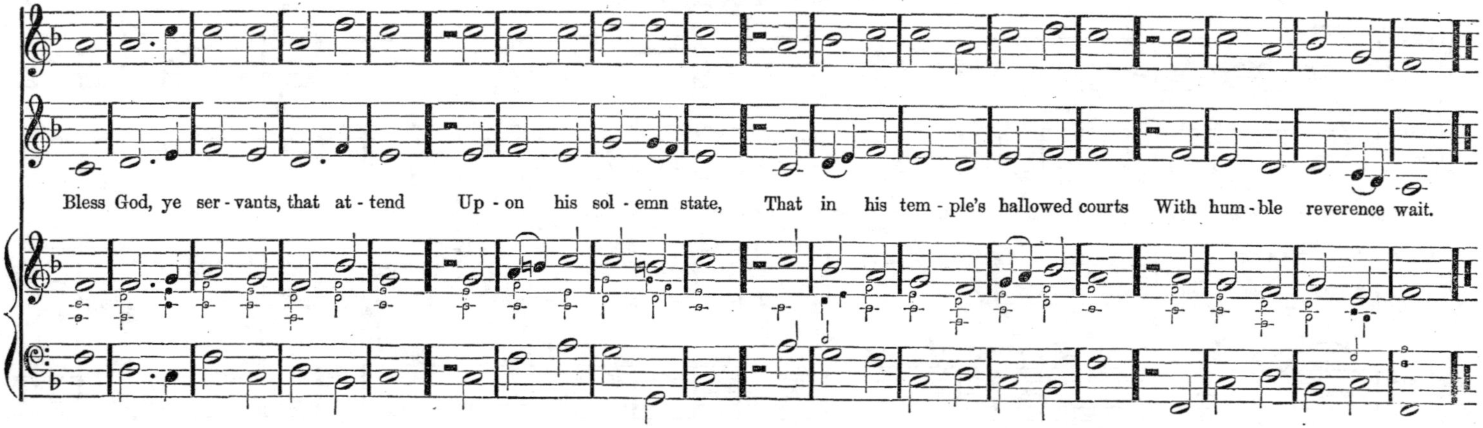

Bless God, ye ser - vants, that at - tend Up - on his sol - emn state, That in his tem - ple's hallowed courts With hum - ble reverence wait.

LAUD. C. M.

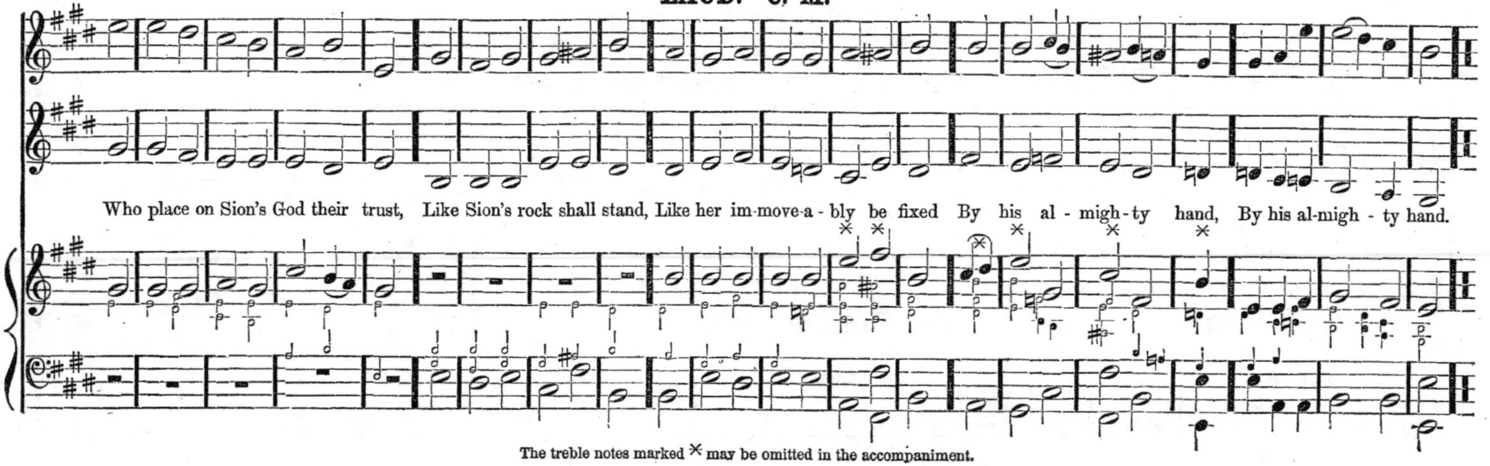

Who place on Sion's God their trust, Like Sion's rock shall stand, Like her im-move-a - bly be fixed By his al - migh - ty hand, By his al-migh - ty hand.

The treble notes marked ✕ may be omitted in the accompaniment.

RANDAL. C. M.

To our Re - deem - er's glo - rious name A-wake the sa - cred song! O, may his love (im - mor - tal flame!) Tune ev - ery heart and tongue.
CHESTERFIELD. C. M.
Father, what - e'er of earth - ly bliss Thy sovereign will de - nies, Ac - cept - ed at thy throne, let this, My hum - ble prayer a - rise.

DITCHLING. C. M.

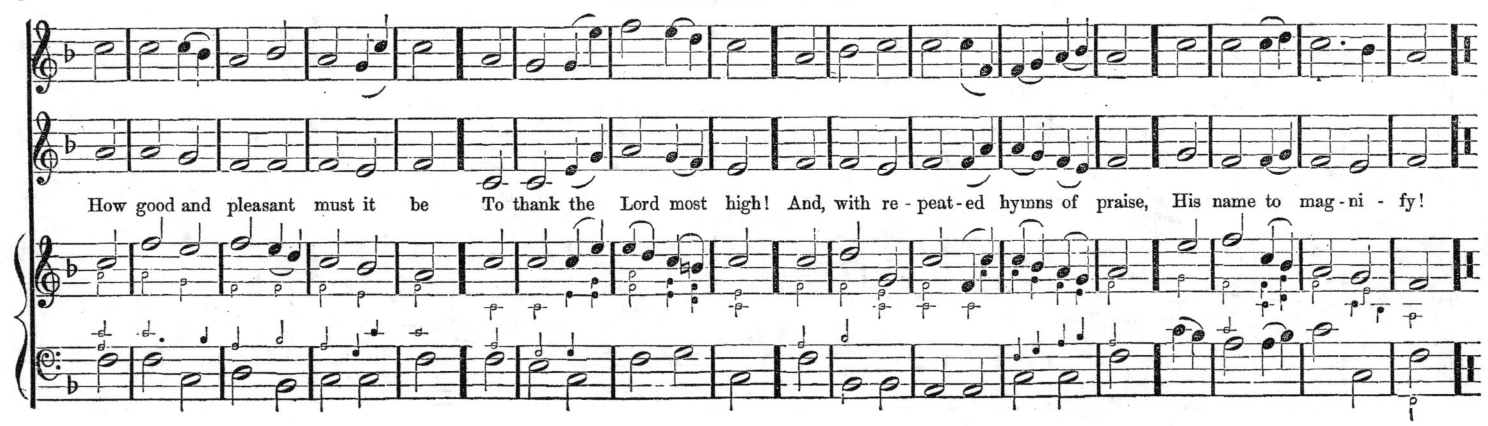

HORNE. C. M.

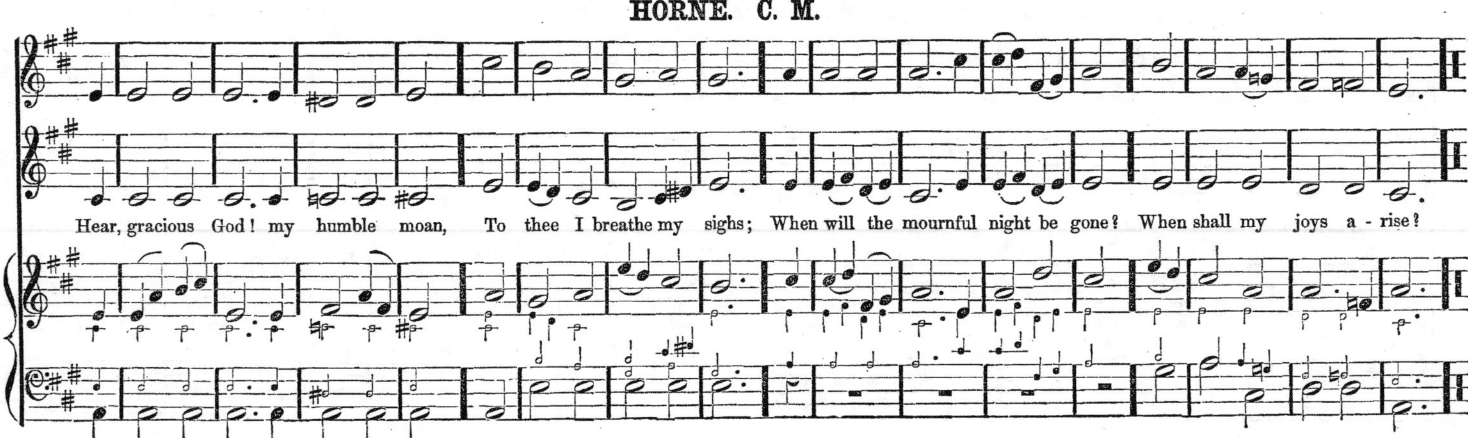

CRUCIFIXION. C. M.
Thy chastening wrath, O Lord, re-strain, Though I deserve it all; Nor let on me the heavy storm Of thy displeasure fall.
KEN. C. M.
Ye humble souls, approach your God With songs of sa - cred praise, For he is good, su - premely good, And kind are all his ways.

DOWLAND. C. M.

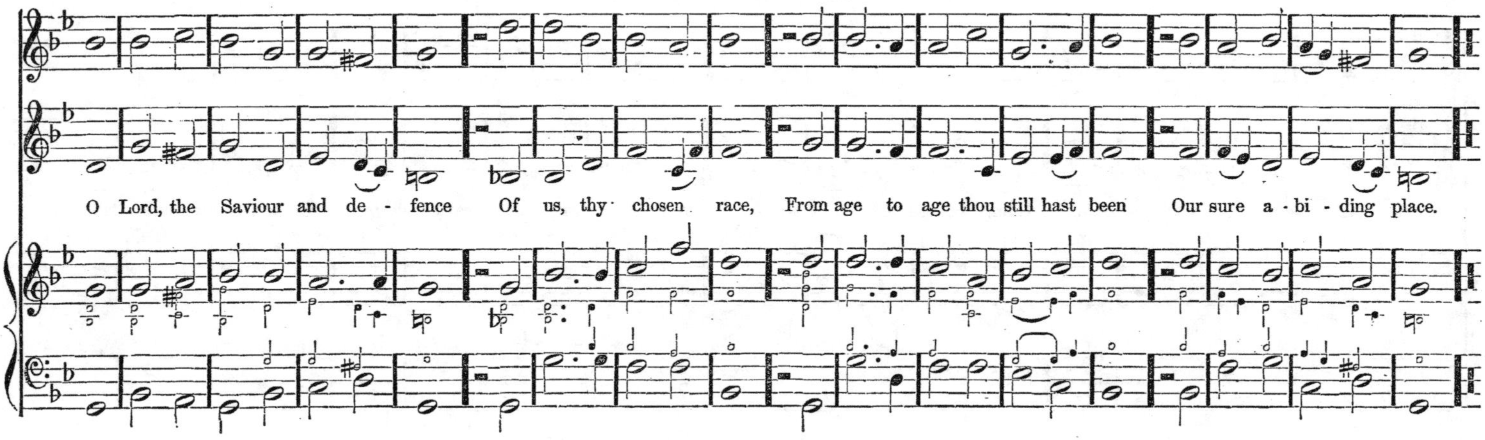

O Lord, the Saviour and de - fence Of us, thy chosen race, From age to age thou still hast been Our sure a - bi - ding place.

FROME. C. M.

Fa - ther of mer - cies! in thy word What end - less glo - ry shines! Forev - er be thy name a - dored, For these ce - les - tial lines.

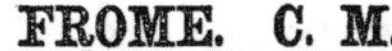

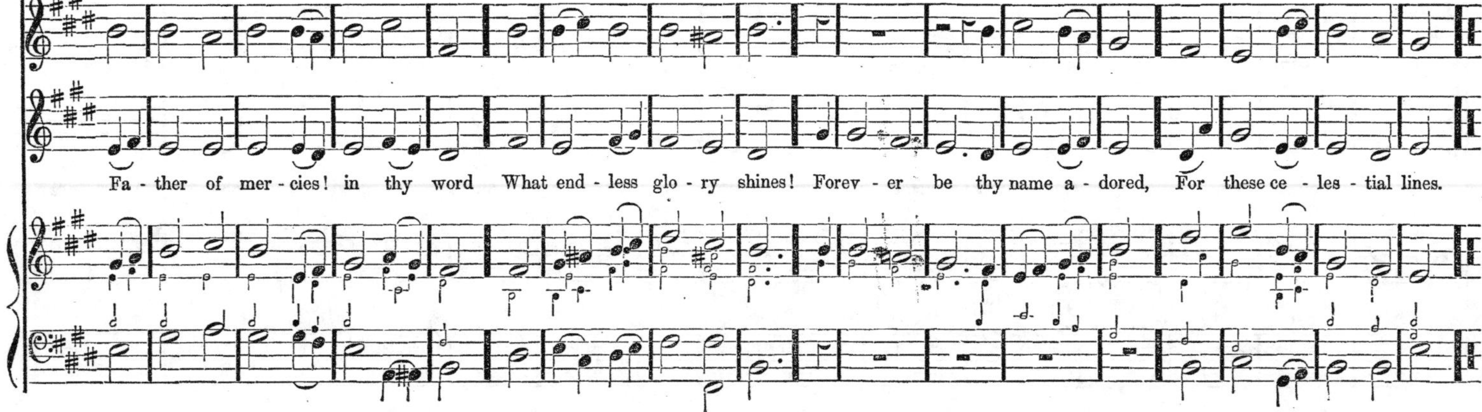

BELLEFIELD. C. M.

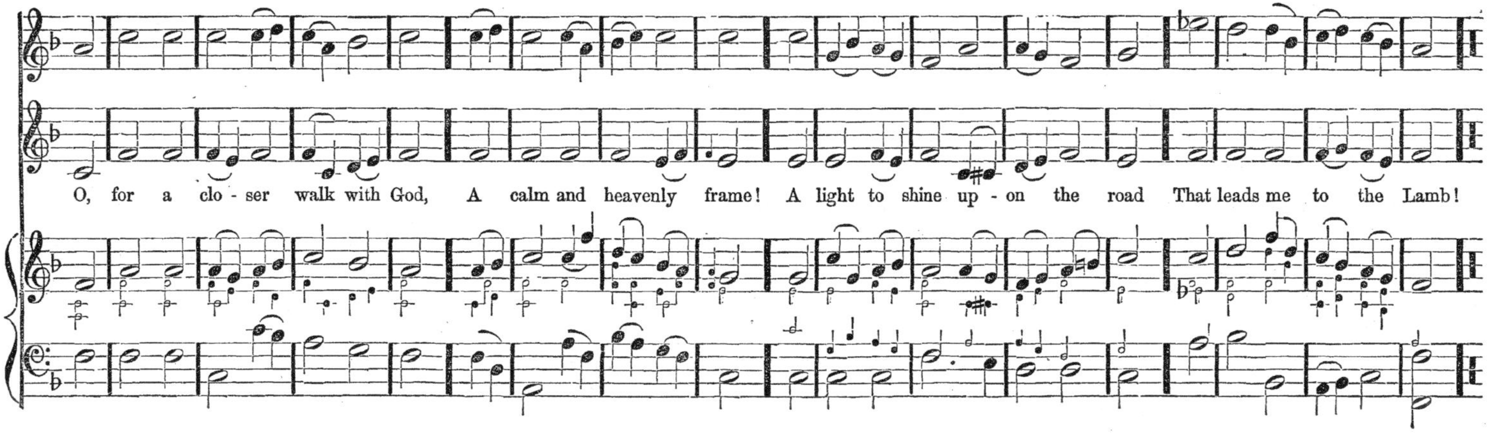
O, for a clo - ser walk with God, A calm and heavenly frame! A light to shine up - on the road That leads me to the Lamb!

ST. CECILIA. C. M.

Lord! tho' at times surprised by fear, On danger's first a - larm, Yet still for suc - cor I de - pend On thy al - mighty arm.

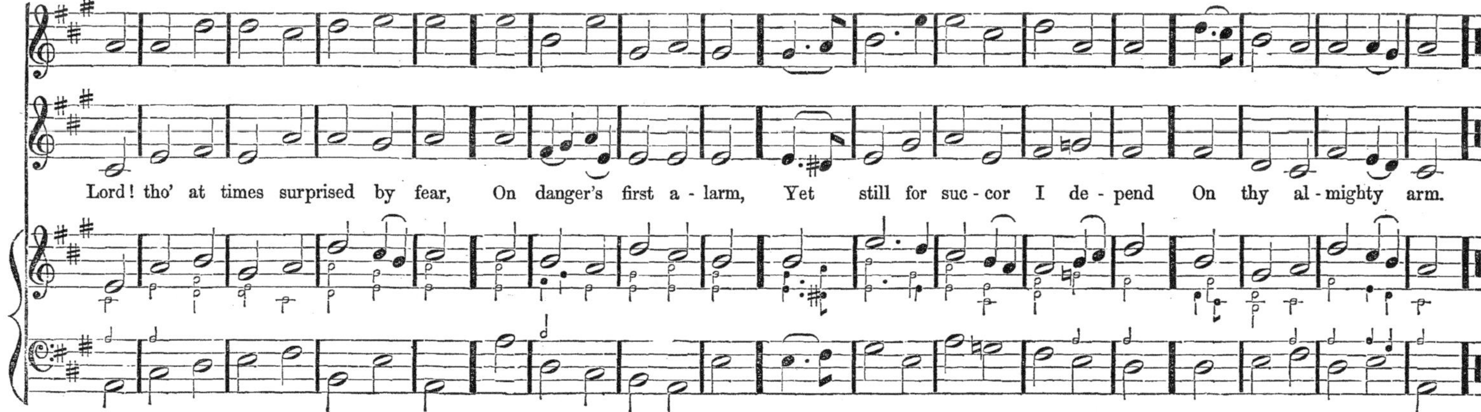

ARABIA. C. M.

When I can read my ti - tle clear To man - sions in the skies, I'll bid fare - well to ev - ery fear,
And wipe my weep - ing eyes, I'll bid fare - well to ev - ery fear, And wipe my weep - ing eyes.

NORTON. C. M.

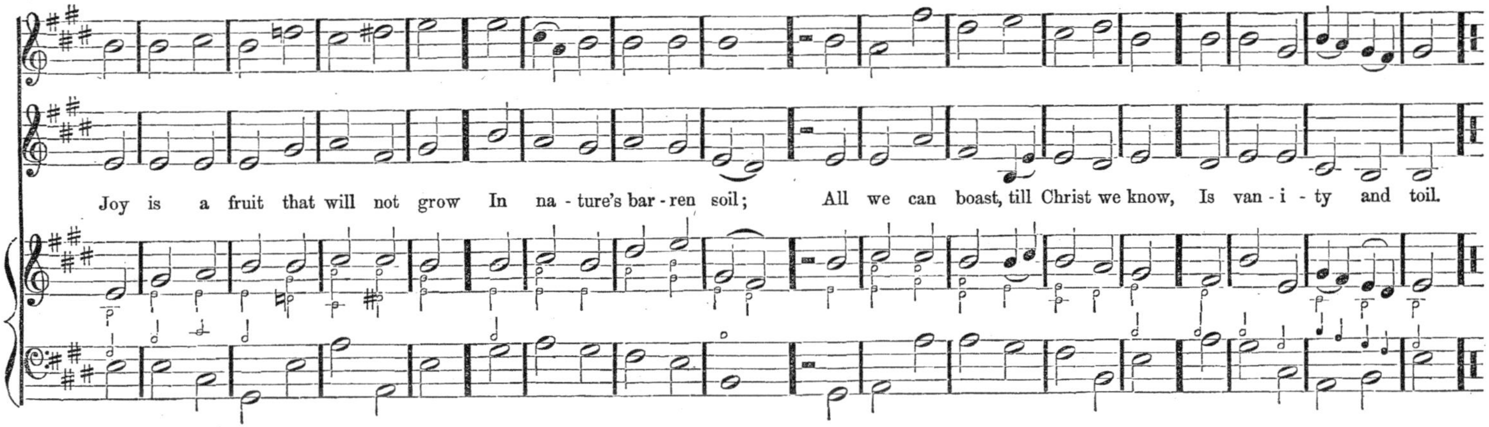

Joy is a fruit that will not grow In na - ture's bar - ren soil; All we can boast, till Christ we know, Is van - i - ty and toil.

YORK. C. M.

The man is blest that fears the Lord, Nor on - ly wor - ship pays, But keeps his steps confined with care To his ap - point - ed ways.

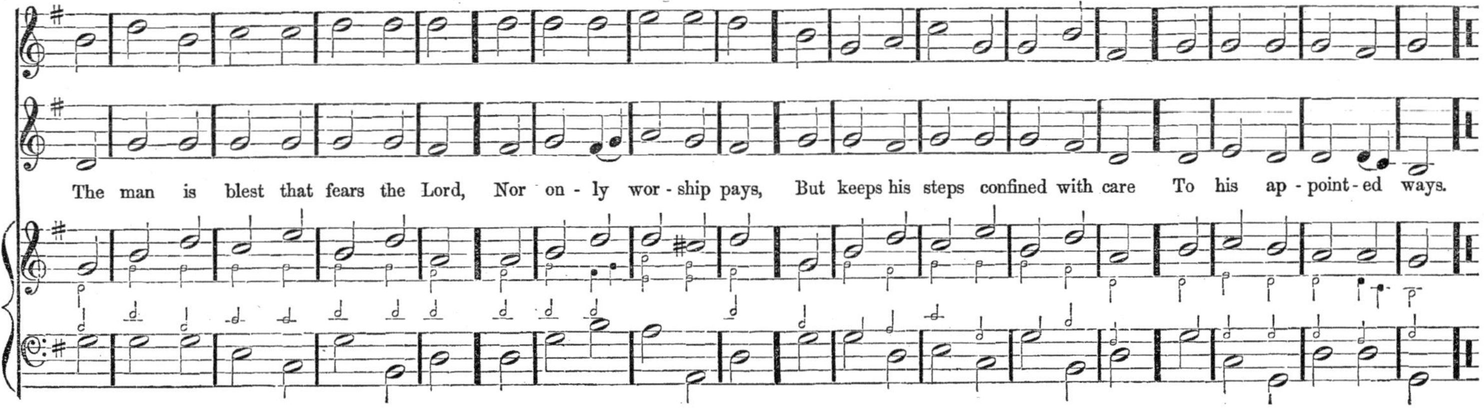

COLET. C. M. Double.

CHRISTMAS. C. M.

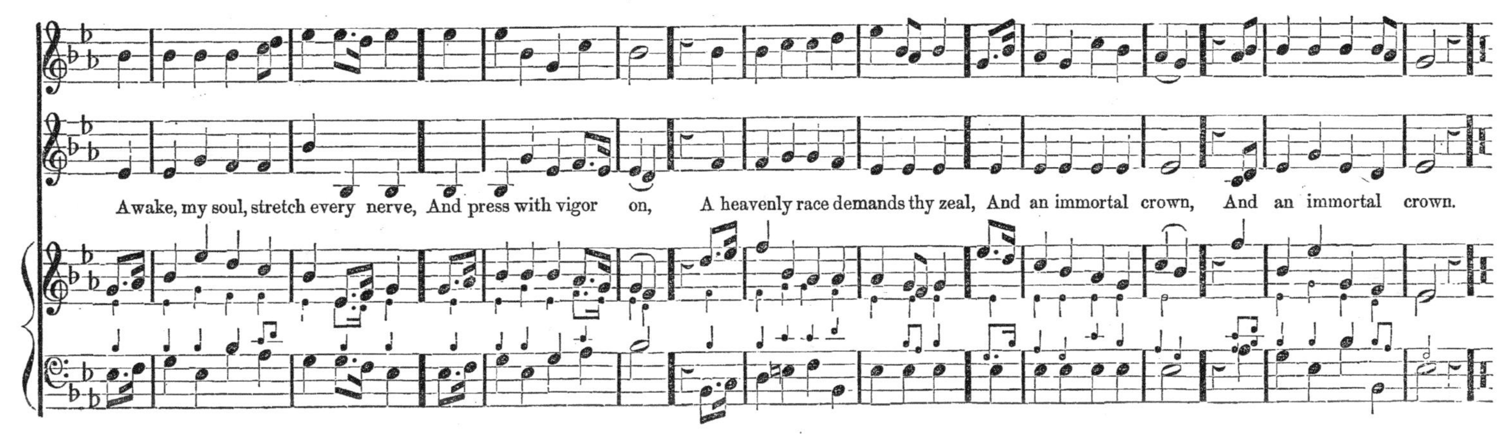

WARWICK. C. M.

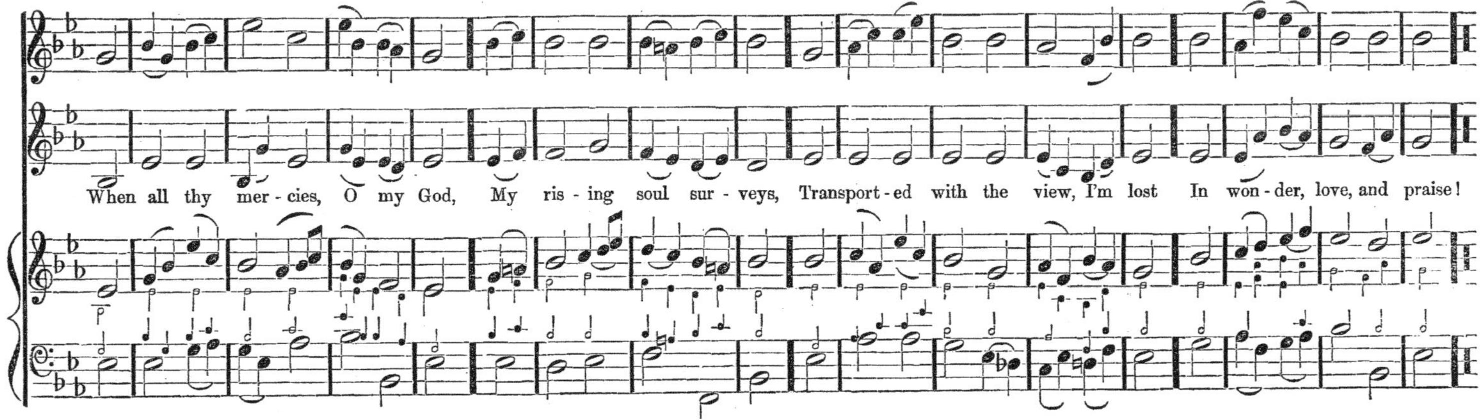

ST. MAGNUS. C. M.

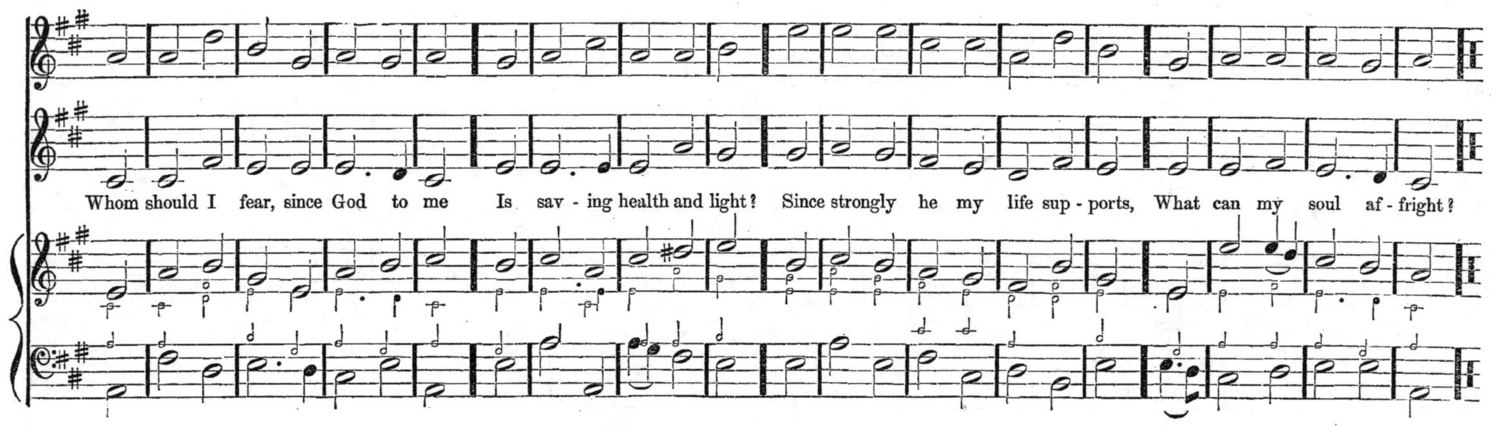

COUPAR. C. M.

TIVERTON. C. M.

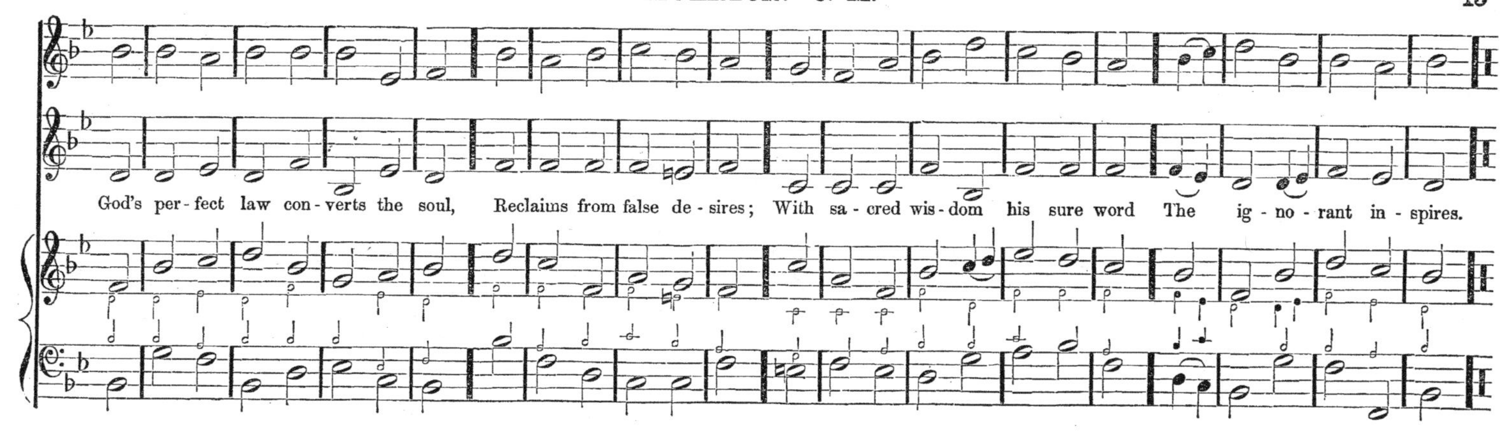

MEDFIELD. C. M.

TURNHAM GREEN. C. M.

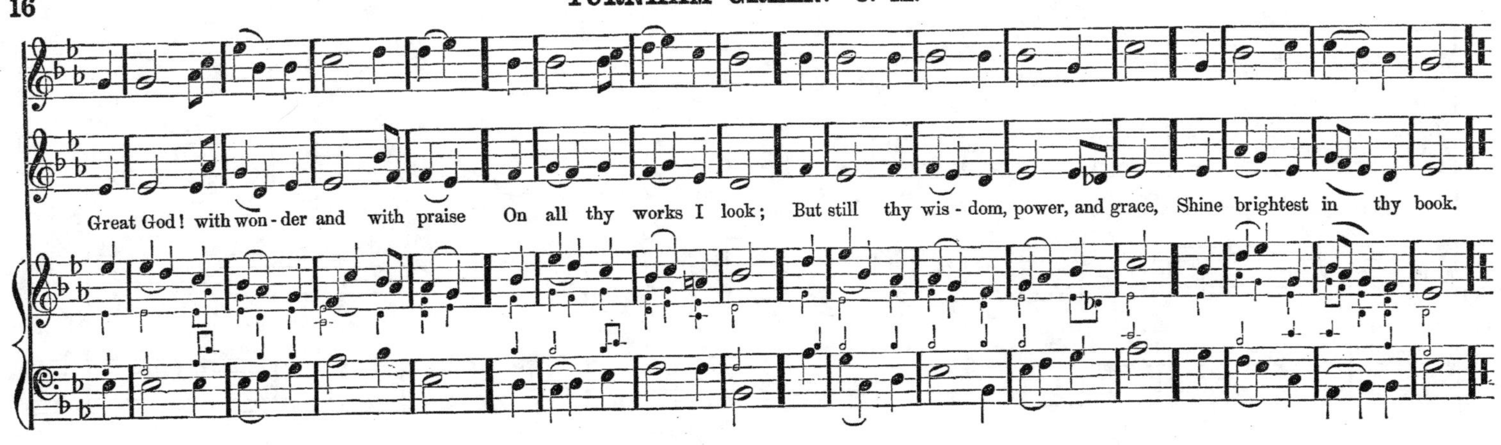

BANGOR. C. M.

LYDIA. C. M.

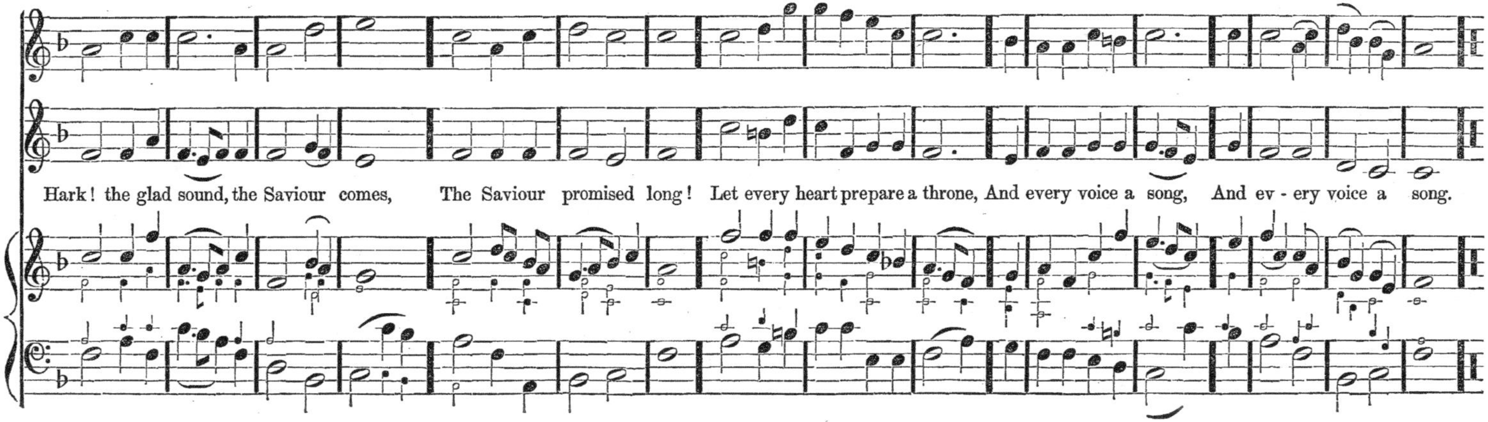

Hark! the glad sound, the Saviour comes, The Saviour promised long! Let every heart prepare a throne, And every voice a song, And ev - ery voice a song.

REPTON. C. M.

O, with due rev - erence, let us all To God's a - bode re - pair: And, prostrate at his foot - stool fallen, Pour out our hum - ble prayer.

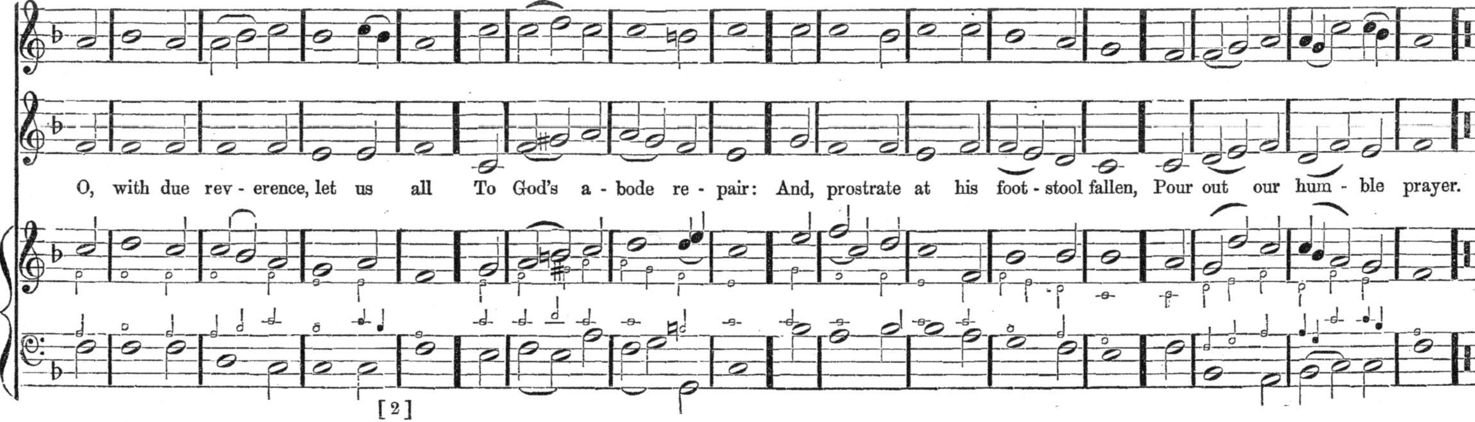

ELTHAM. C. M.

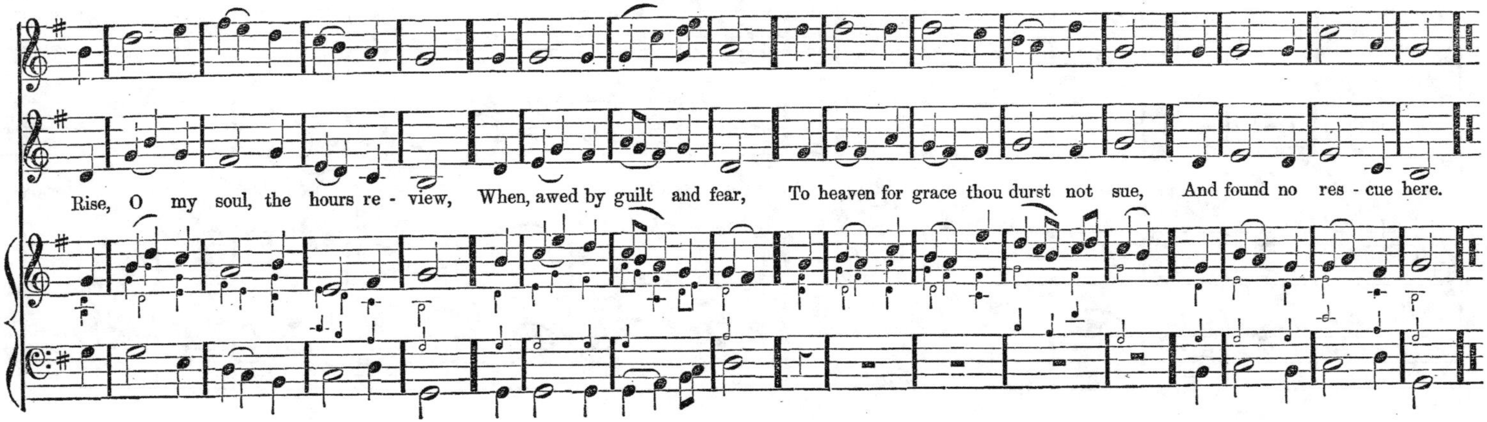

Rise, O my soul, the hours re - view, When, awed by guilt and fear, To heaven for grace thou durst not sue, And found no res - cue here.

LULLINGTON. C. M.

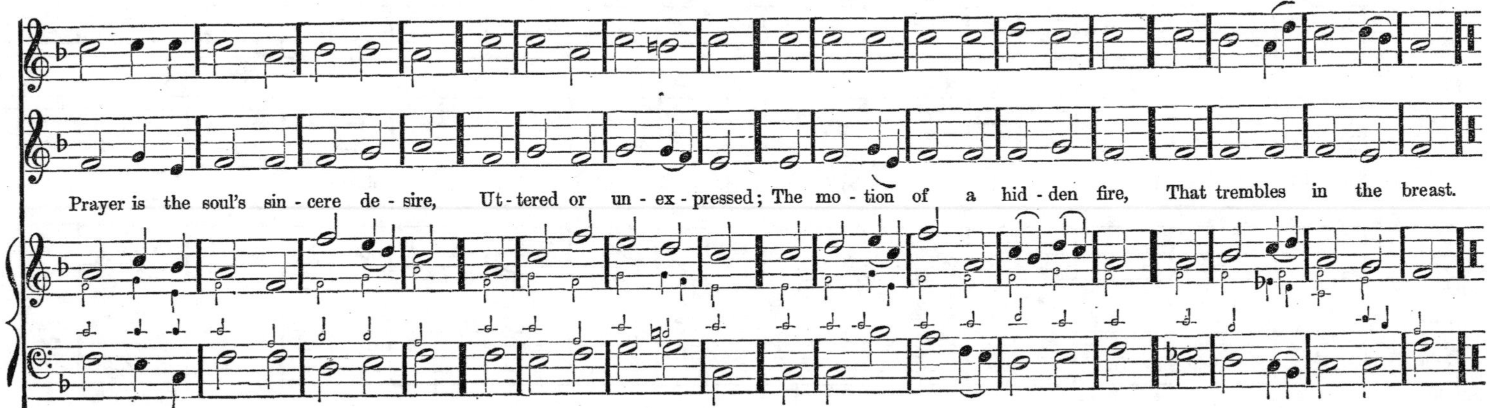

LONDON NEW. C. M.

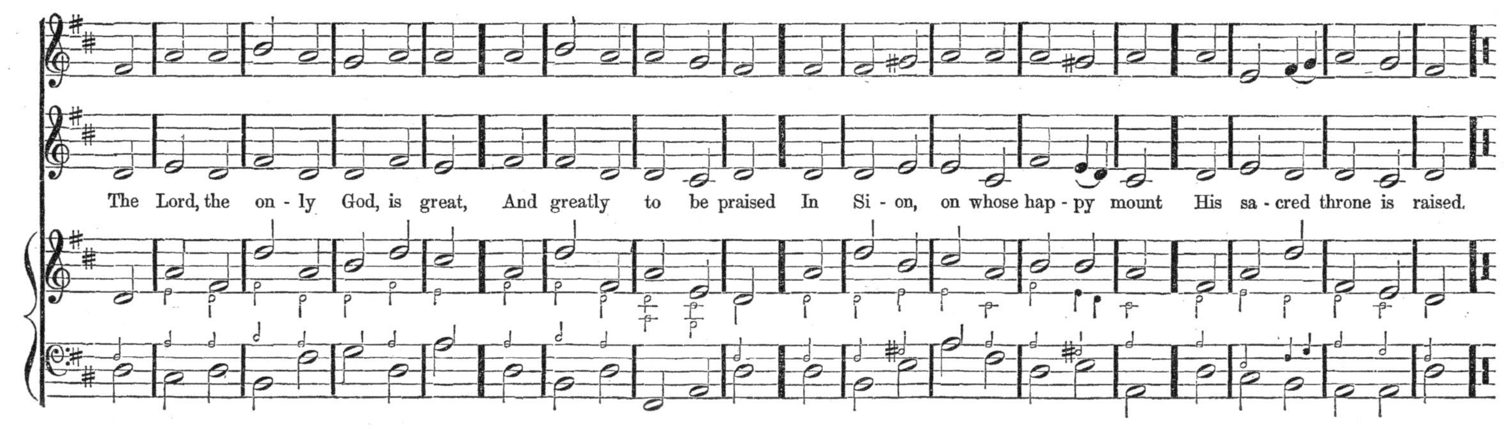

ABRIDGE. C. M.

MEAR. C. M.

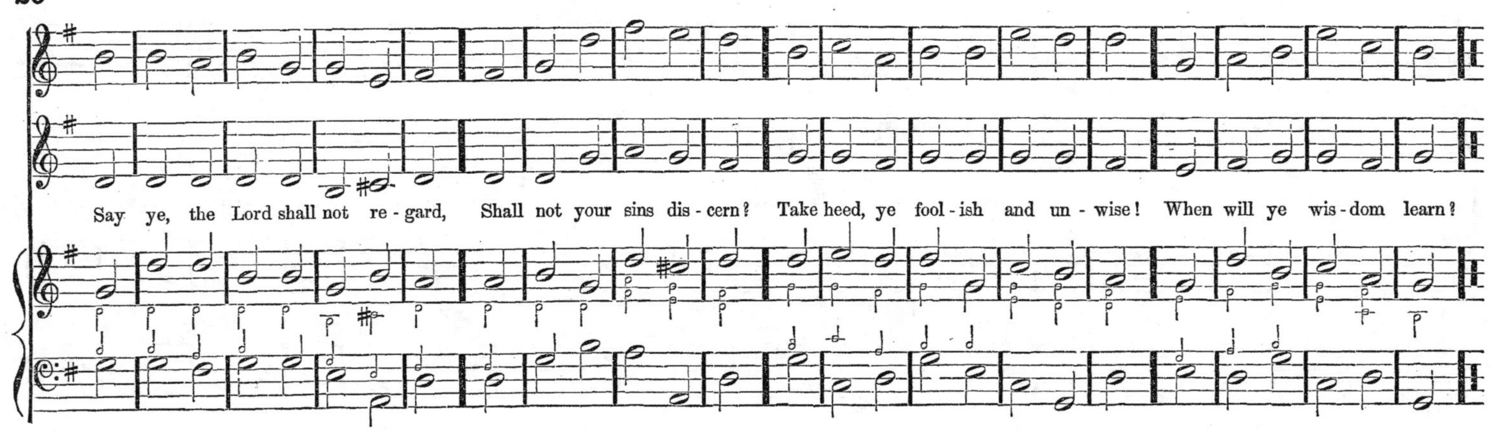

NAYLAND. C. M.

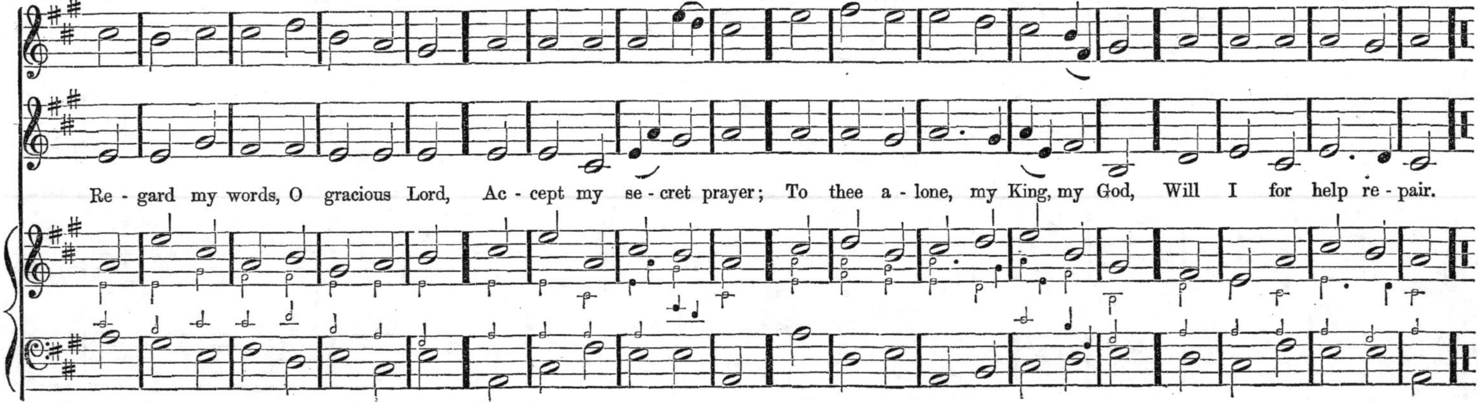

ST. DAVID'S. C. M.

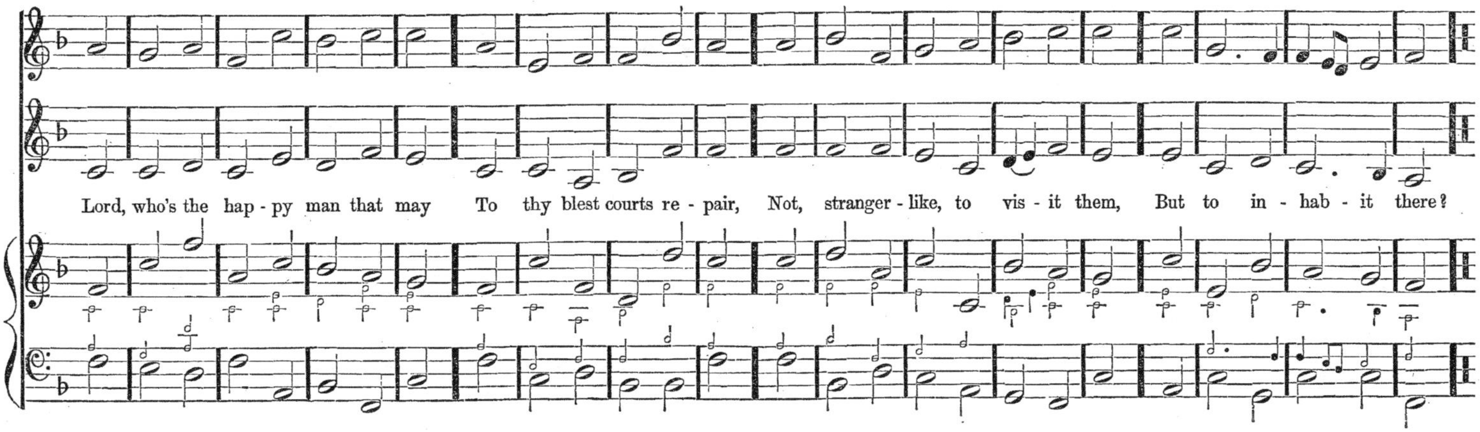
Lord, who's the hap - py man that may To thy blest courts re - pair, Not, stranger - like, to vis - it them, But to in - hab - it there?

WINCHESTER. C. M.

Je - ho - vah reigns: let therefore all The guilt - y na - tions quake; On cherub's wings he sits enthroned; Let earth's foun - da - tions shake.

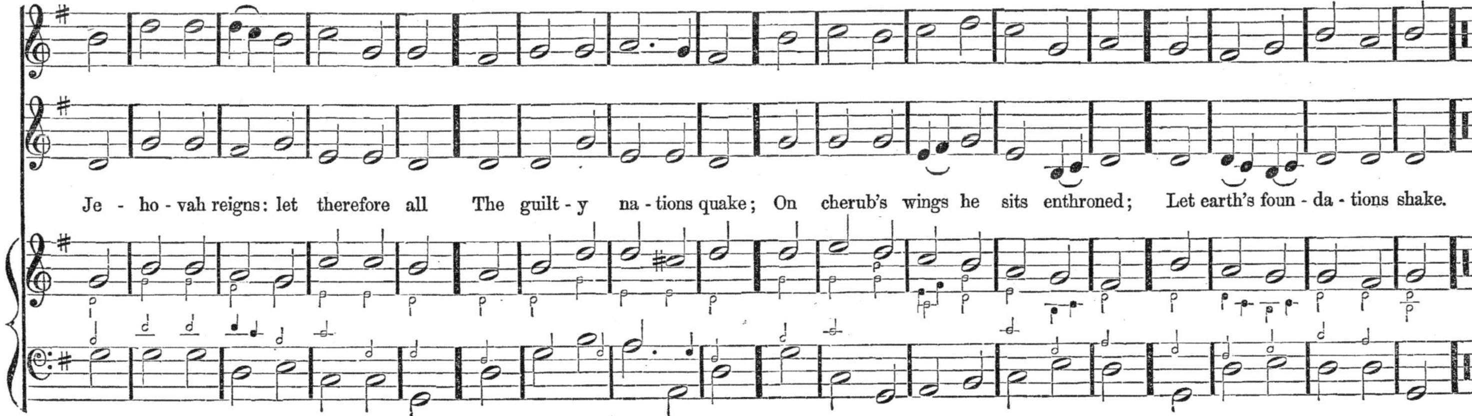

ST. JAMES'S. C. M.

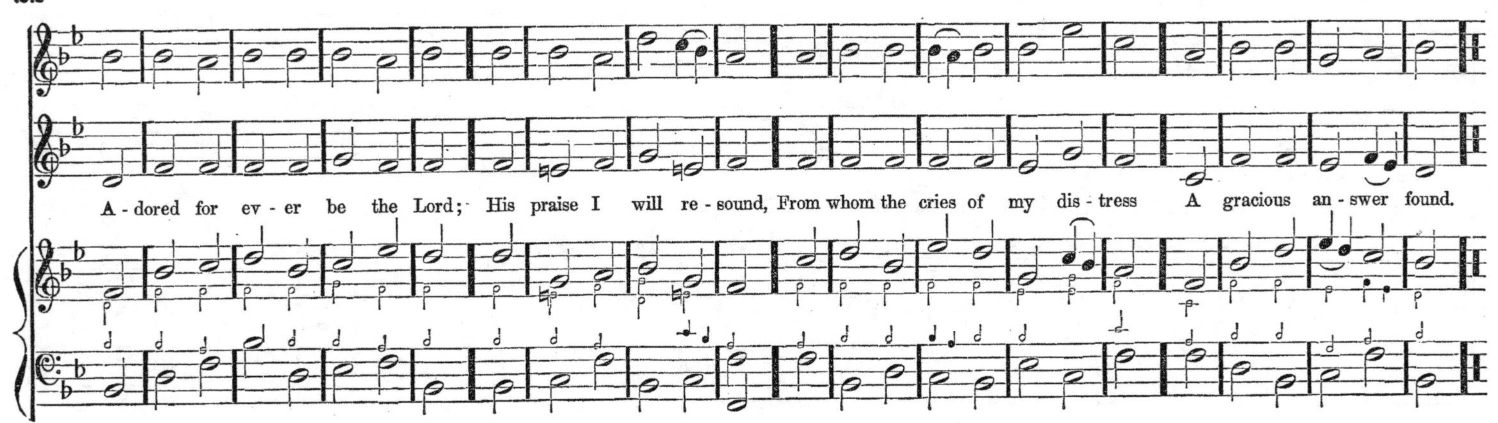

ZURICH. C. M.

ST. GREGORIUS. C. M.

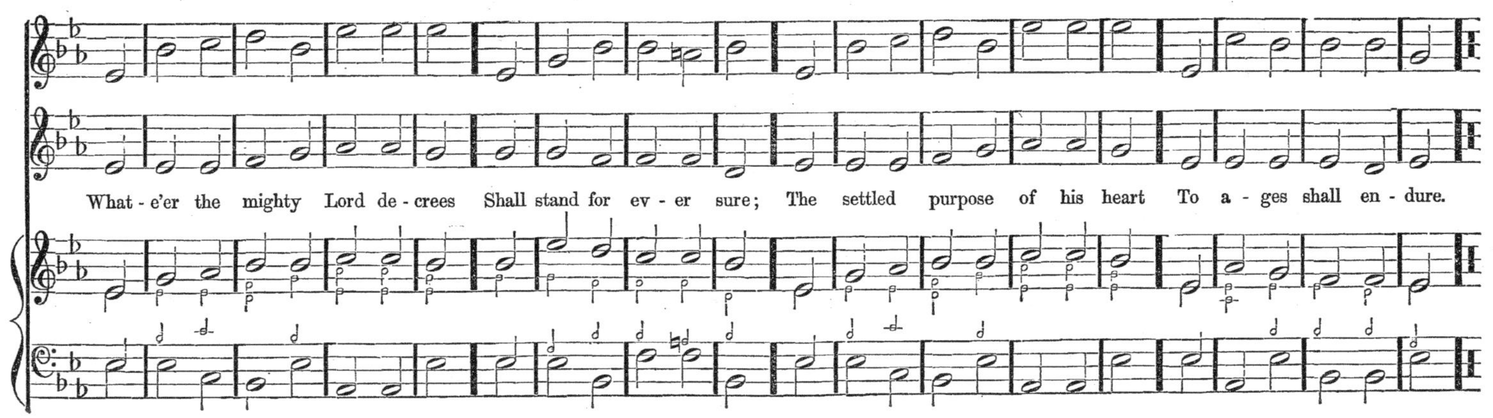

CARLEYLE. C. M.

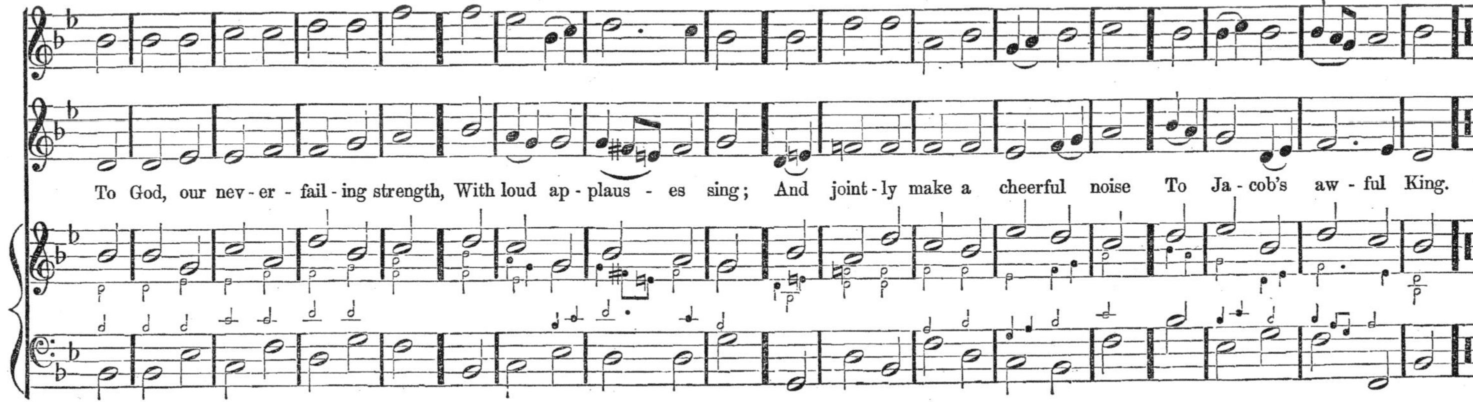

NORWOOD. C. M.

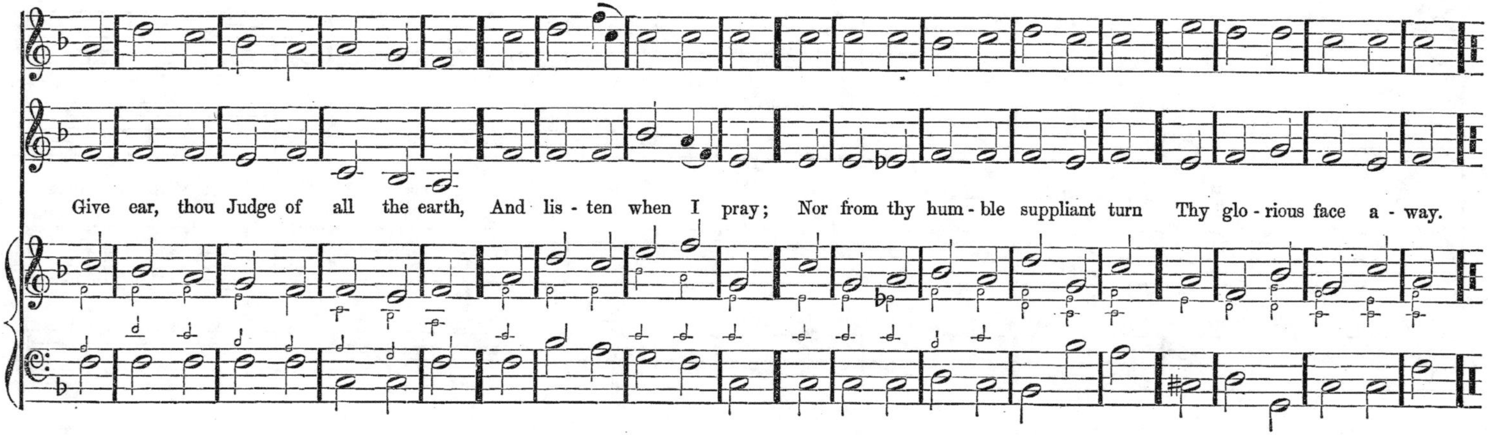

Give ear, thou Judge of all the earth, And lis - ten when I pray; Nor from thy hum - ble suppliant turn Thy glo - rious face a - way.

GORTON. C. M.

Lord, to my brethren I'll de - clare The tri - umphs of thy name: In presence of as - sem - bled saints Thy glo - ry thus pro - claim.

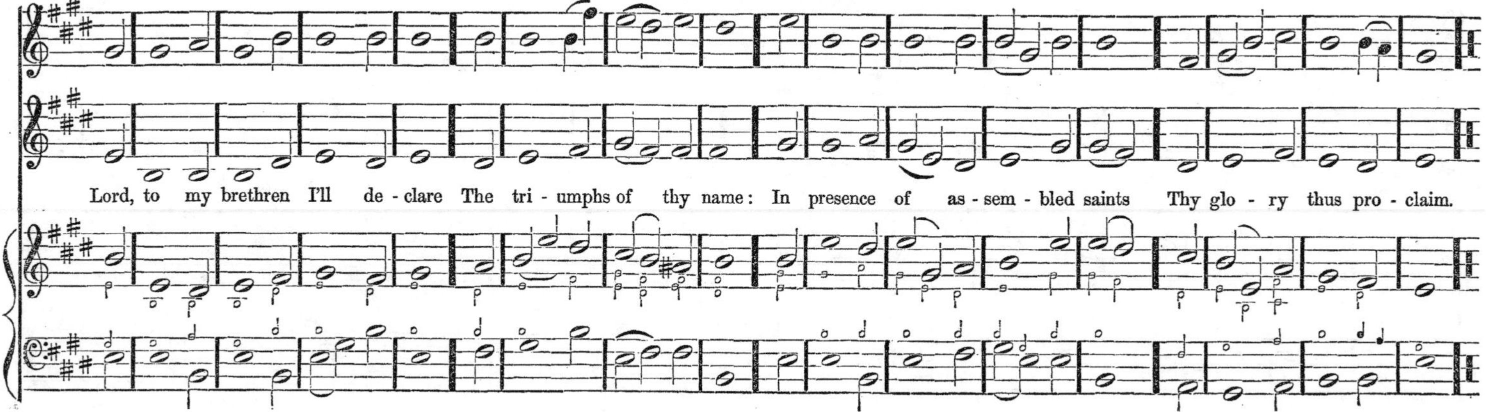

ANGMERING. C. M.

LEWES. C. M.

BURLINGTON. C. M.

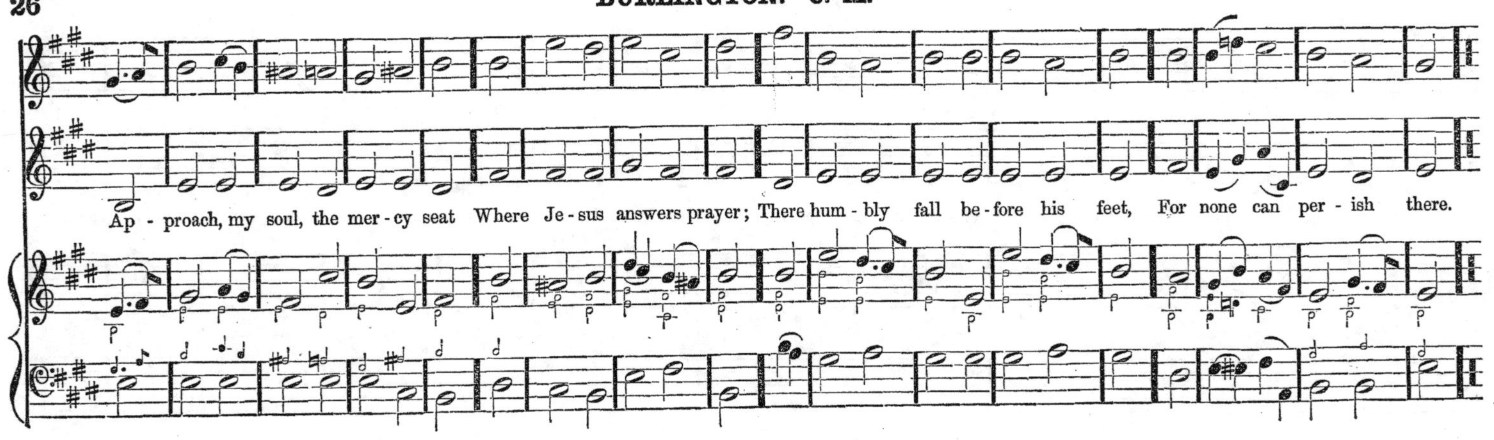

SHROPSHIRE. C. M.

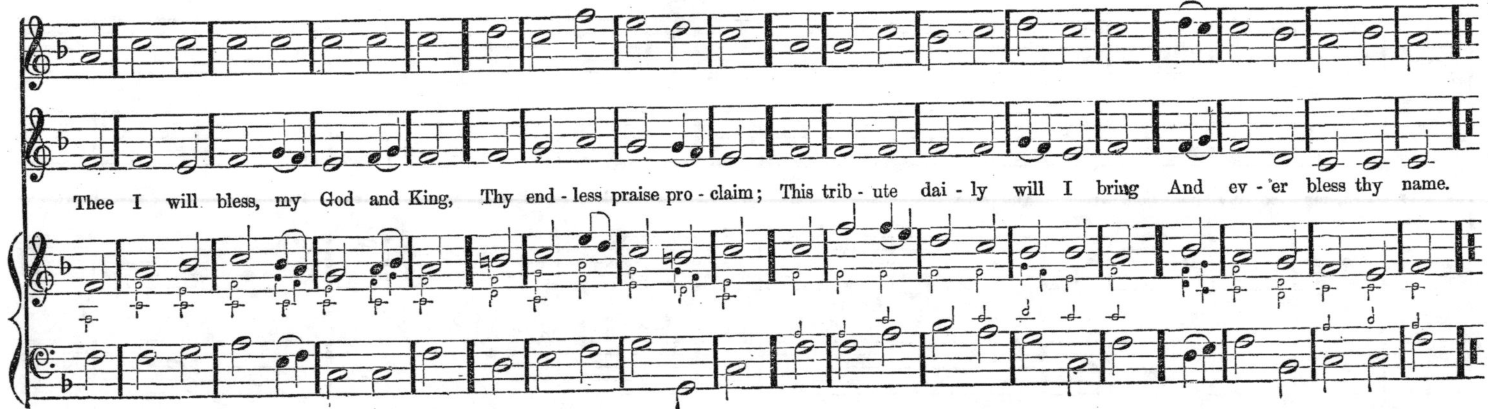

DUNDEE. C. M.

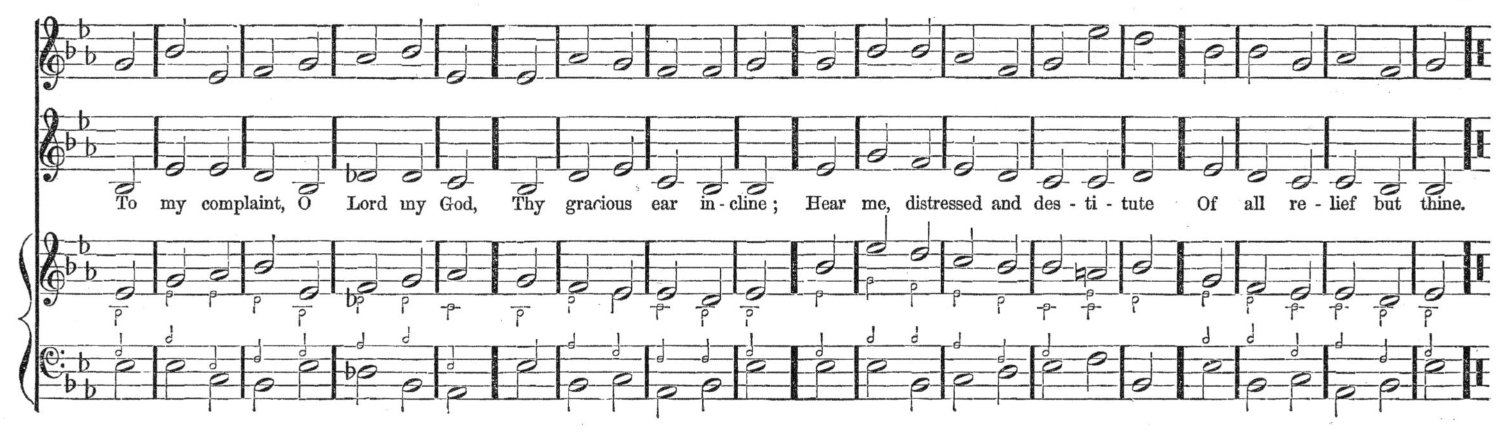

MARLOW. C. M.

ST. MARY'S. C. M.

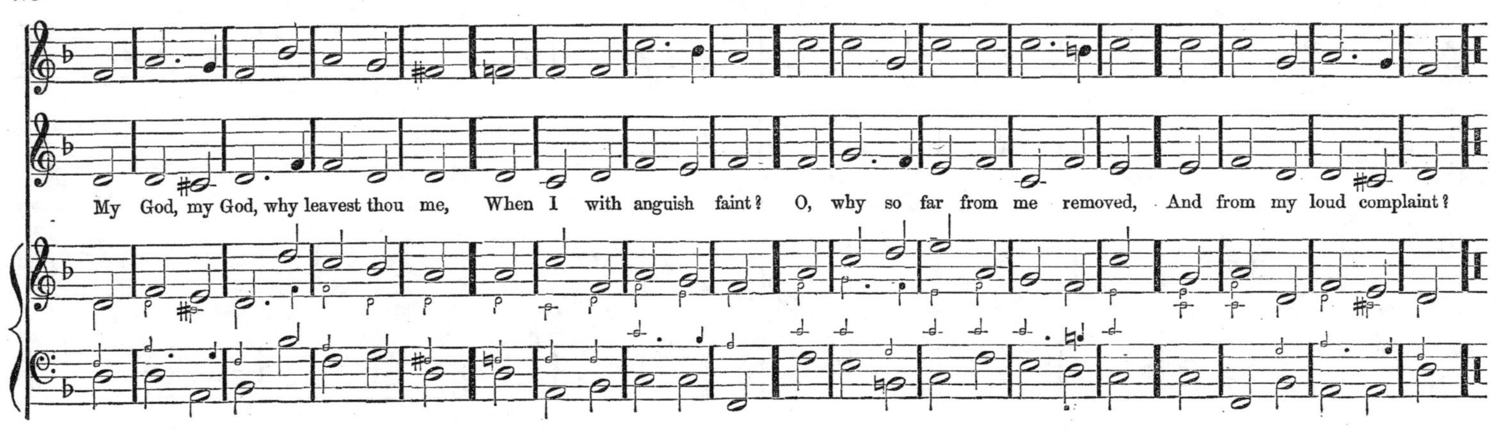

DEDHAM. C. M.

WINDSOR. C. M.

OLD COMMON TUNE. C. M.

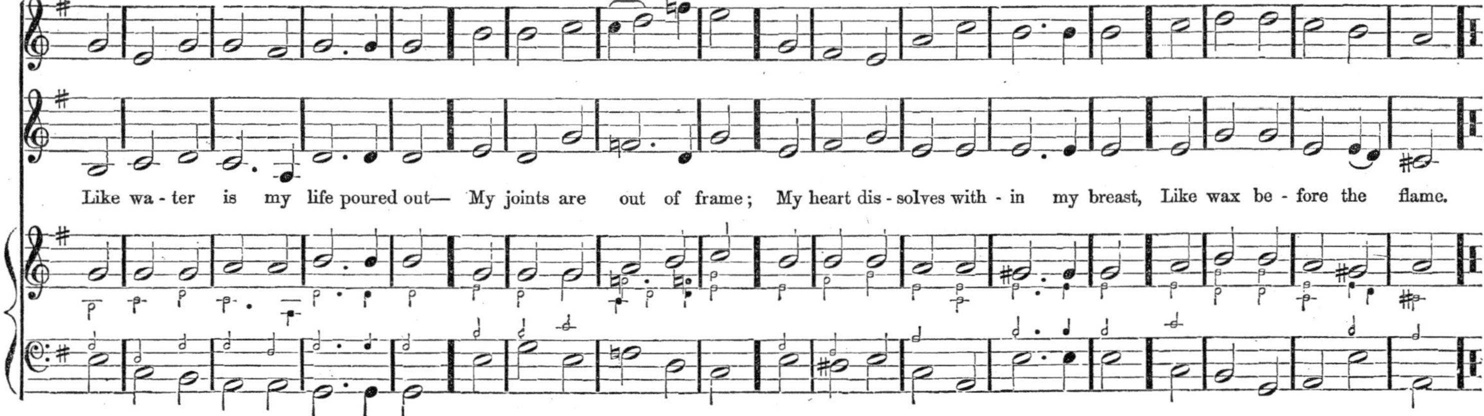

MANCHESTER. C. M.

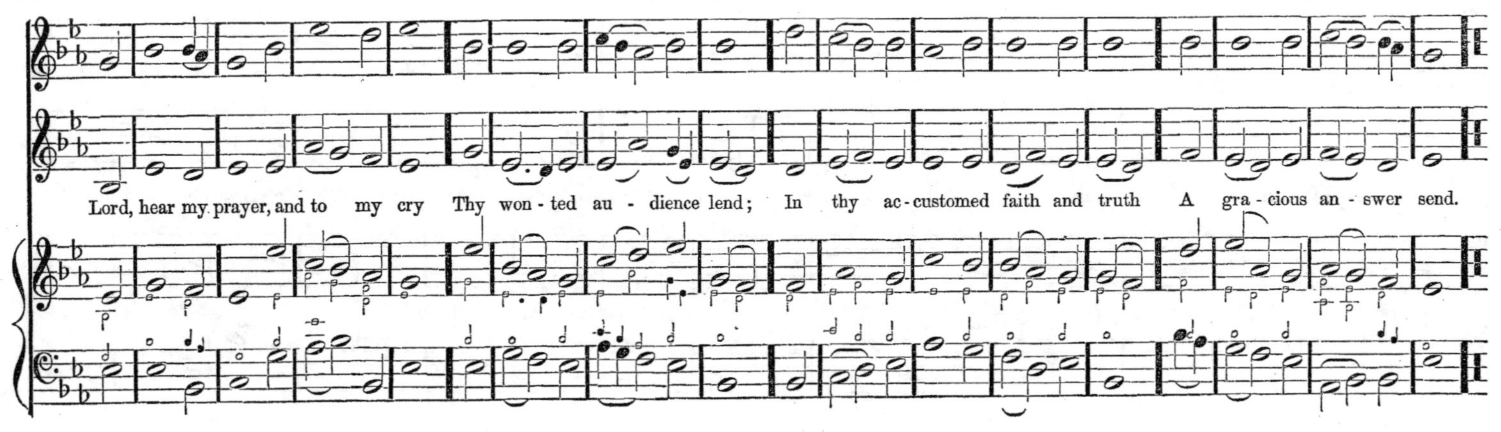

BEDFORD. C. M.

GOWER. C. M.

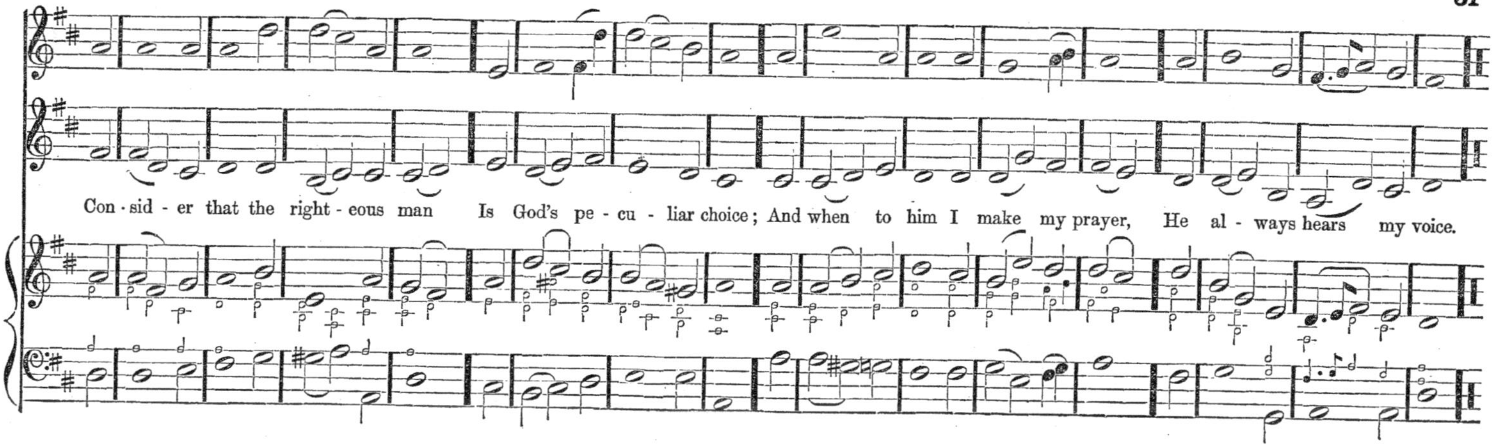

Con - sid - er that the right - eous man Is God's pe - cu - liar choice; And when to him I make my prayer, He al - ways hears my voice.

HOBART. C. M.

Come, Ho - ly Spir - it, heavenly Dove! With all thy quickening powers, Kin - dle a flame of sa - cred love In these cold hearts of ours.

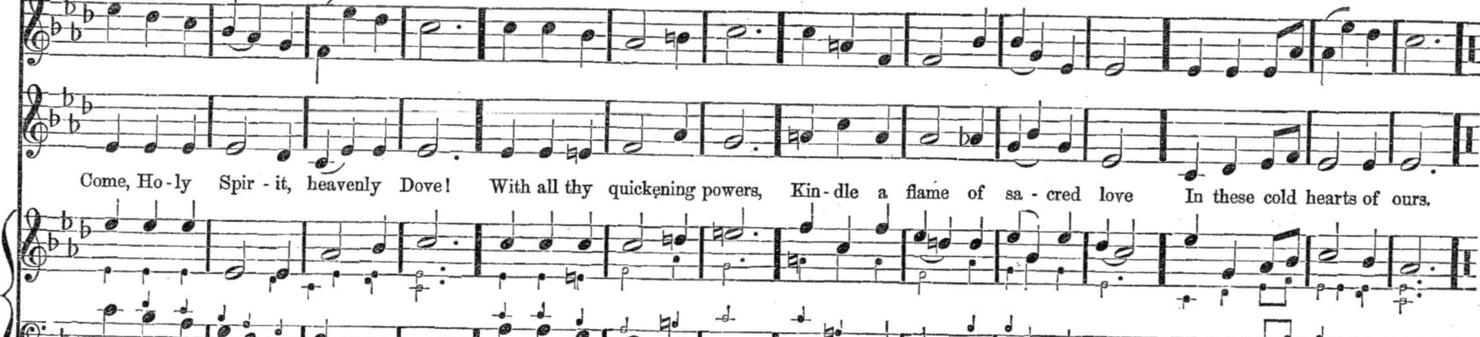

ST. MATTHEWS. C. M. Double.

LATIMER. C. M.

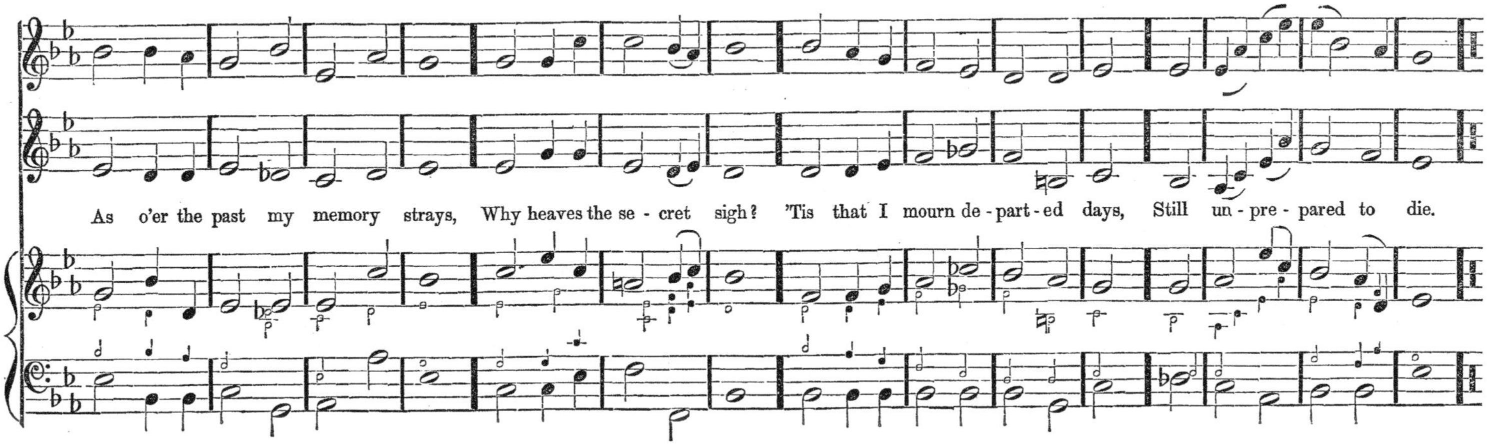
As o'er the past my memory strays, Why heaves the se - cret sigh? 'Tis that I mourn de - part - ed days, Still un - pre - pared to die.

ADAMS. C. M.

Come, Ho - ly Ghost! Cre - a - tor, come, In - spire these souls of thine; Till ev - ery heart which thou hast made Be filled with grace di - vine.

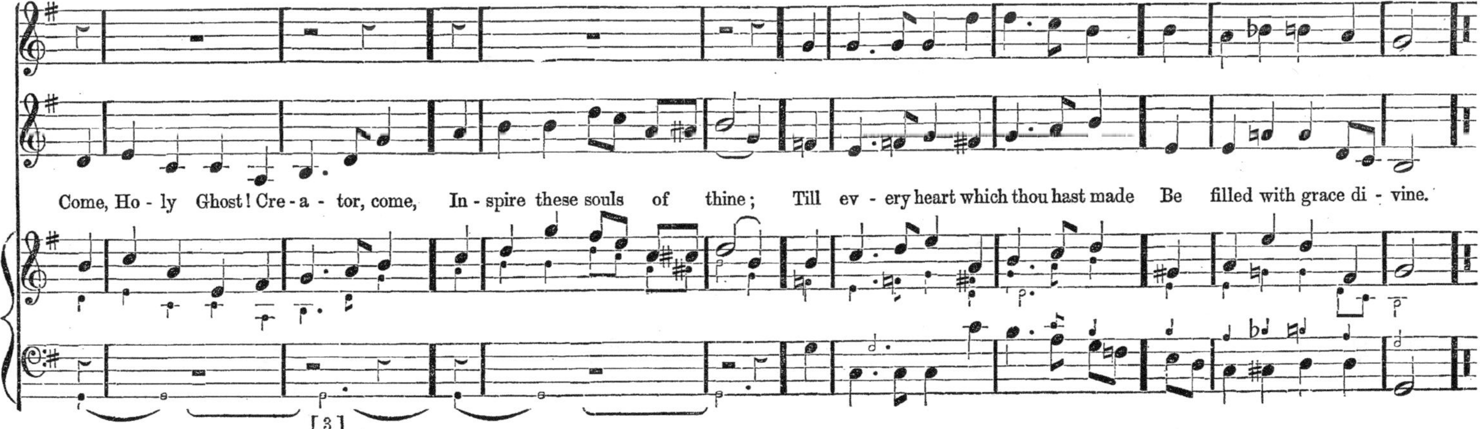

STAFFORD. C. M.

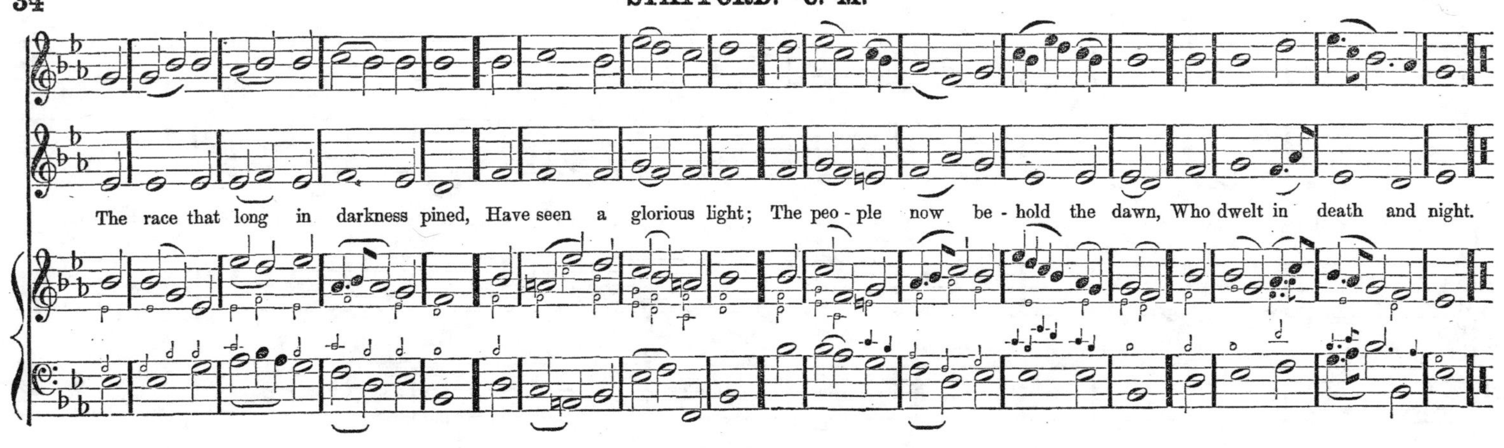

MARTYRDOM. C. M.

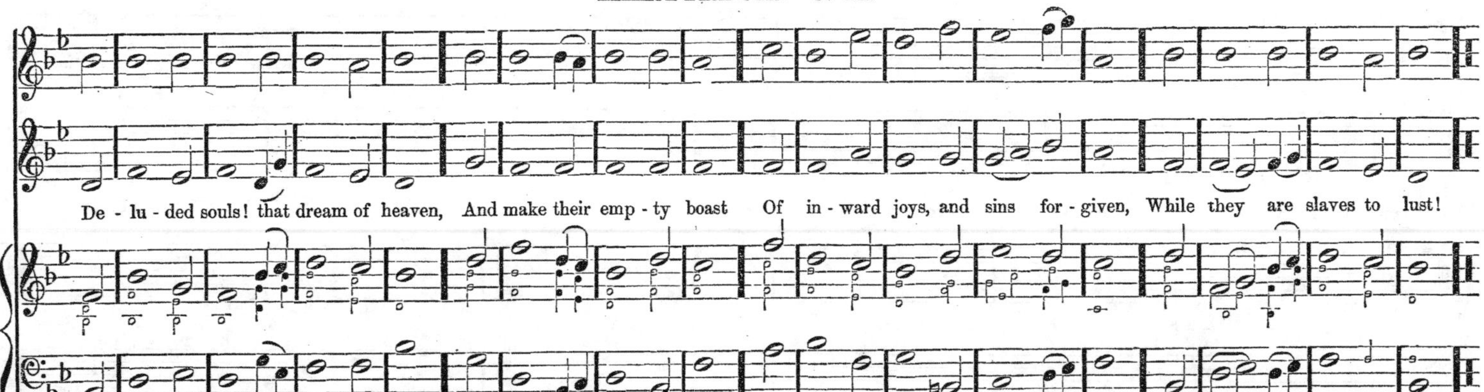

AXBRIDGE. C. M.

In Thee I put my stead - fast trust: De - fend me, Lord, from shame; In - cline thine ear, and

save my soul, For right - - eous is thy name, For right - eous is thy name.

MANOAH. C. M.

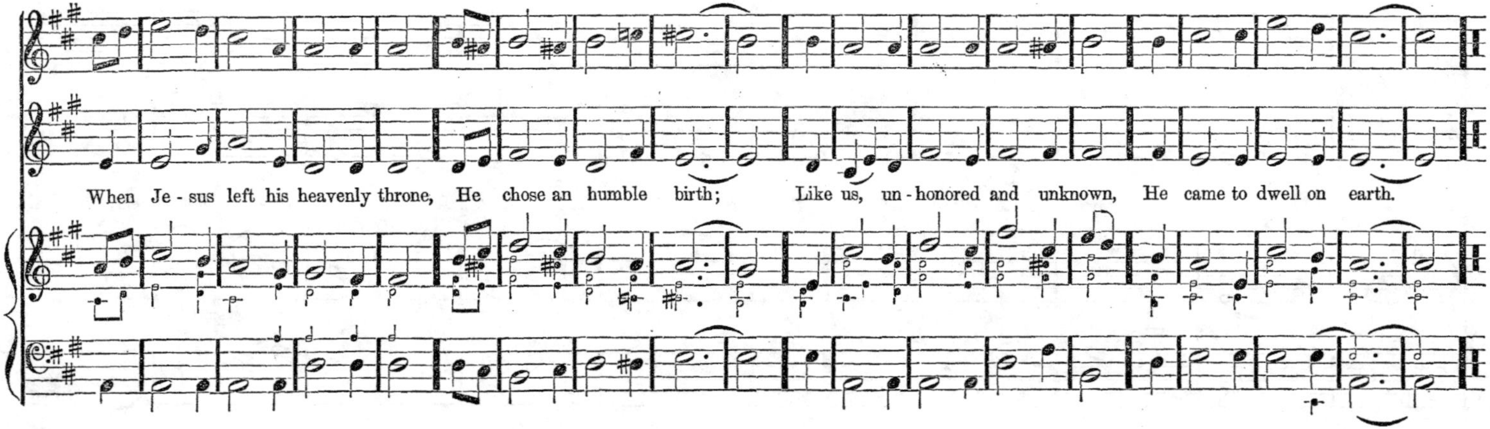

When Je - sus left his heavenly throne, He chose an humble birth; Like us, un - honored and unknown, He came to dwell on earth.

ST. MICHAEL. C. M.

O praise the Lord, for he is good, His mer - cies ne'er de - cay; That his kind fa - vors ev - er last, Let thankful Is - rael say.

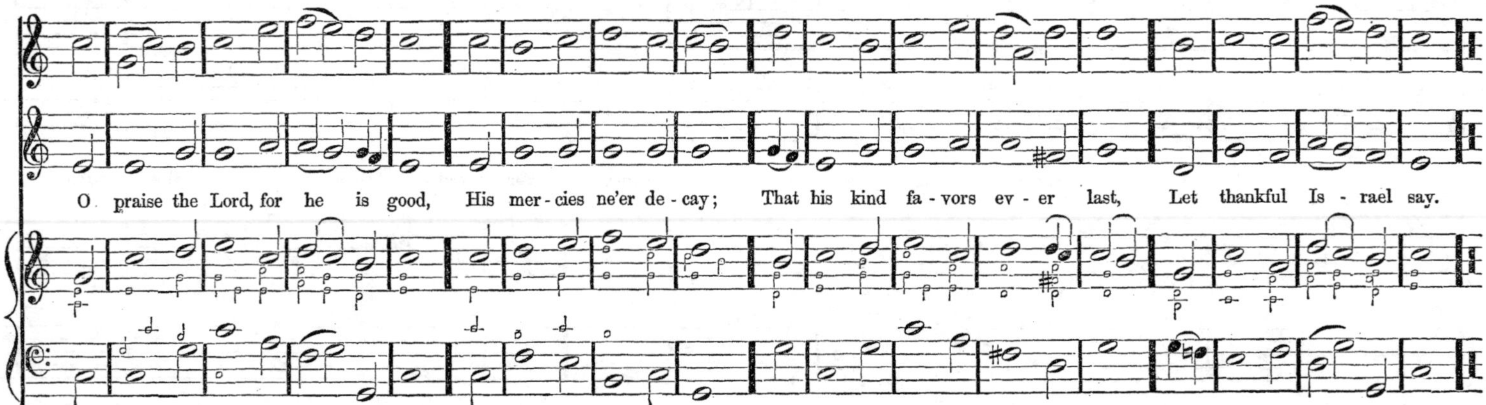

BISHOPTHORP. C. M.

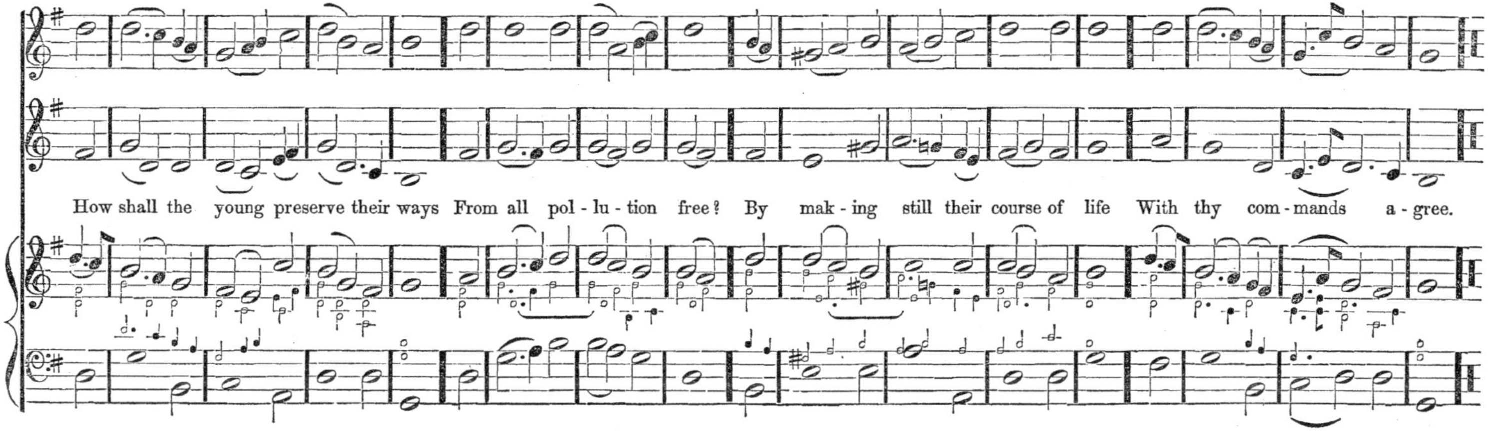

How shall the young preserve their ways From all pol - lu - tion free? By mak - ing still their course of life With thy com - mands a - gree.

CLEMENS. C. M.

How oft, alas! this wretched heart Has wandered from the Lord! How oft my roving thoughts de - part, For - get - ful of his word! Forgetful of his word!

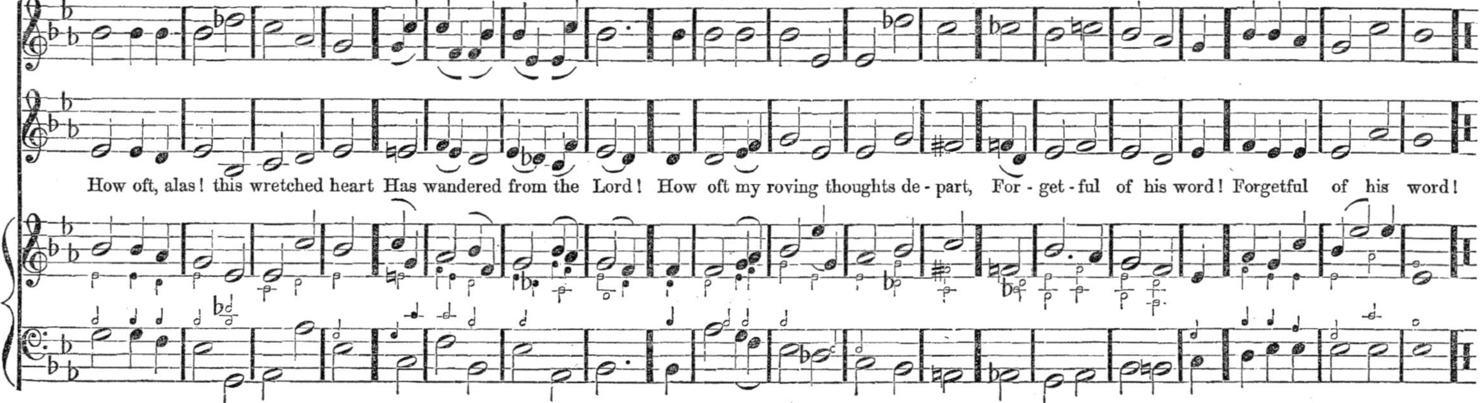

MESSIAH. C. M.

Be - hold the Sa - viour of man - kind Nailed to the shame - ful tree; How vast the love that
him in - clined To bleed and die for me! To bleed and die for me! To bleed and die for me!

OLDER. C. M.

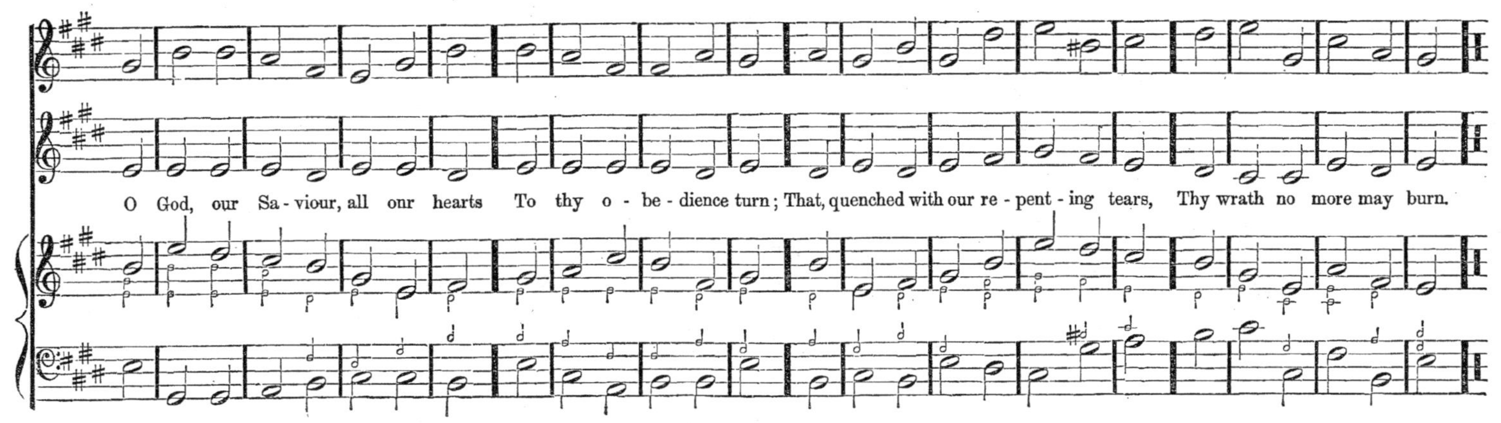

EDEN. C. M.

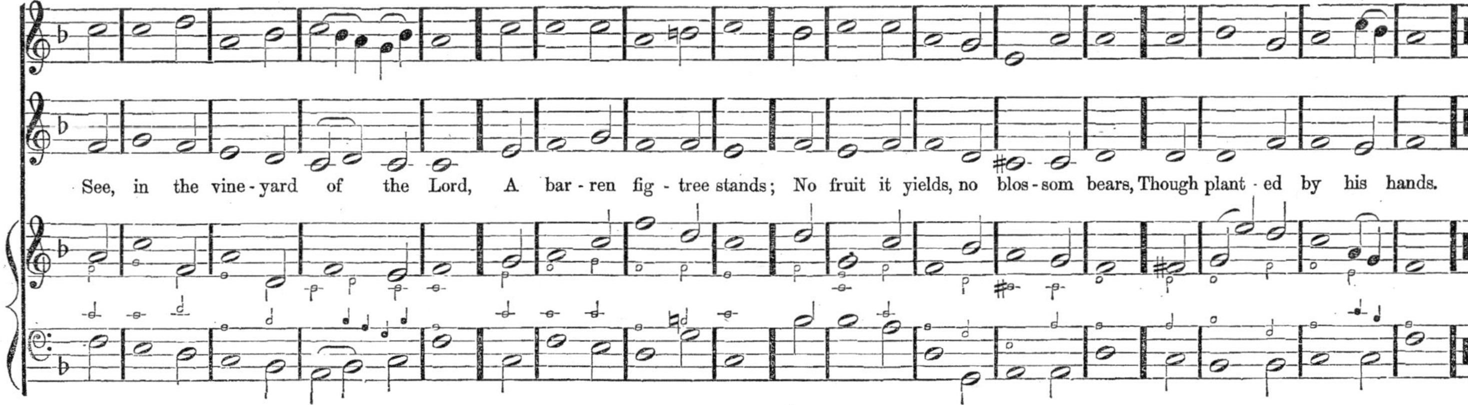

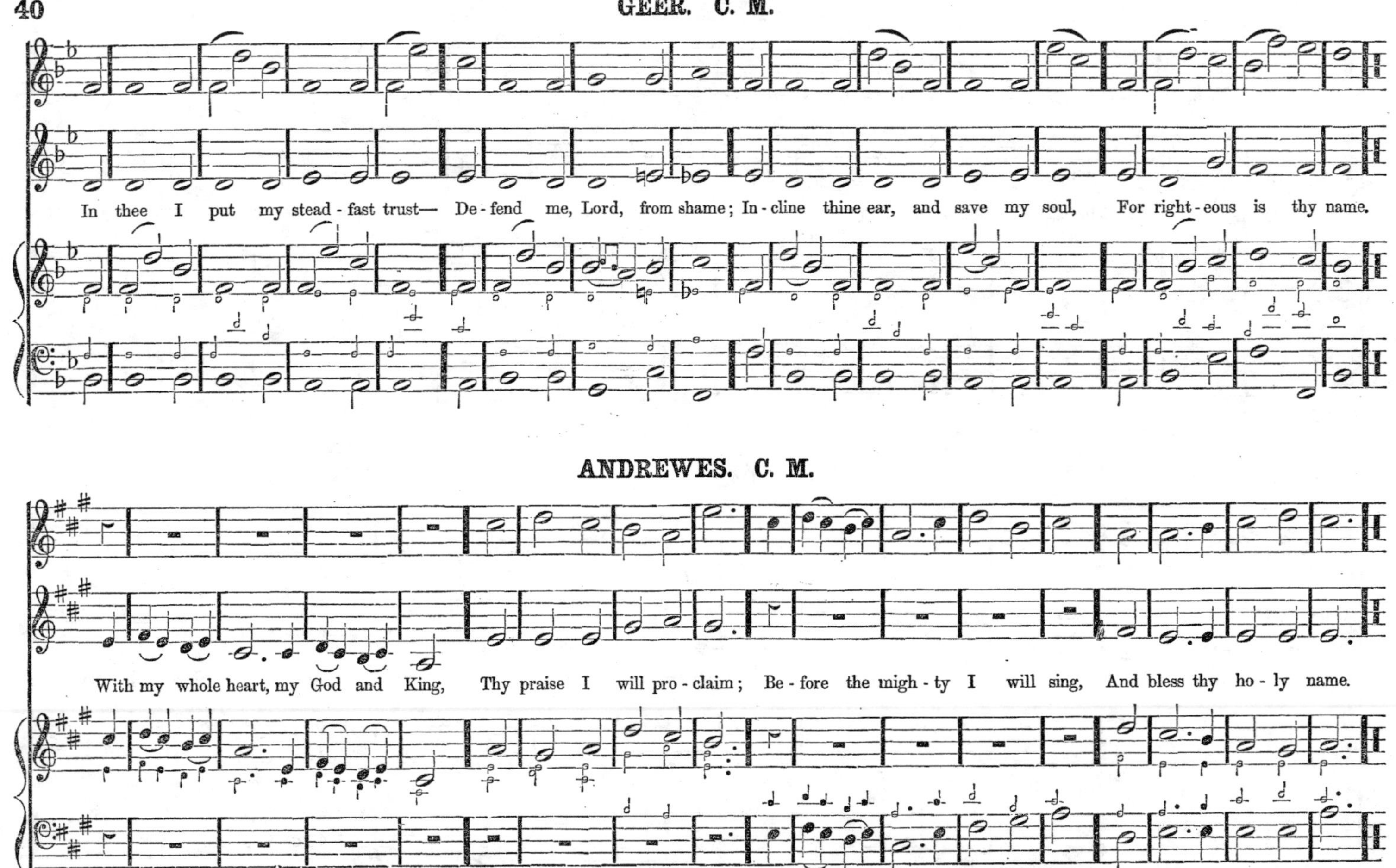
GEER. C. M.
In thee I put my stead - fast trust— De - fend me, Lord, from shame; In - cline thine ear, and save my soul, For right - eous is thy name.
ANDREWES. C. M.
With my whole heart, my God and King, Thy praise I will pro - claim; Be - fore the migh - ty I will sing, And bless thy ho - ly name.

TOTTENHAM. C. M.

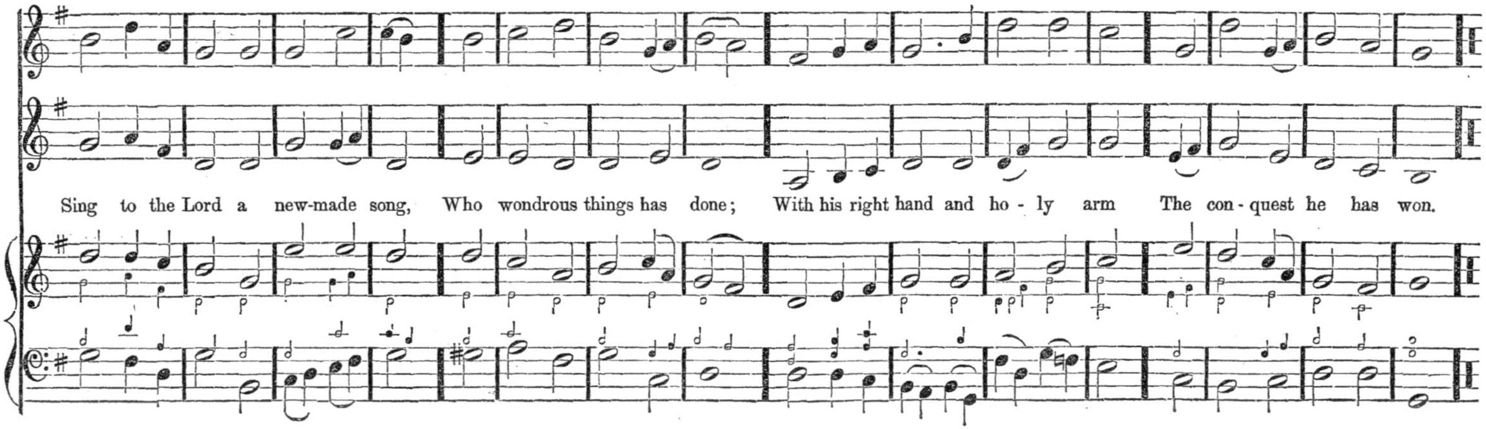

Sing to the Lord a new-made song, Who wondrous things has done; With his right hand and ho - ly arm The con - quest he has won.

BEMERTON. C. M.

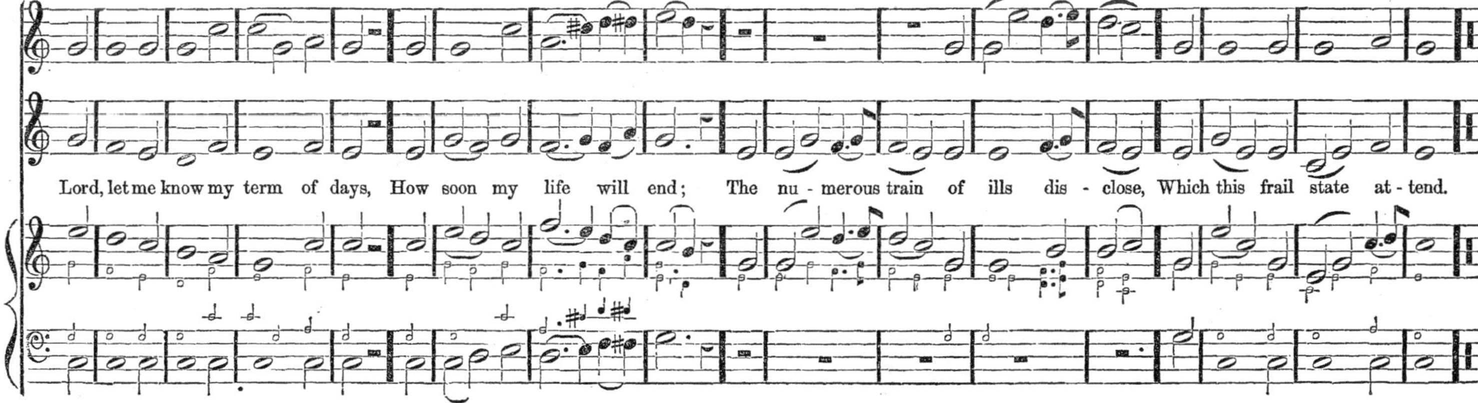

EASTHAM. C. M.

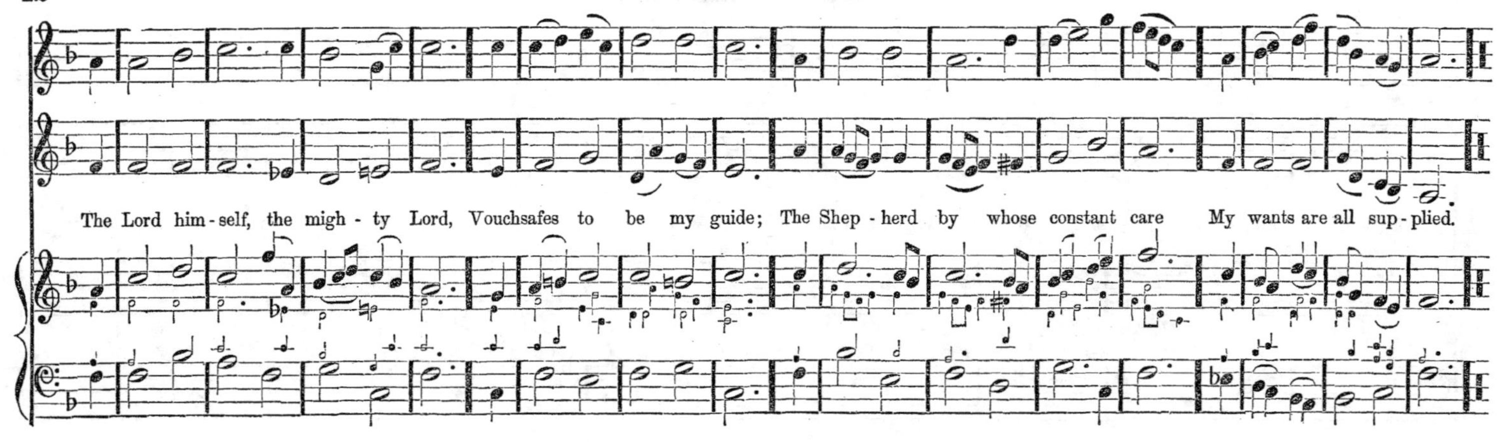

BURTON. C. M.

ST. STEPHEN'S. C. M.

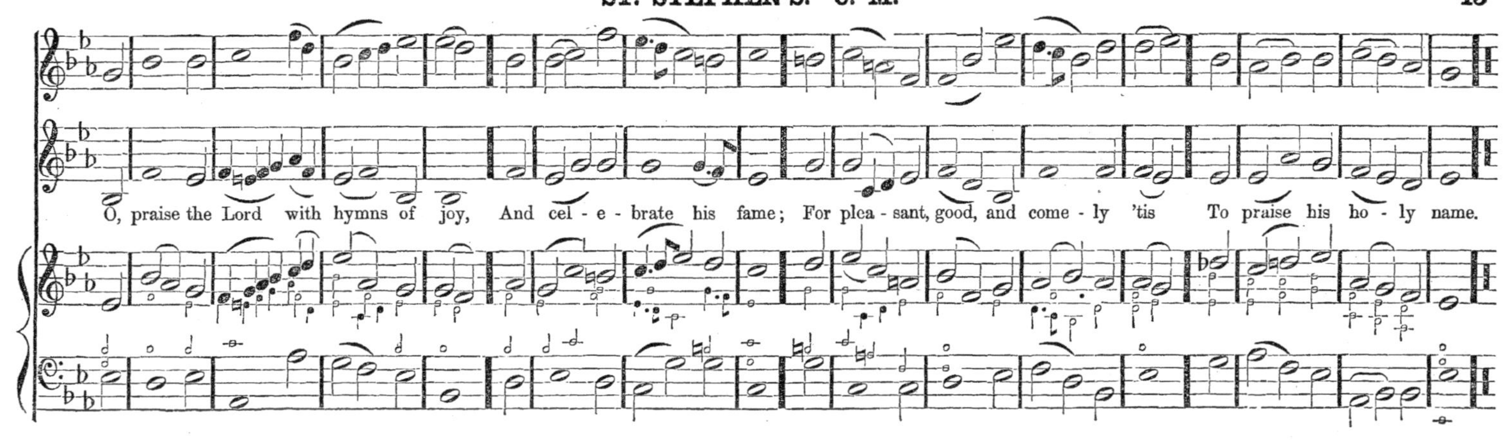

BORNE. C. M.

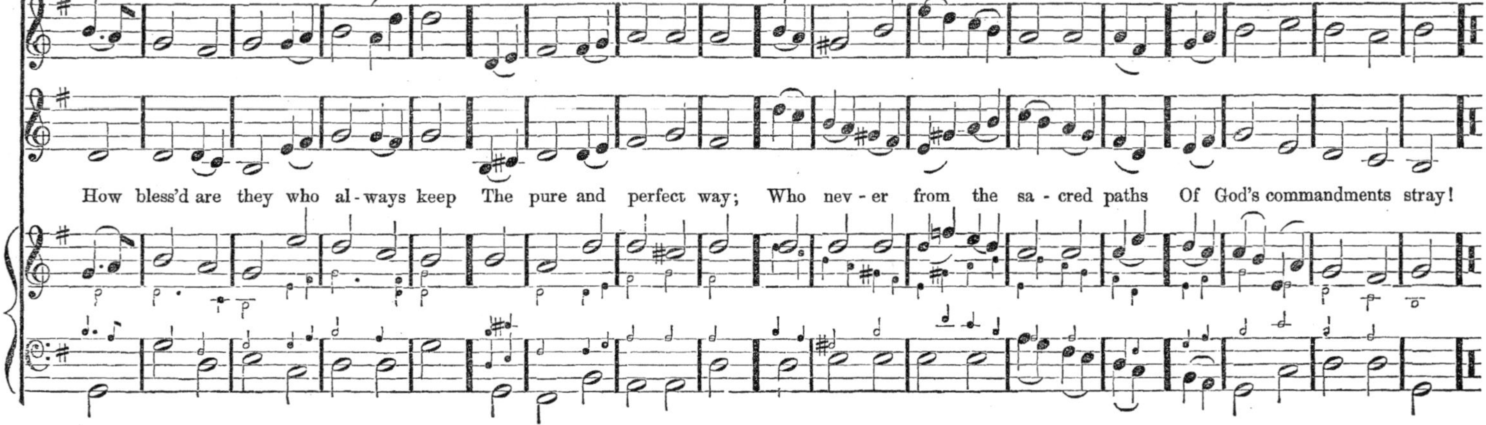

DAYSPRING. C. M.

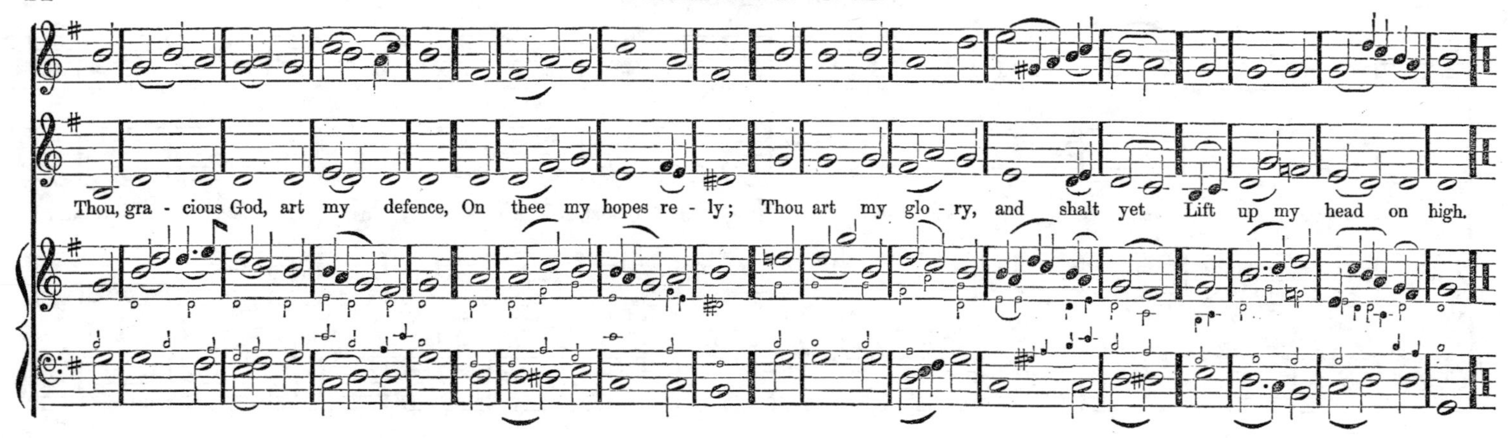

ST. PAUL'S. C. M.

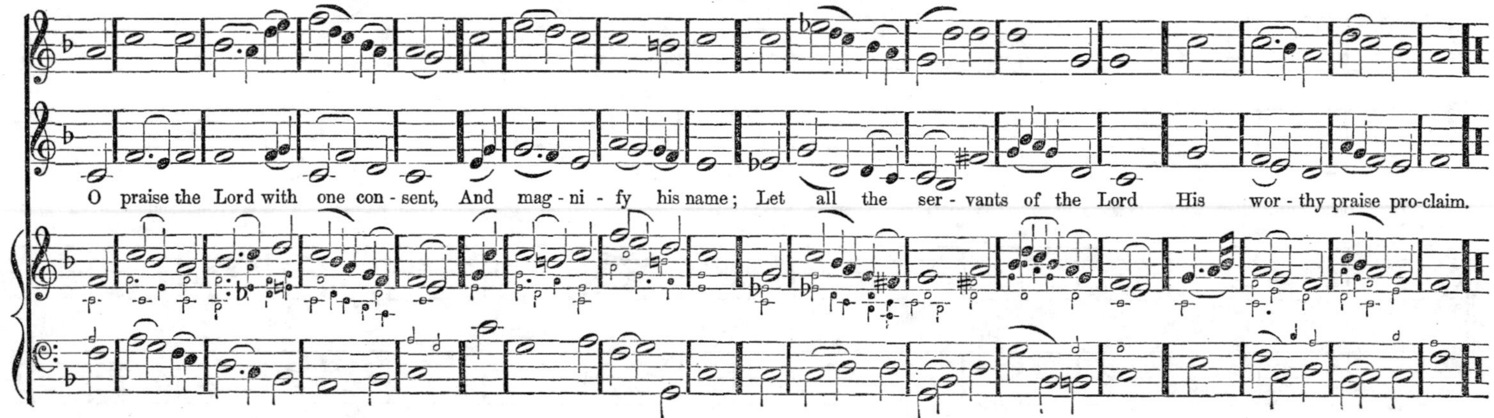

ST. ANSELM. C. M.

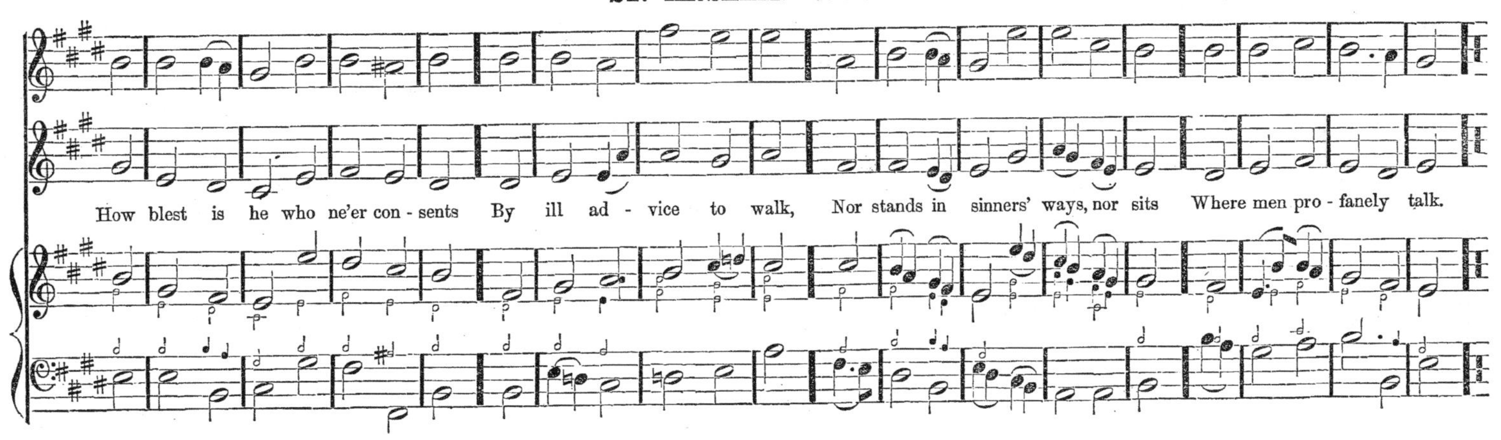

TAYLOR. C. M.

BENONI. C. M.

Do thou, ... O Lord, at - tend;
When I pour out my soul in prayer, Do thou, O Lord, at - tend;
To thy e - ter - nal throne of grace Let my sad cry as - cend, Let my sad cry as - cend.

ST. GEORGE'S. C. M.

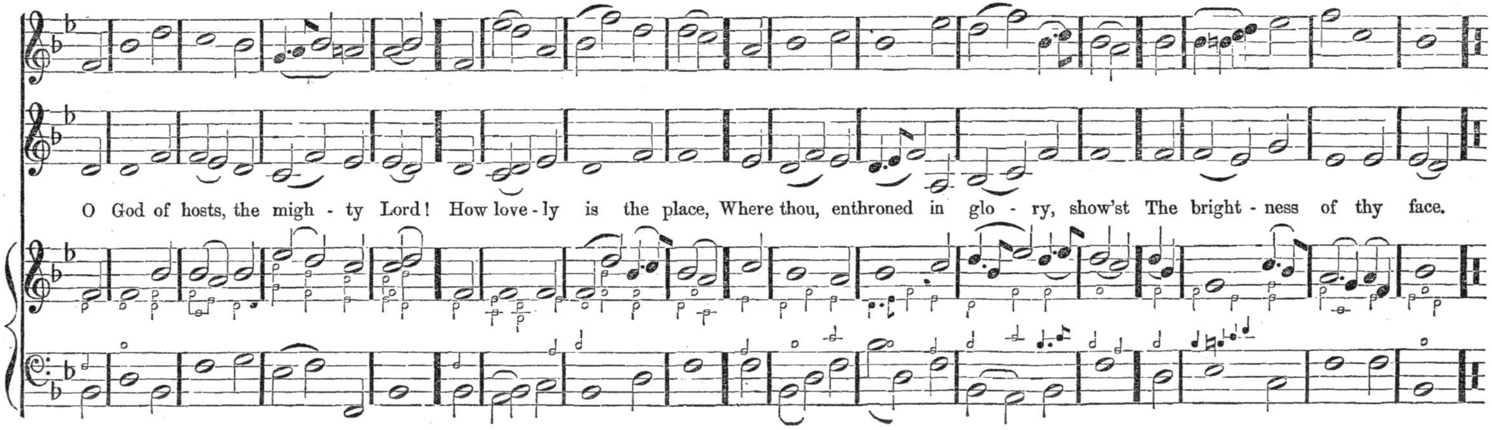
O God of hosts, the migh - ty Lord! How love - ly is the place, Where thou, enthroned in glo - ry, show'st The bright - ness of thy face.

TRENT. C. M.

How long wilt thou for - get me, Lord? Must I for ev - er mourn? How long wilt thou withdraw from me, O! nev - er to re - turn?

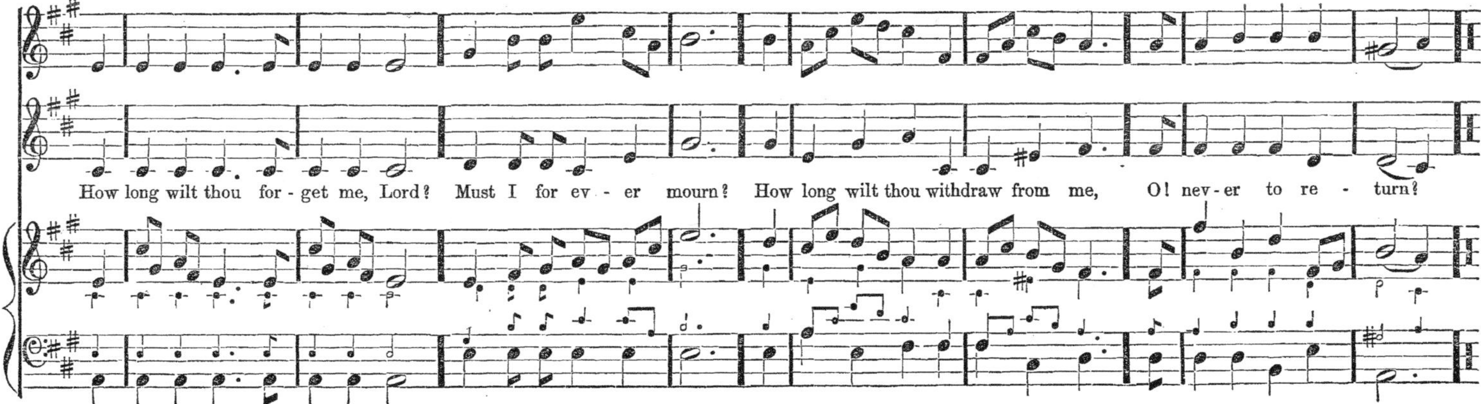

TINTERN ABBEY. C. M.

To my re-quest and earnest cry, At-tend, O gra-cious Lord; In-spire my heart with heavenly skill, Ac-cord-ing to thy word.

CLIFTON. C. M.

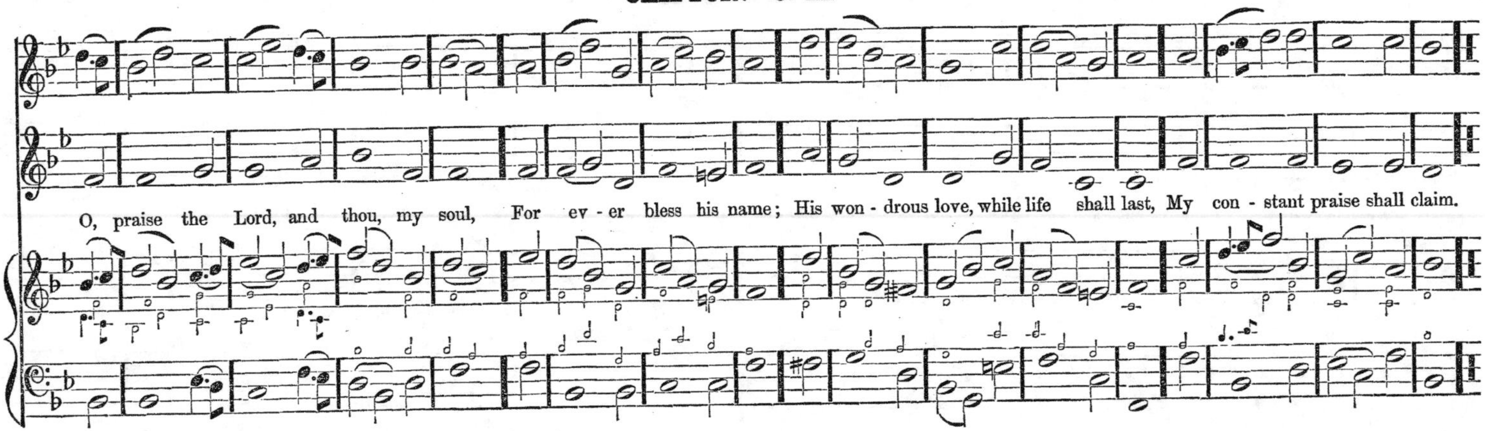

O, praise the Lord, and thou, my soul, For ev-er bless his name; His won-drous love, while life shall last, My con-stant praise shall claim.

ST. MARK'S. C. M.

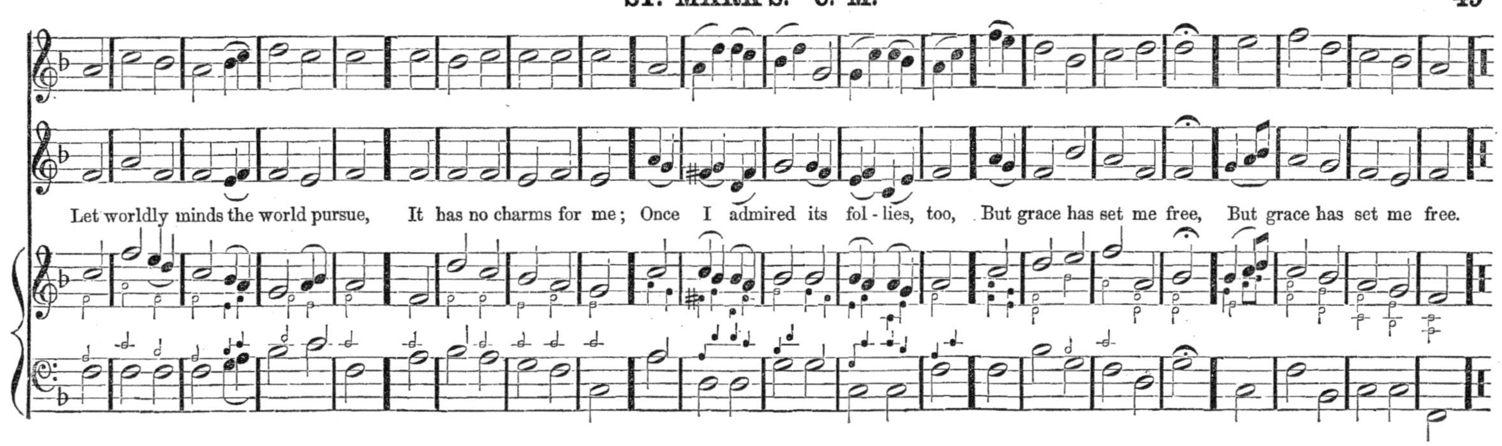

STRASBURGH. C. M.

MANHEIM. C. M.

For ev - er and for ev - er, Lord, Un - changed thou dost re - main; Thy word, es - tab - lished in the heavens,

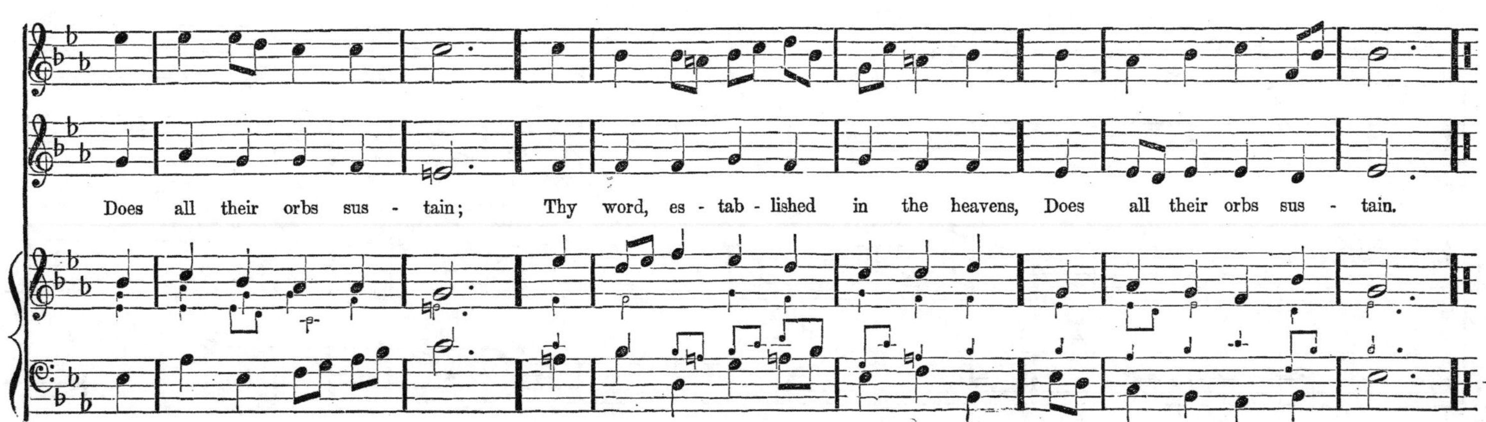
Does all their orbs sus - tain; Thy word, es - tab - lished in the heavens, Does all their orbs sus - tain.

OLD HUNDREDTH. L. M.*

* The Harmony as it was printed in the first English collection of Psalm Tunes, published in 1592.

THE HUNDREDTH PSALM. L. M.

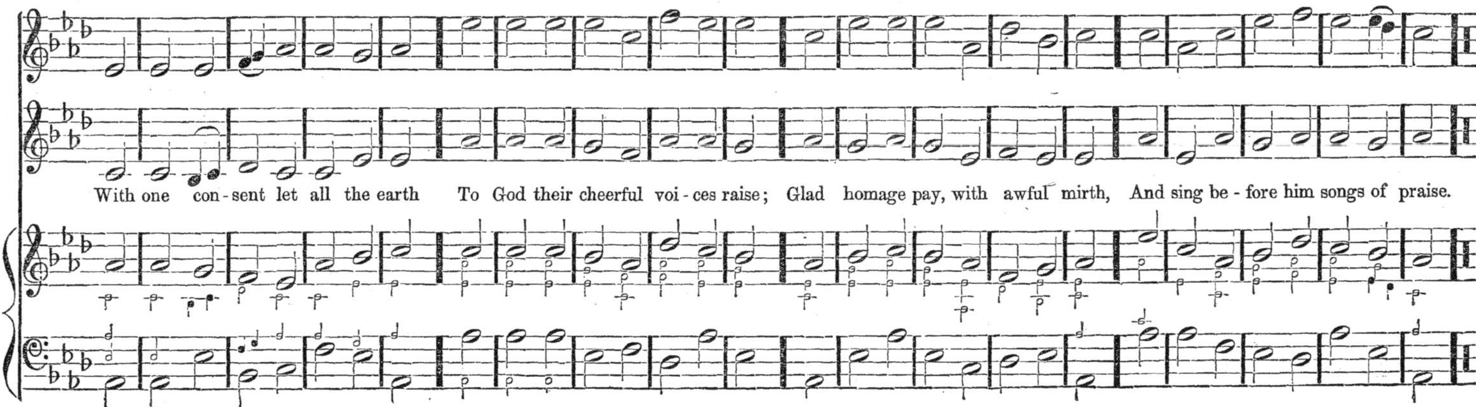

IVY BRIDGE. L. M.

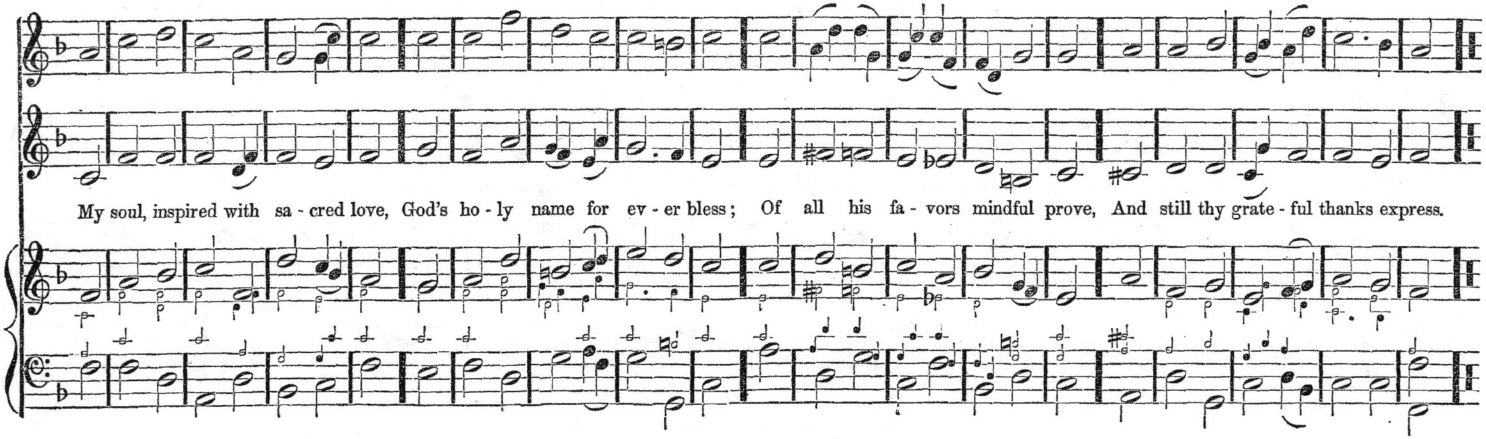
My soul, inspired with sa - cred love, God's ho - ly name for ev - er bless; Of all his fa - vors mindful prove, And still thy grate - ful thanks express.

SUMNER. L. M.

O thou, whom heavenly hosts o - bey, How long shall thy fierce an - ger burn? How long thy suffering people pray, And to their prayers have no re - turn?

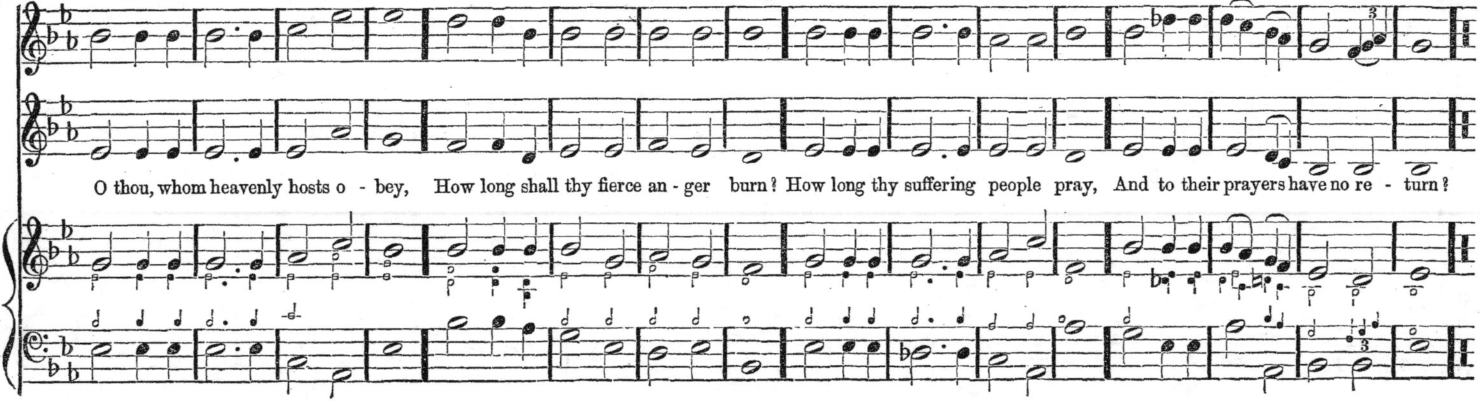

MELCOMBE. L. M.

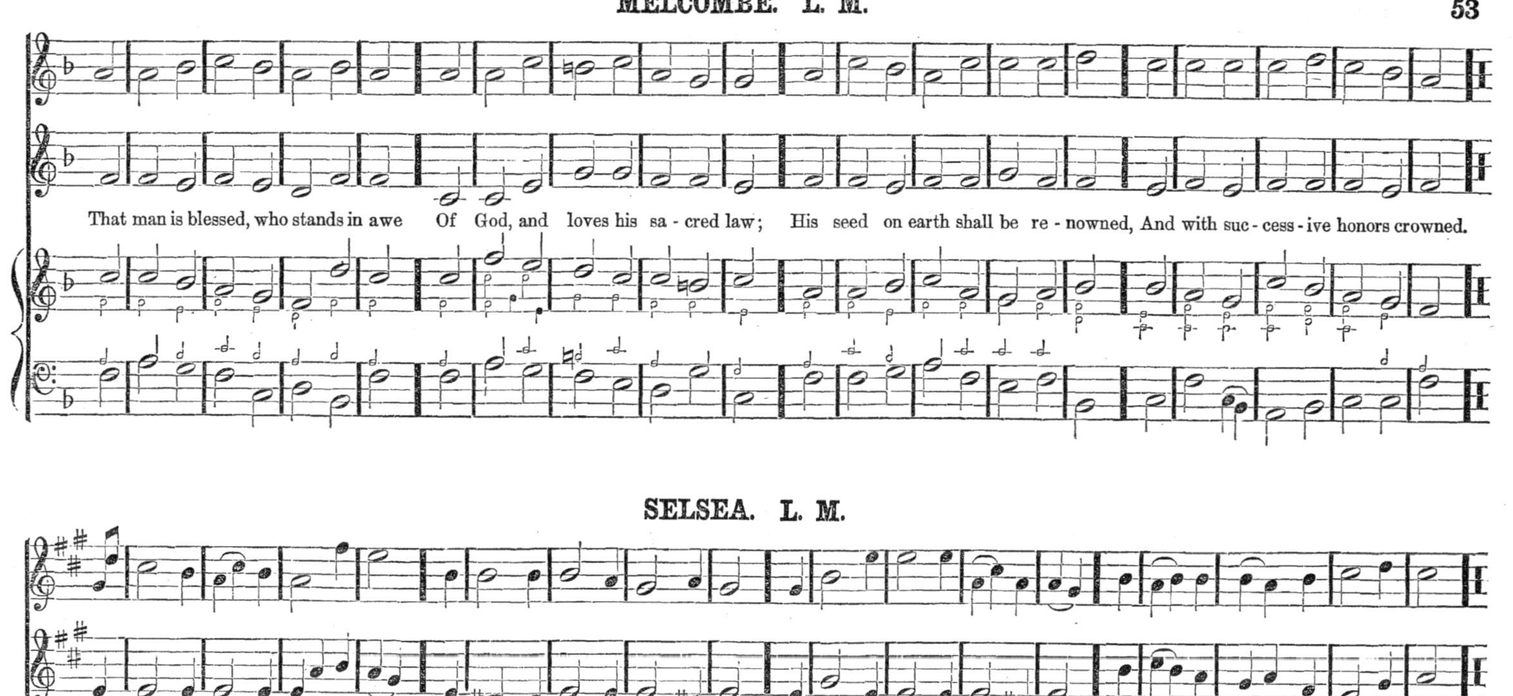

SELSEA. L. M.

I wait - ed meek - ly for the Lord, Till he vouchsafed a kind re - ply; Who did his gracious ear af - ford, And heard from heaven my humble cry.

ANGEL'S SONG. L. M.

FERRAR. L. M.

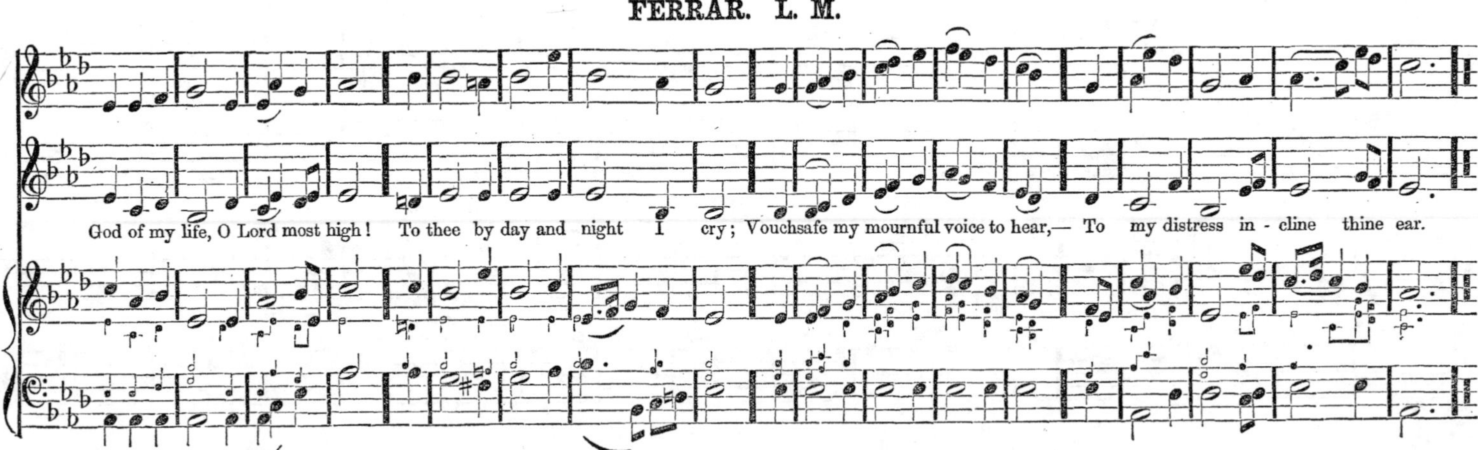

ST. BEDE. L. M.

Let me with light and truth be blessed, Be these my guides to lead the way; Till on thy ho - ly hill I rest, And in thy sacred tem - ple pray.

SALVATION. L. M.

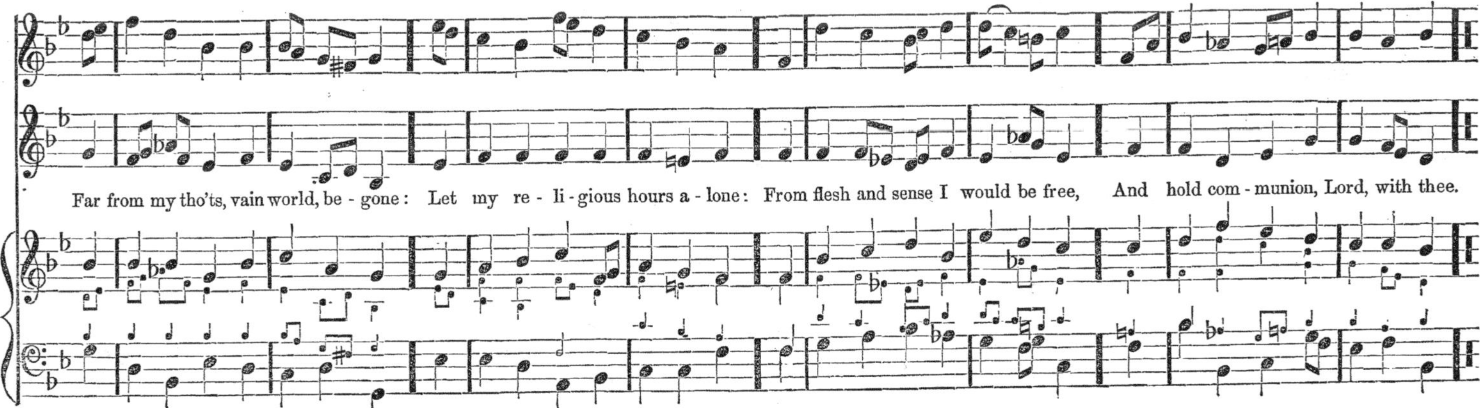

WAREHAM. L. M.

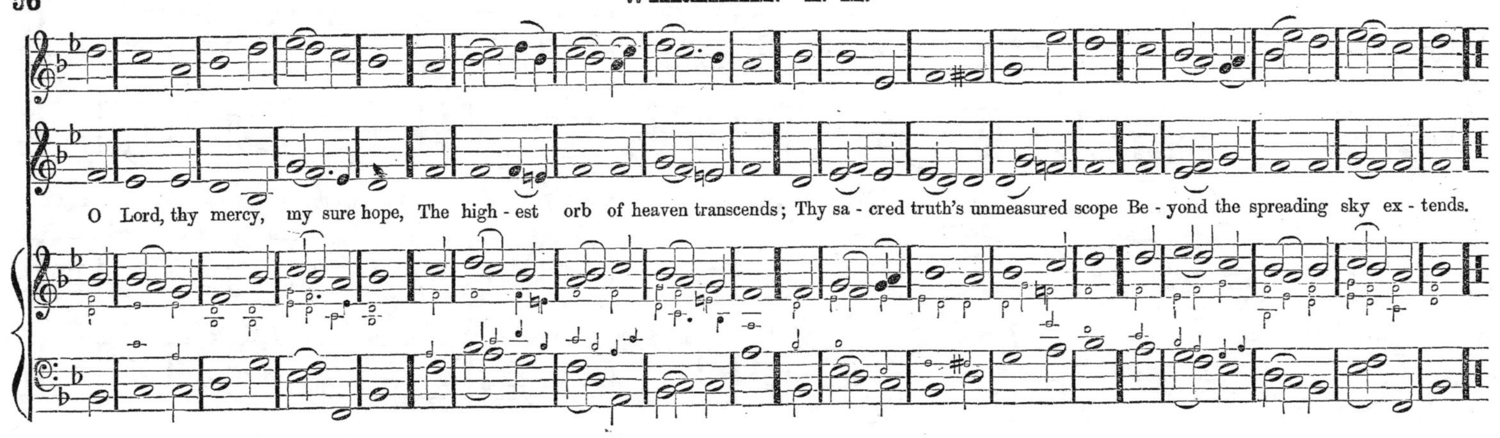

MARLBOROUGH. L. M.

ST. PANCRAS. L. M.

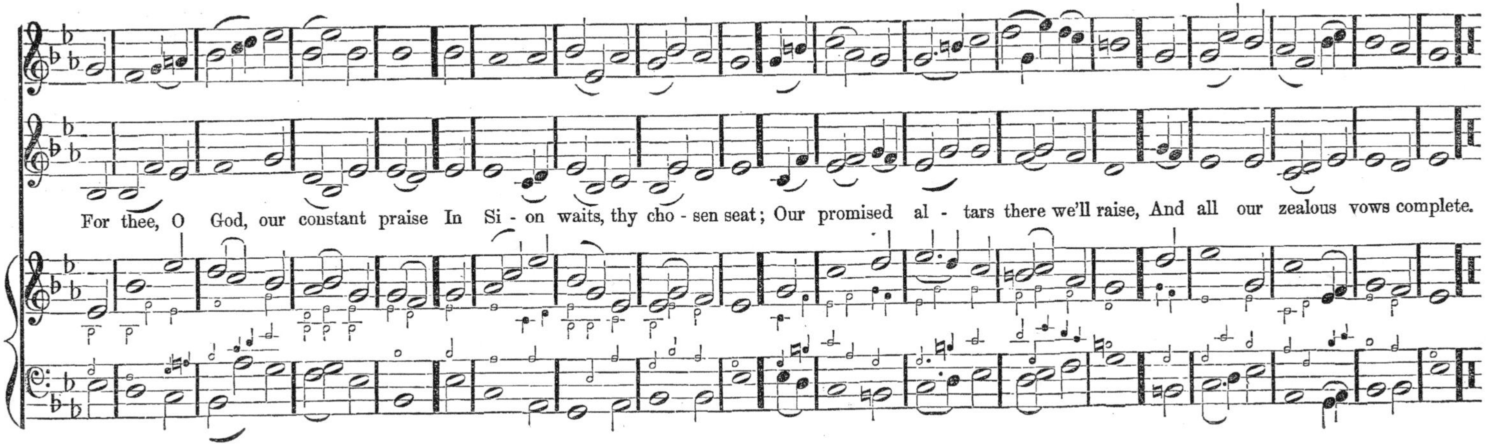

For thee, O God, our constant praise In Si - on waits, thy cho - sen seat; Our promised al - tars there we'll raise, And all our zealous vows complete.

ST. OLAVE'S. L. M.

Praise ye the Lord! our God to praise My soul her utmost power shall raise; With private friends, and in the throng Of saints, his praise shall be my song.

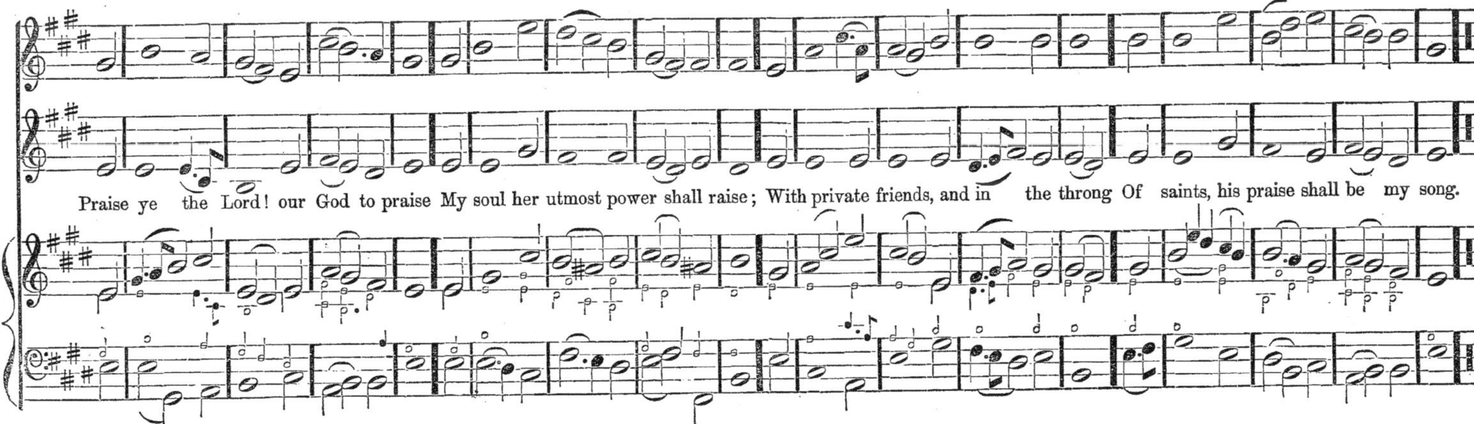

ROCKINGHAM. L. M.

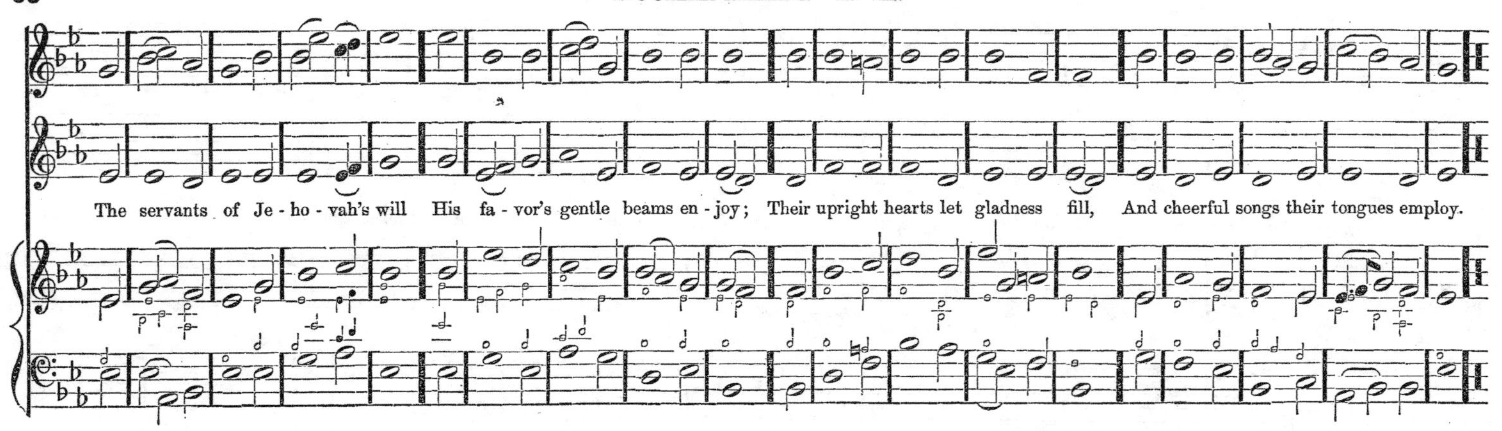

GROSTETE. L. M.

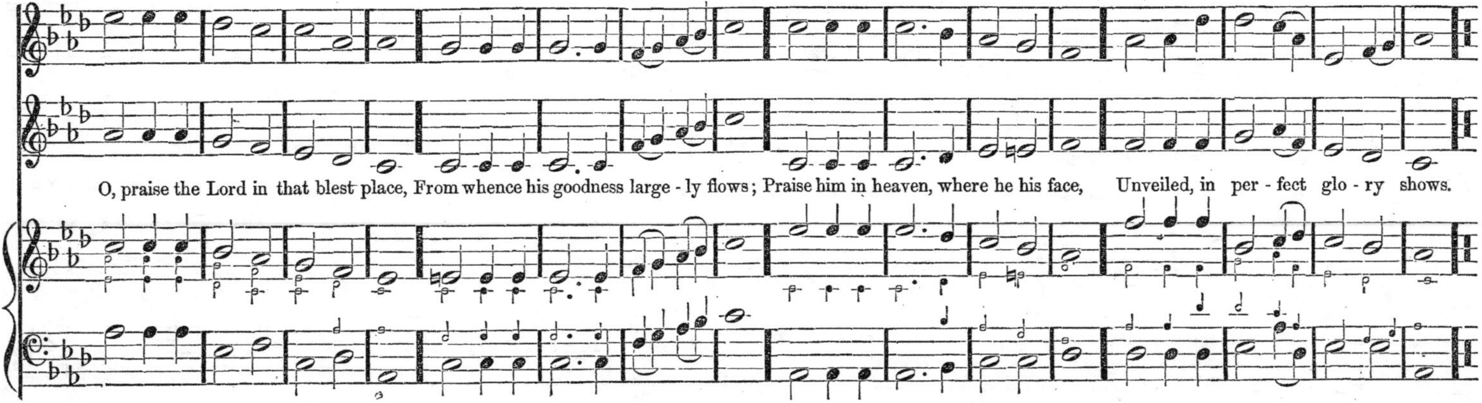

ST. AUSTIN. L. M.

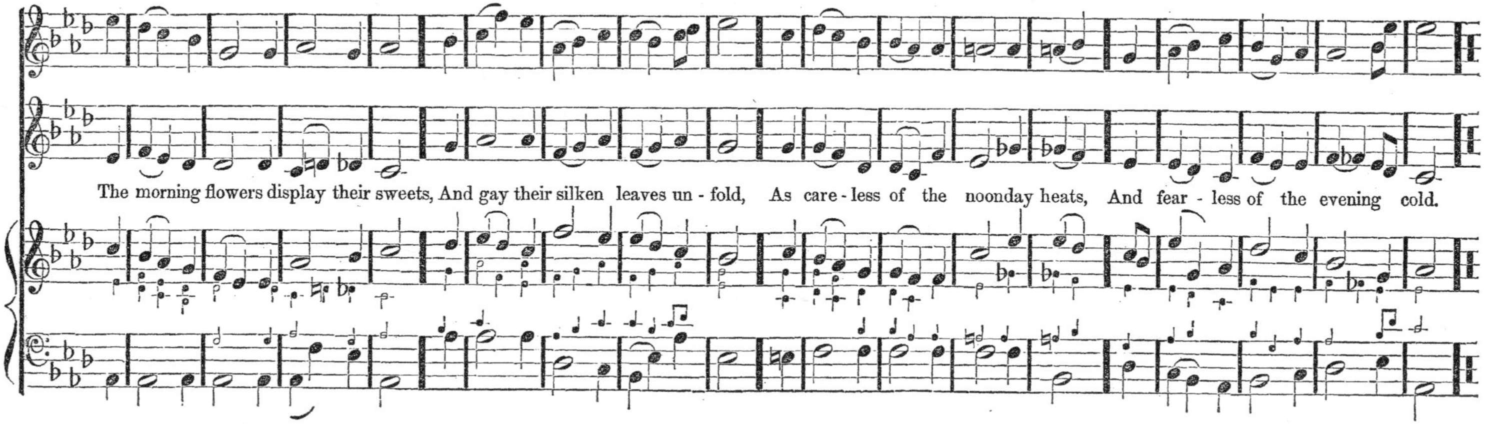
The morning flowers display their sweets, And gay their silken leaves un - fold, As care - less of the noonday heats, And fear - less of the evening cold.

WILLINGTON. L. M.

Thy presence, Lord, hath me supplied, Thou my right hand support dost give; Thou first shalt with thy counsel guide, And then to glo - ry me receive.

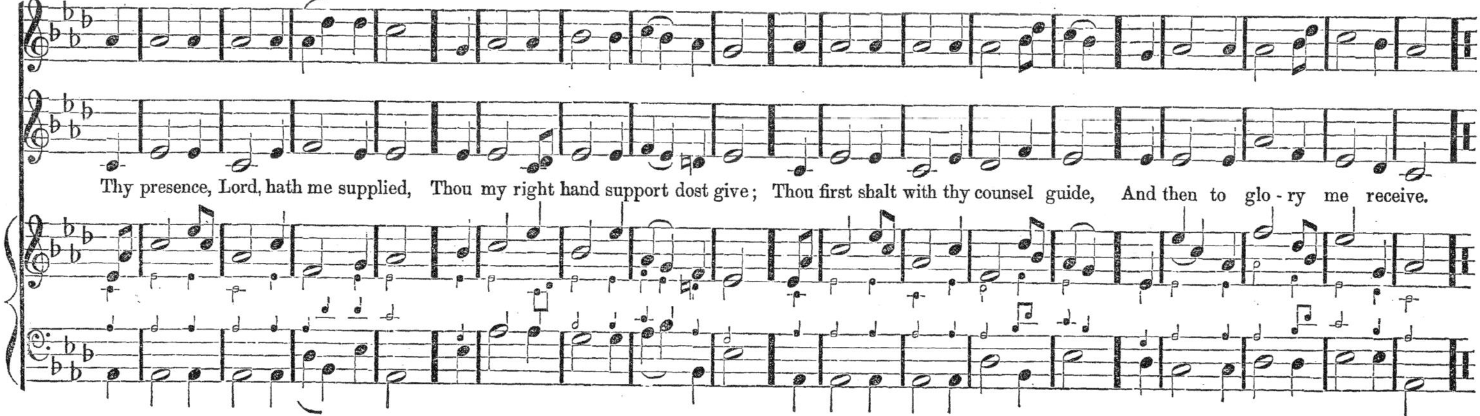

MONMOUTH. L. M.

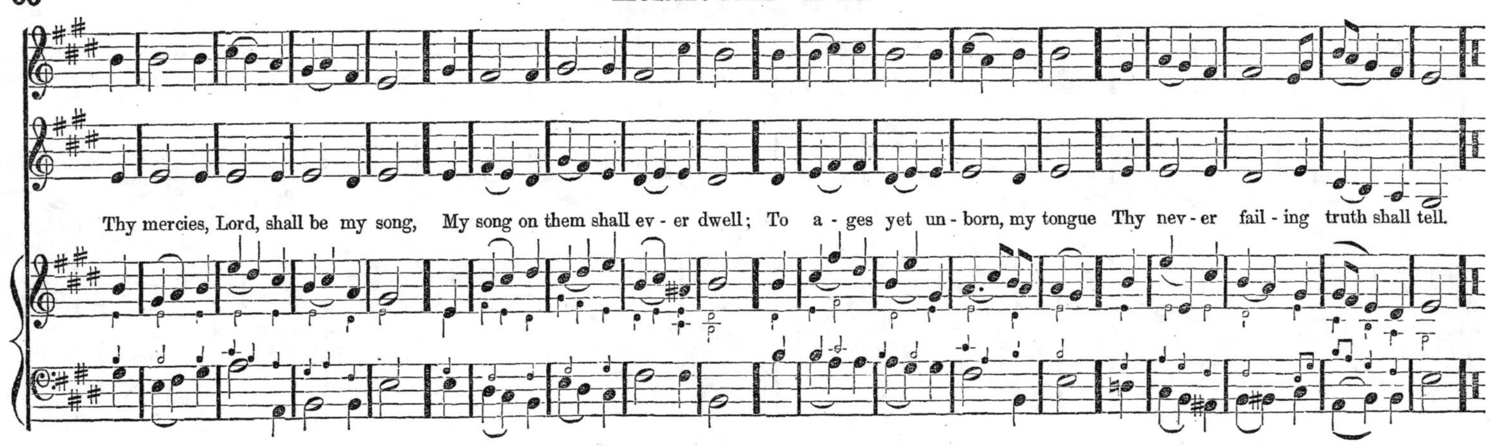

EPPING. L. M.

WESLEY. L. M.

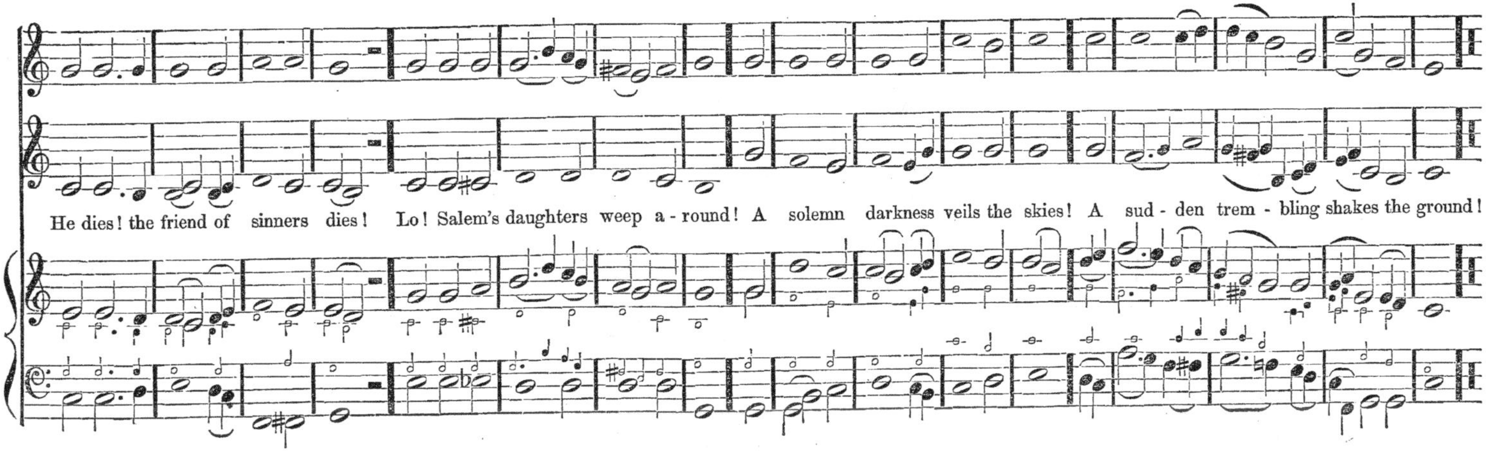

He dies! the friend of sinners dies! Lo! Salem's daughters weep a - round! A solemn darkness veils the skies! A sud - den trem - bling shakes the ground!

LANCASTER. L. M.

How various, Lord, thy works are found, For which thy wisdom we a - dore! The earth is with thy treasure crowned, Till nature's hand can grasp no more.

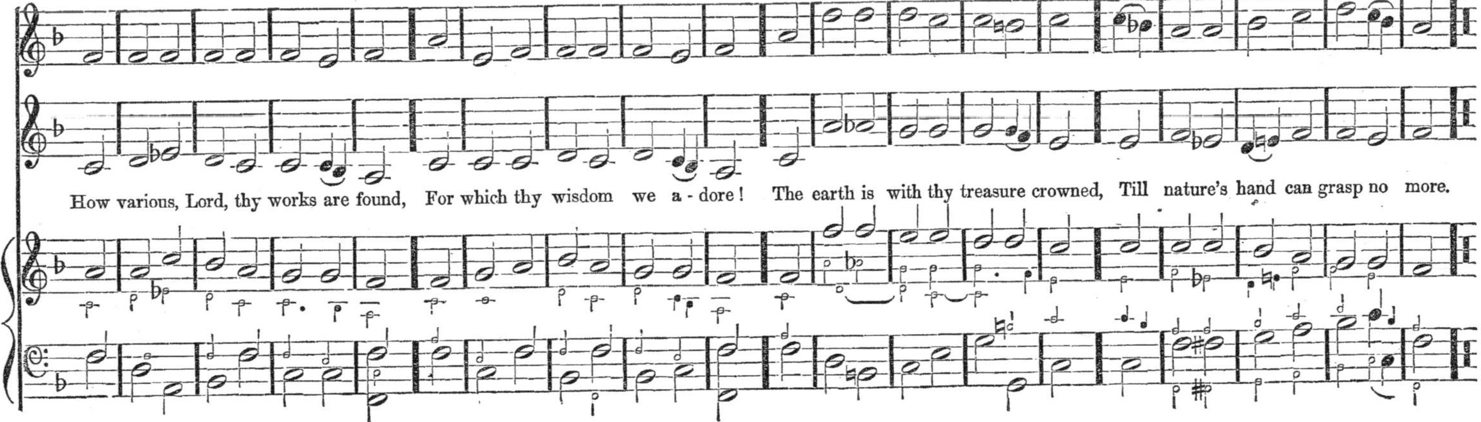

WALTHAMSTOW. L. M.

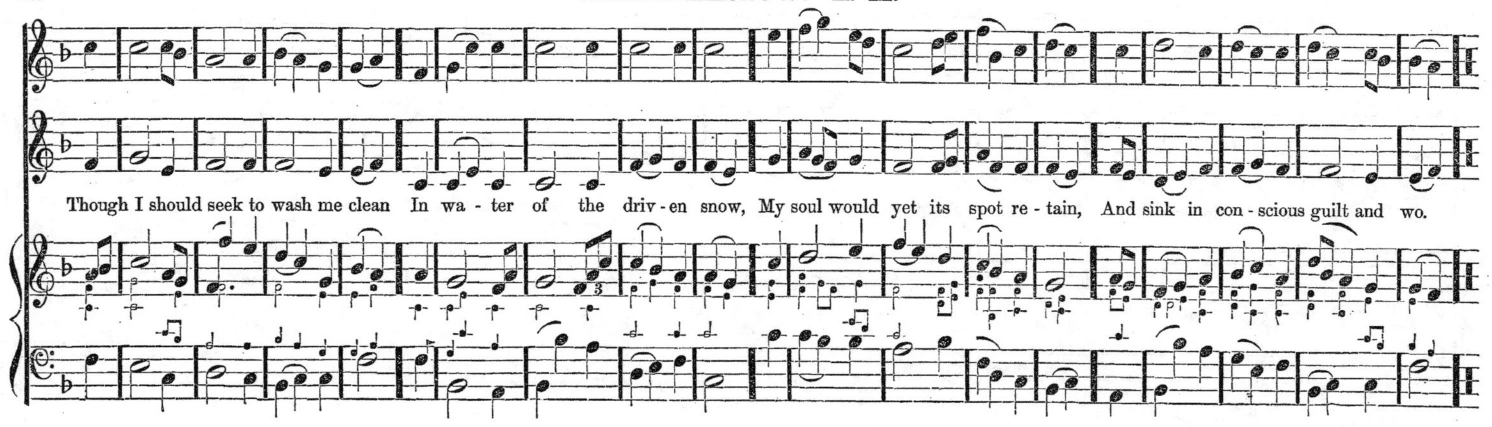

REST. L. M.

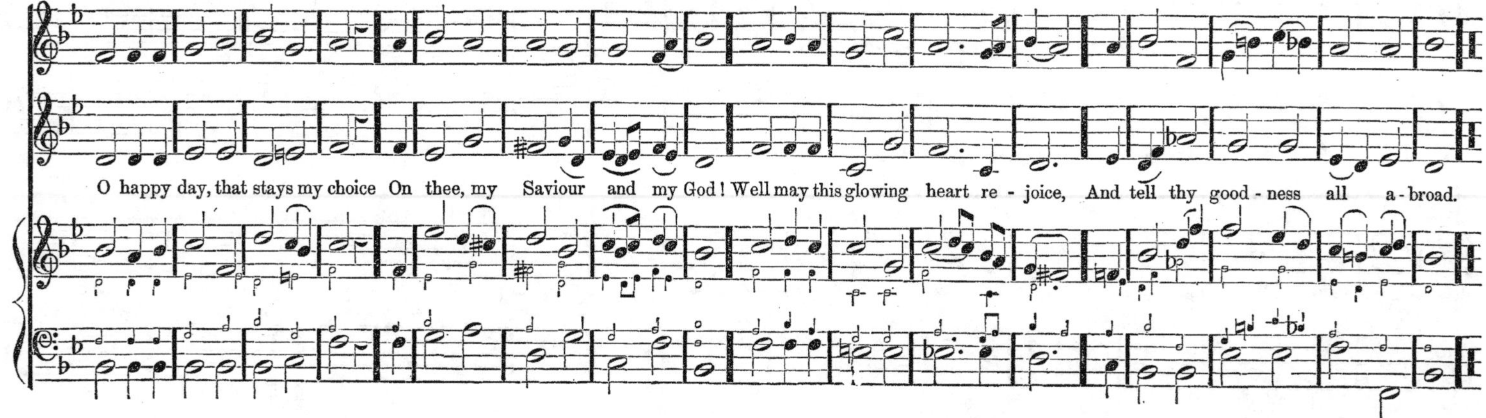

PECKHAM. L. M.

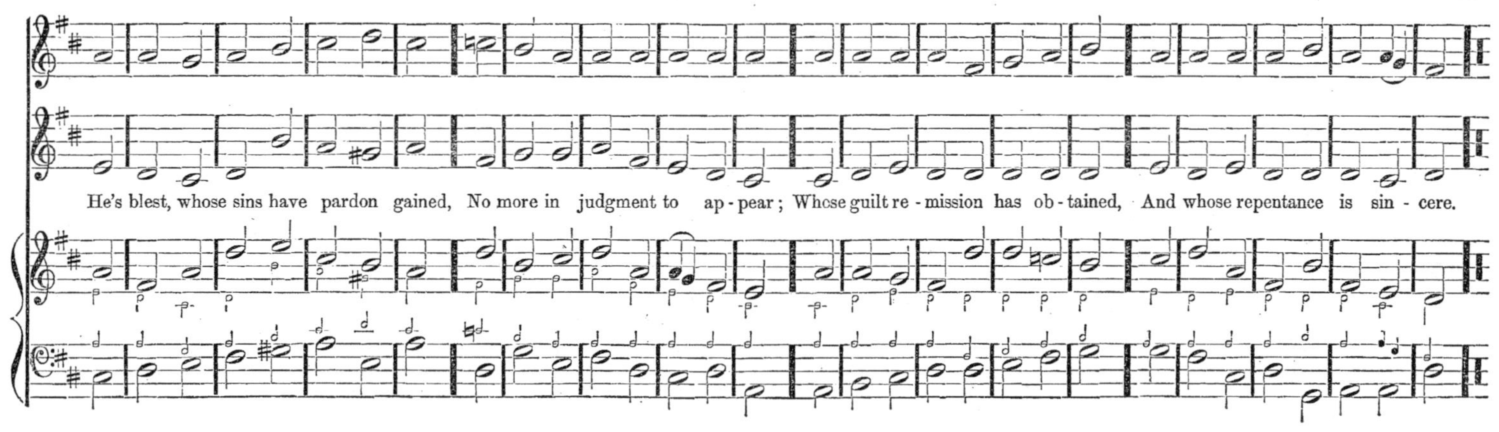

GERMANY. L. M.

BELSHAZZAR. L. M.

DREW. L. M.

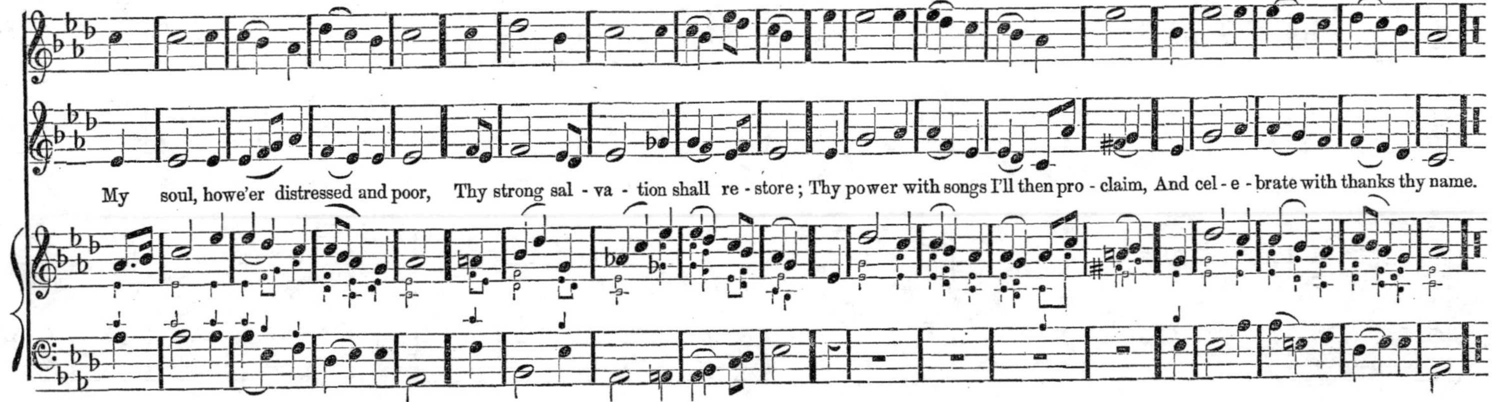

HIGHGATE. L. M.

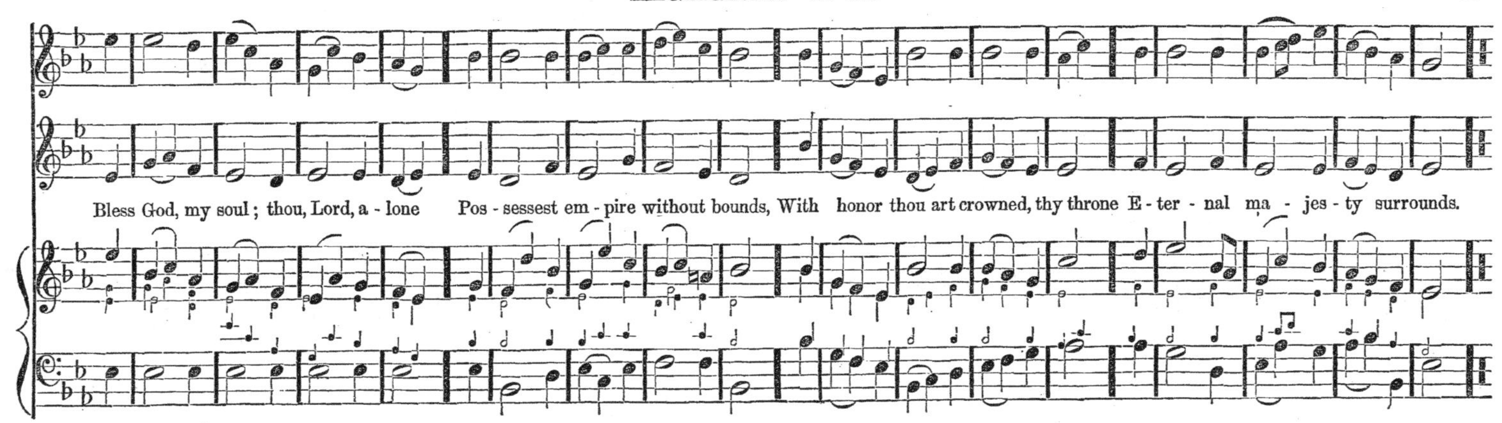

OXFORD. L. M.

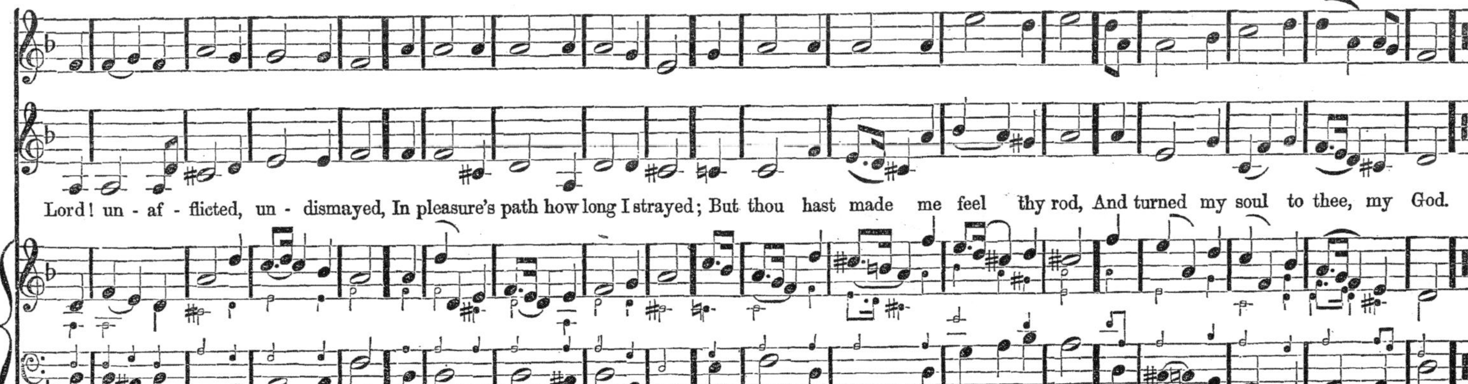

ST. CUTHBERT. L. M.

WILHELM. L. M.

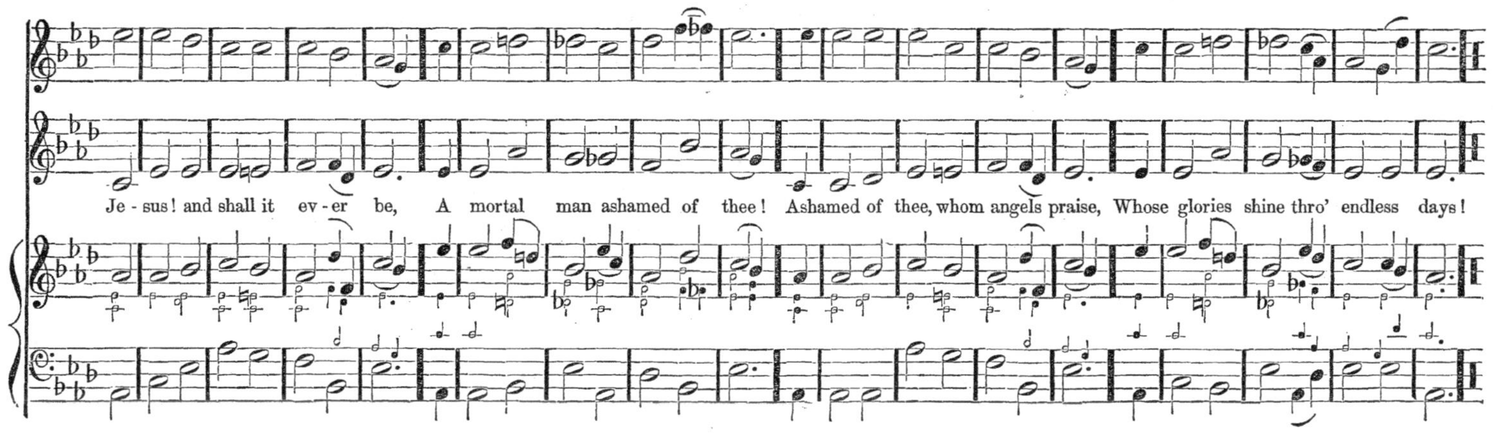

BAUN. L. M.

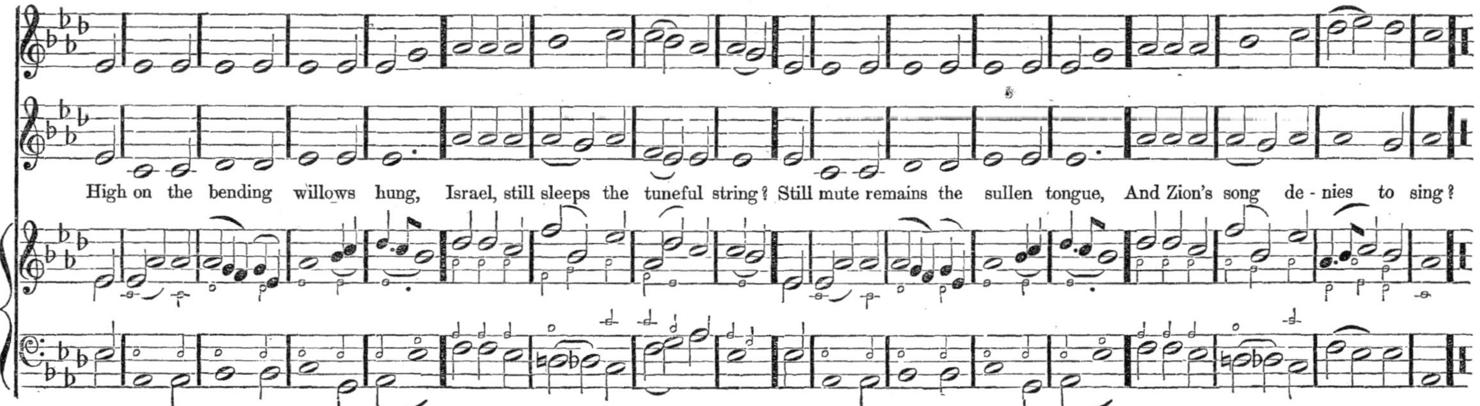

TRURO. L. M.

Ye, that in might and power excel, Your grateful sa - cri - fice pre - pare ; God's glorious actions loud - ly tell, His wondrous power to all de - clare.

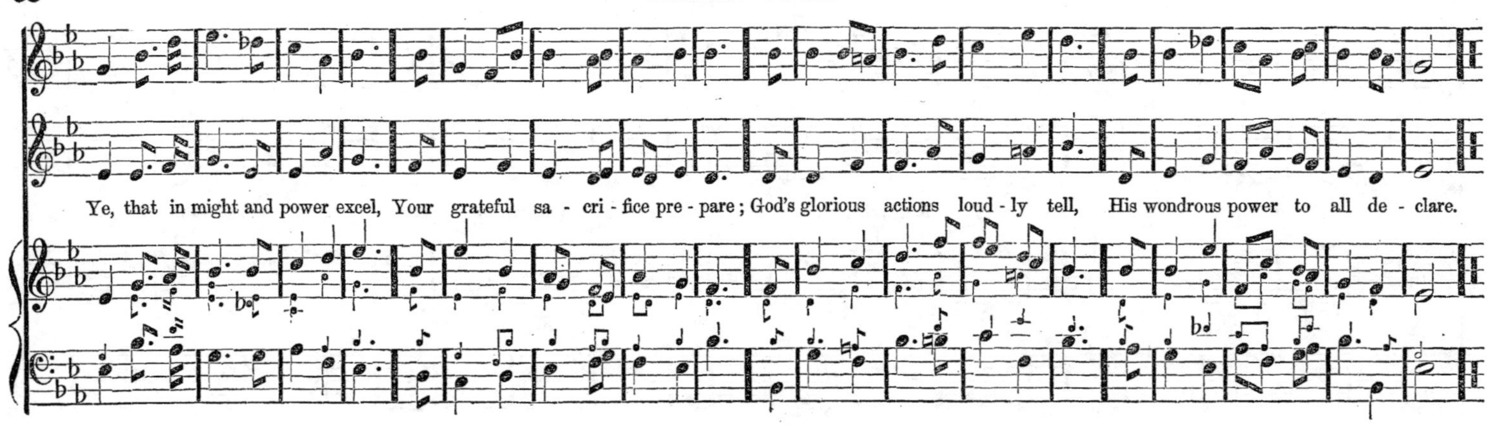

ALFRETON. L. M.

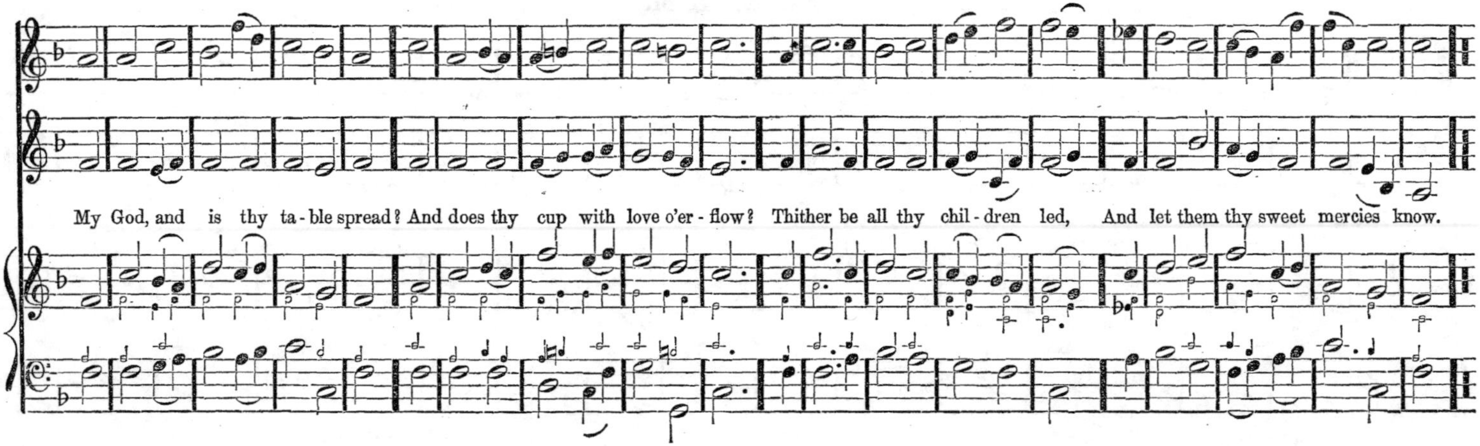
My God, and is thy ta - ble spread? And does thy cup with love o'er - flow? Thither be all thy chil - dren led, And let them thy sweet mercies know.

ROCHESTER. L. M.

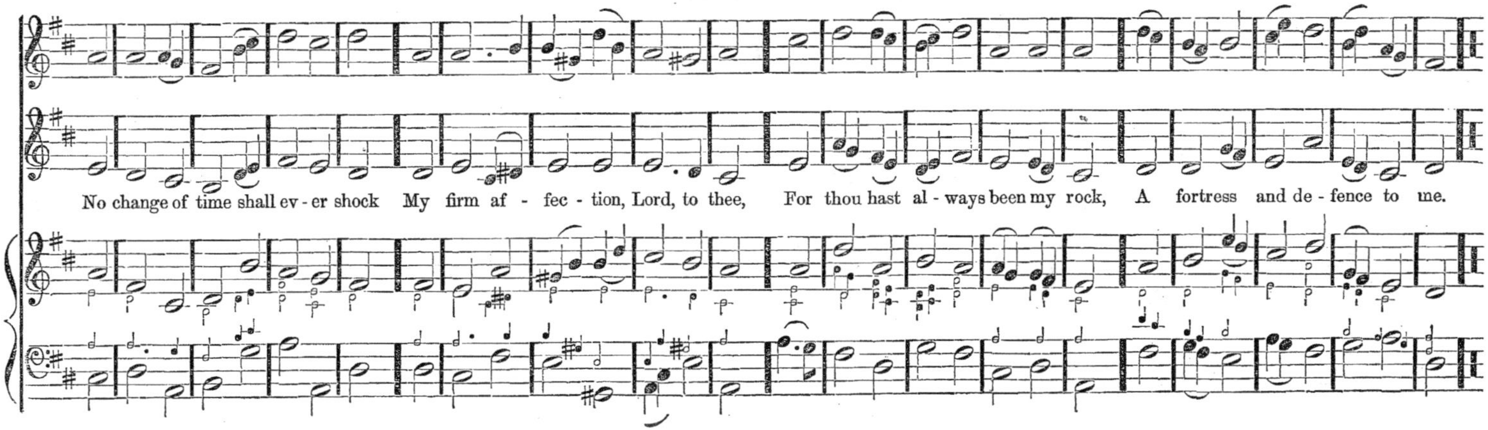
No change of time shall ev - er shock My firm af - fec - tion, Lord, to thee, For thou hast al - ways been my rock, A fortress and de - fence to me.

LOWTH. L. M.

When I sur - vey the wondrous cross On which the Prince of glo - ry died, My richest gain I count but loss, And pour contempt on all my pride.

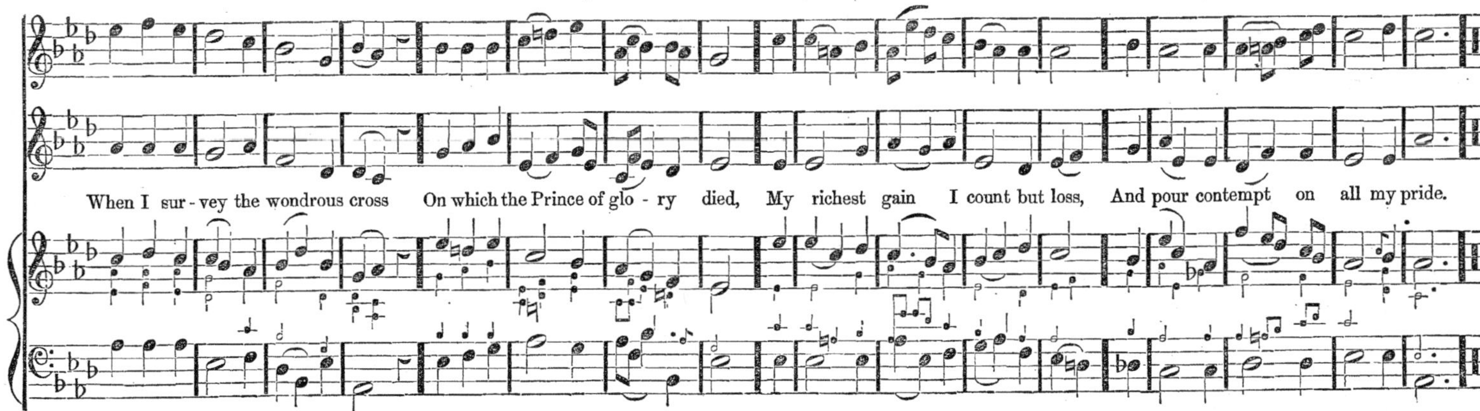

SACRAMENT. L. M.

ST. NEOT'S. L. M.

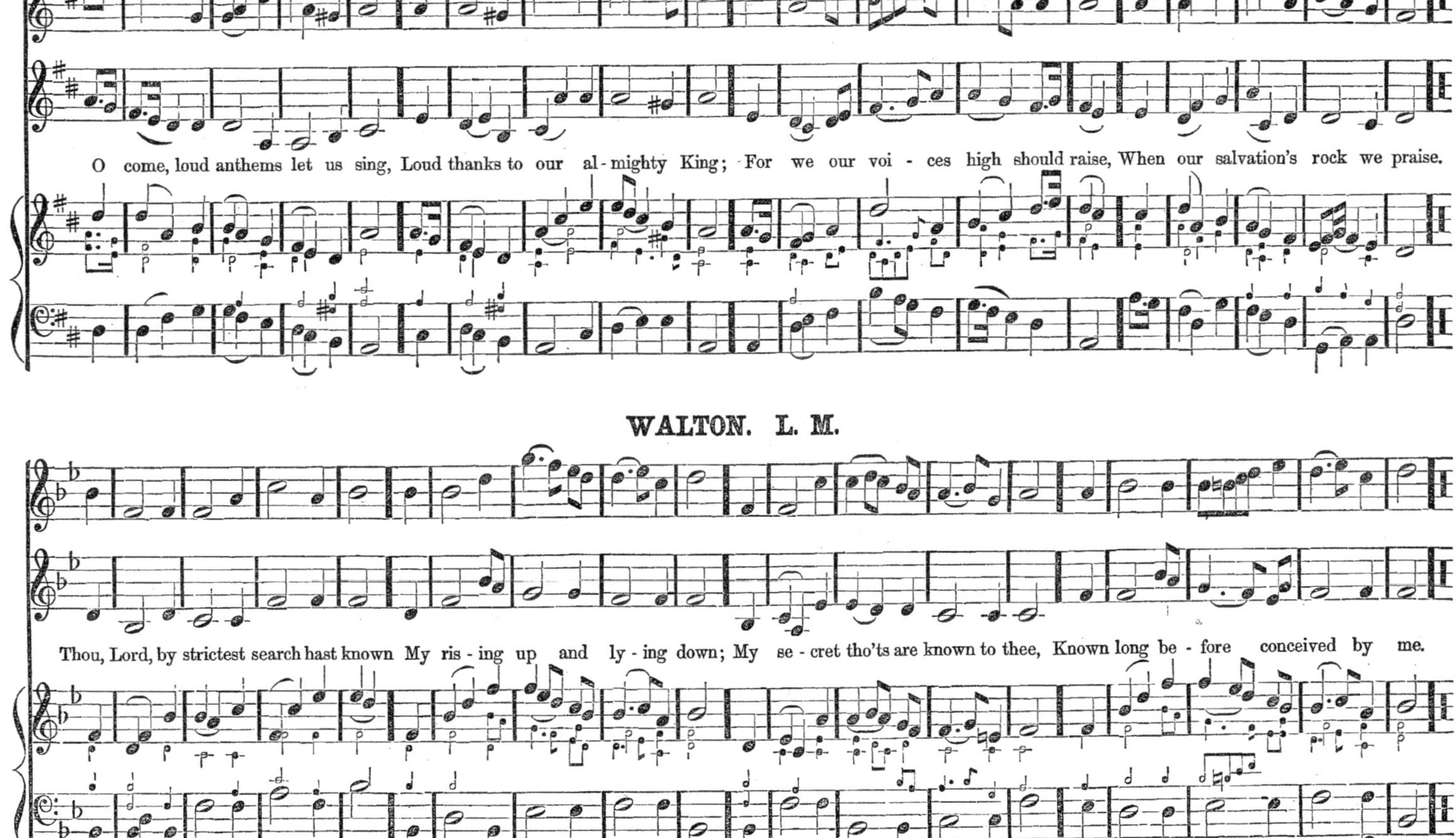
MAGDALEN. L. M.
O come, loud anthems let us sing, Loud thanks to our al - mighty King; For we our voi - ces high should raise, When our salvation's rock we praise.
WALTON. L. M.
Thou, Lord, by strictest search hast known My ris - ing up and ly - ing down; My se - cret tho'ts are known to thee, Known long be - fore conceived by me.

DUNLUCE. L. M.

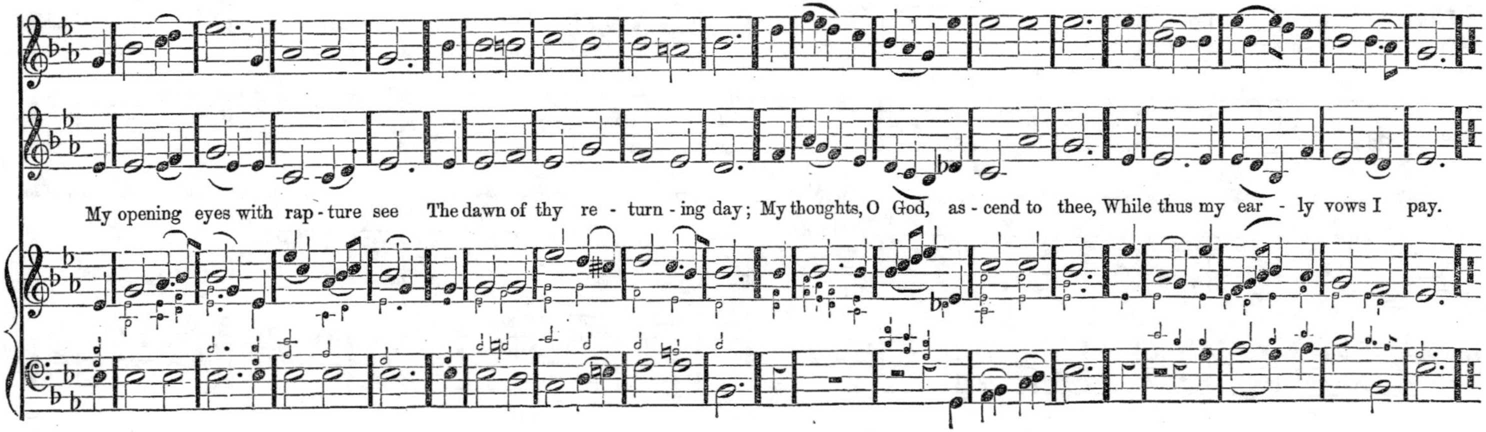
My opening eyes with rap - ture see The dawn of thy re - turn - ing day; My thoughts, O God, as - cend to thee, While thus my ear - ly vows I pay.

VINER. L. M.

My soul, for help on God re - ly, On him a - lone thy trust re - pose; My rock and health will strength supply To bear the shock of all my foes.

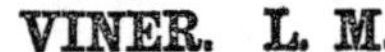

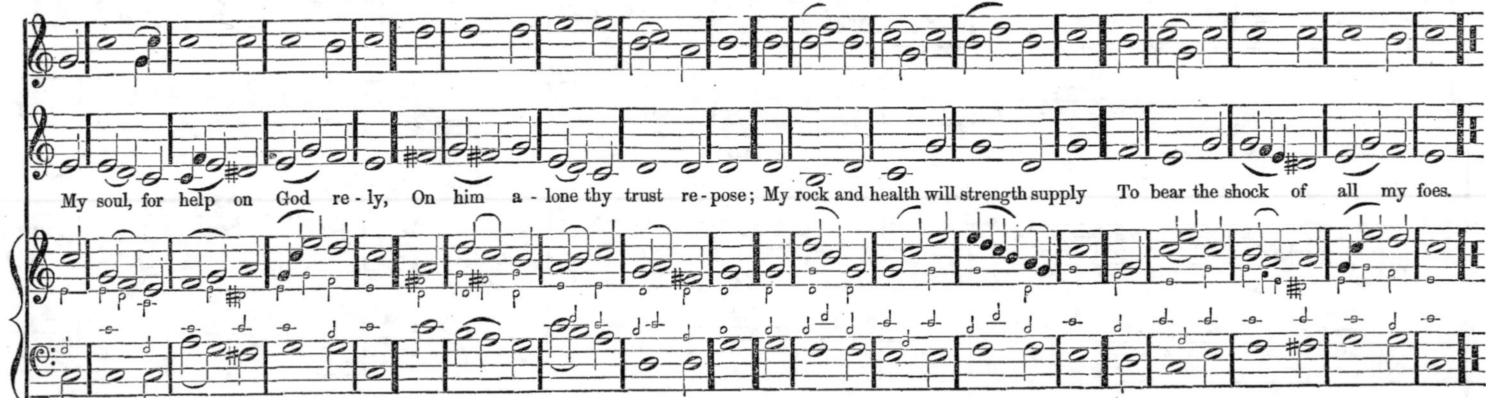

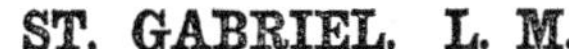

ST. GABRIEL. L. M.

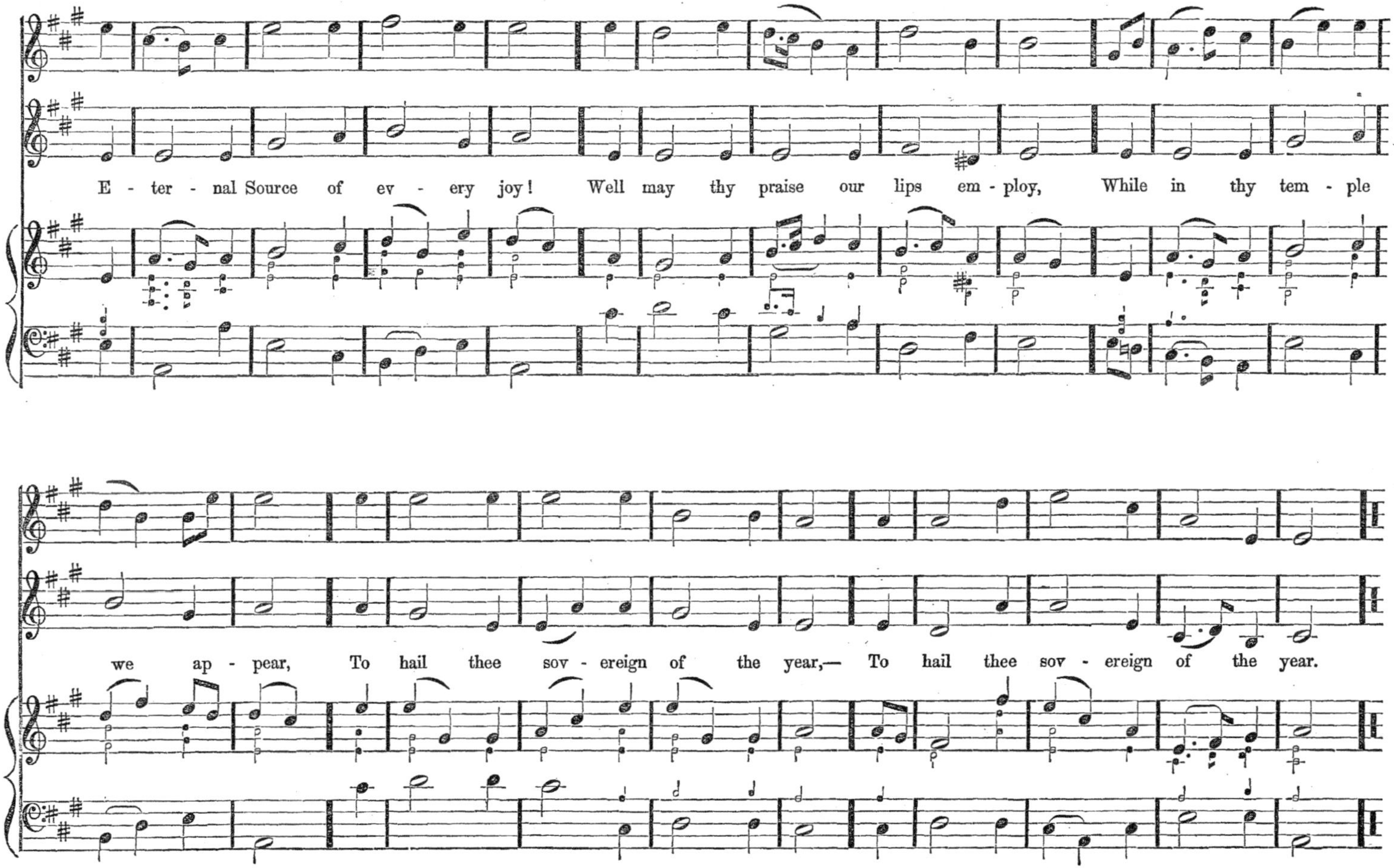

E - ter - nal Source of ev - ery joy! Well may thy praise our lips em - ploy, While in thy tem - ple
we ap - pear, To hail thee sov - ereign of the year,— To hail thee sov - ereign of the year.

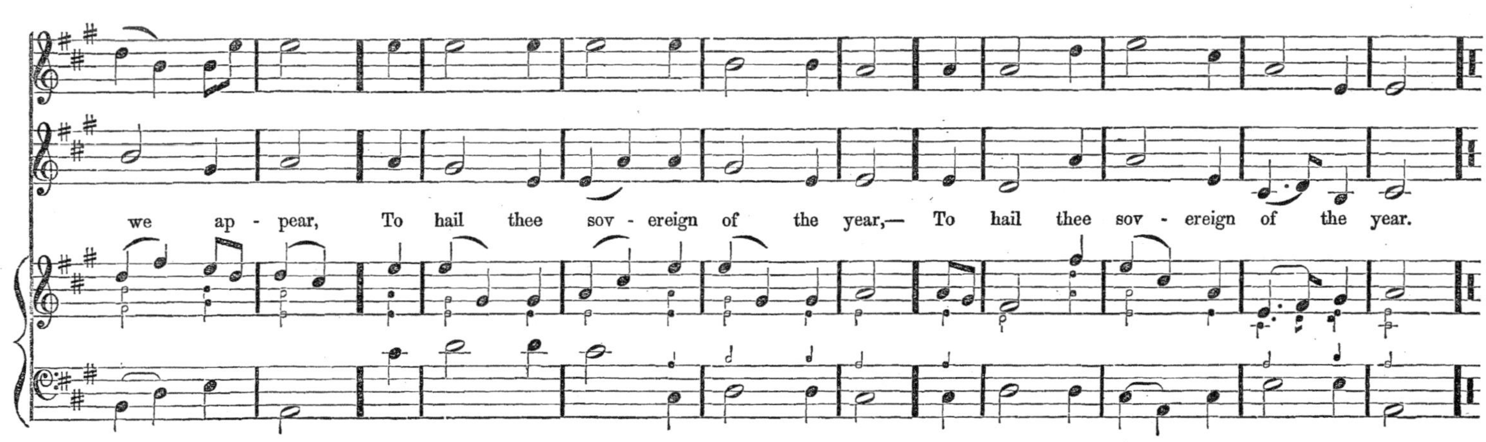

MORNING HYMN. L. M.

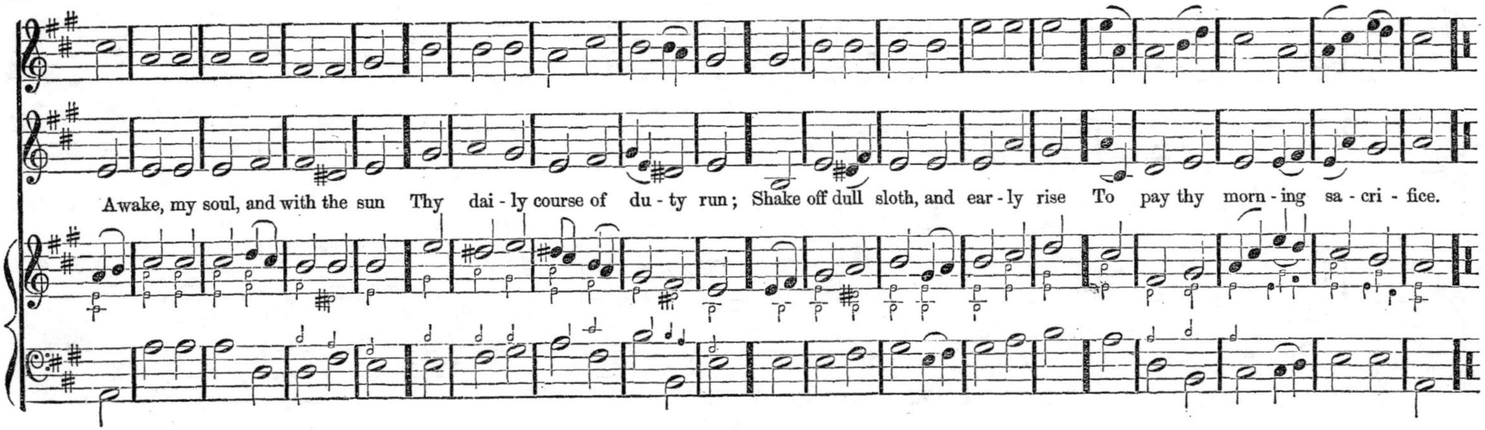

Awake, my soul, and with the sun Thy dai - ly course of du - ty run; Shake off dull sloth, and ear - ly rise To pay thy morn - ing sa - cri - fice.

EVENING HYMN. L. M.

Glo - ry to thee, my God, this night, For all the blessings of the light; Keep me, O keep me, King of kings, Un - der thine own al - migh - ty wings.

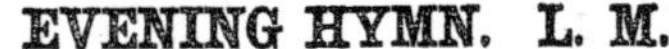

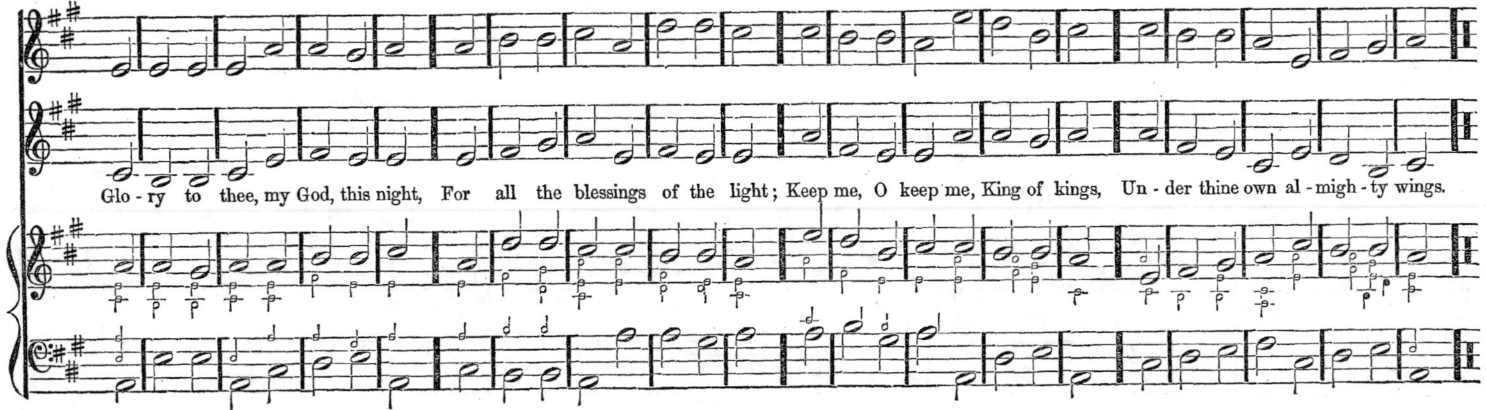

'Tis finished— so the Sa - viour cried, And meekly bowed his head and died; 'Tis finished— yes, the
work is done, The bat - tle fought, the vic - tory won,— The bat - tle fought, the vic - tory won.

WIMBORNE. L. M.

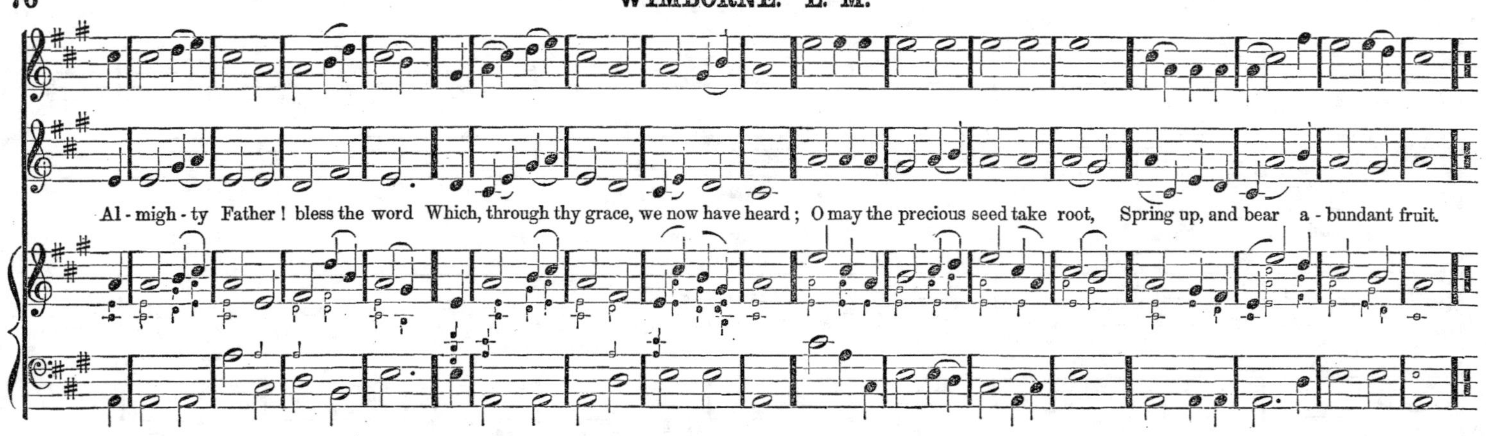

BALCLUTHA. L. M.

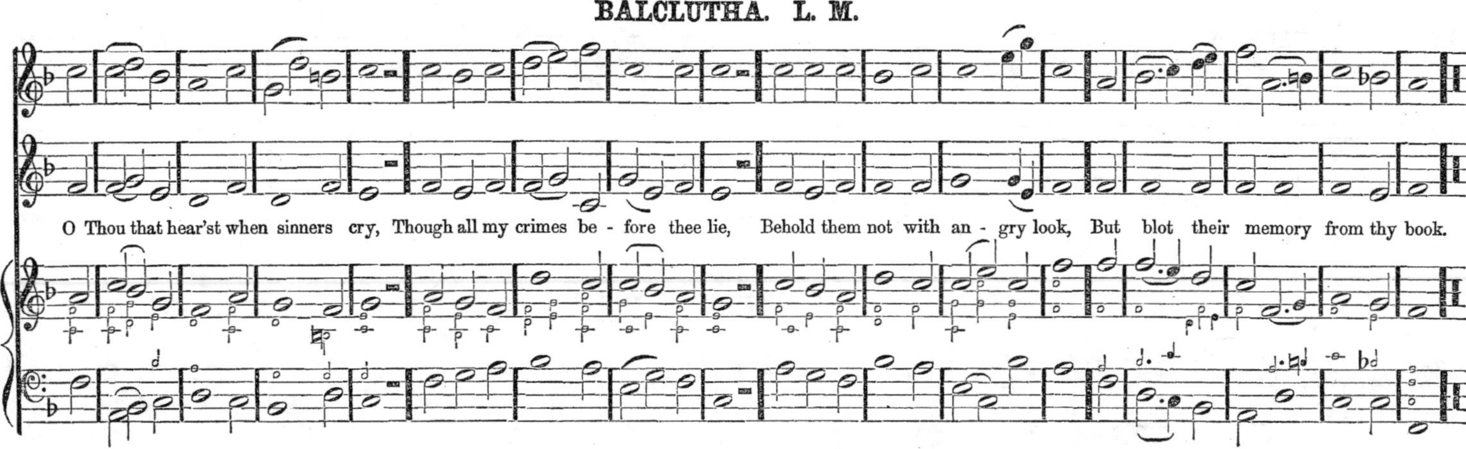

Sa - viour! when night in - volves the skies, My soul, a - dor - ing, turns to thee,— Thee, self - a - based, in
mor - tal guise, And wrapt in shades of death for me,— And wrapt in shades of death for me.

DEEP RIVER. L. M.

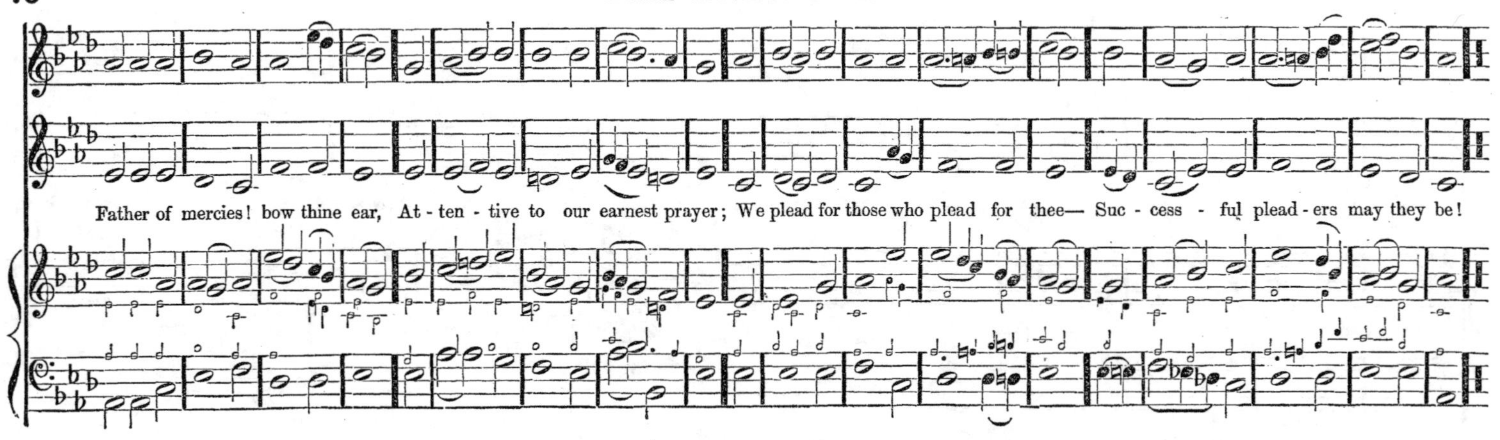

BRETBY. L. M.

CHRIST CHURCH. S. M.

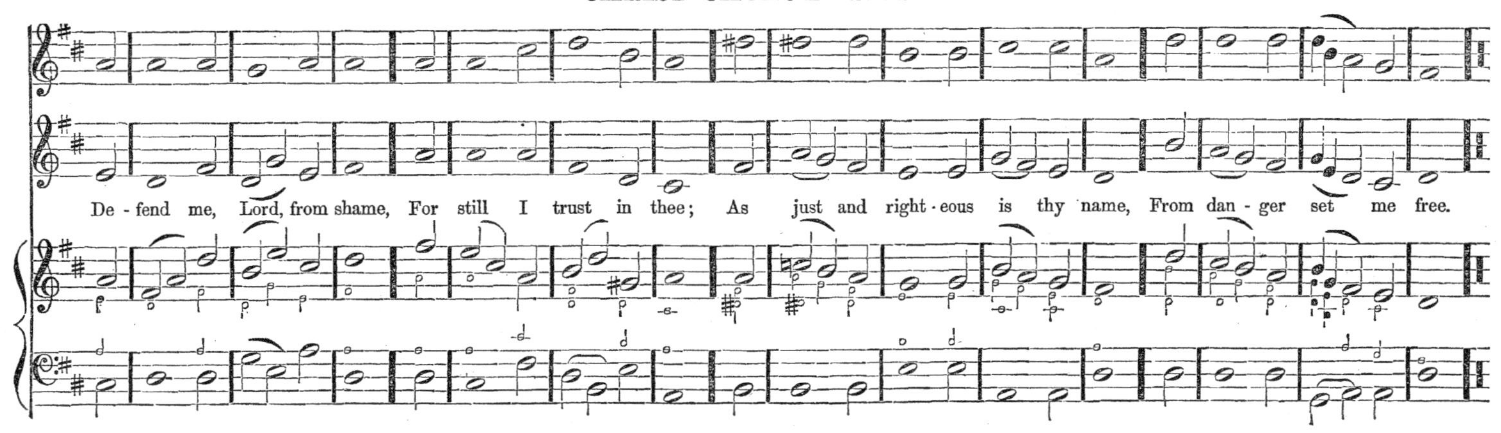

KIRKDALE. S. M.

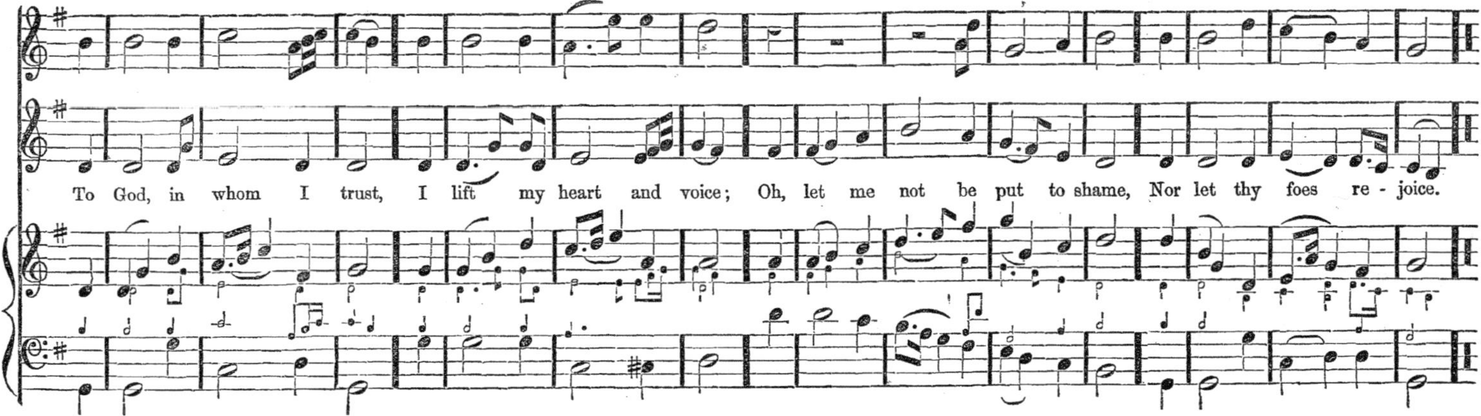

TUTBURY. S. M.

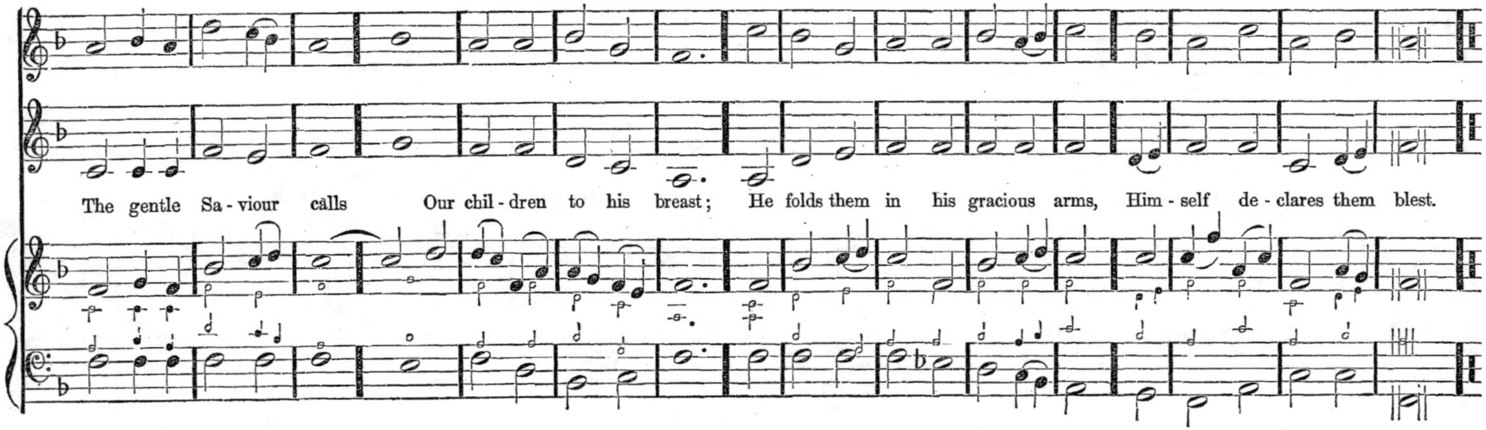

The gentle Sa - viour calls Our chil - dren to his breast; He folds them in his gracious arms, Him - self de - clares them blest.

BRANSTON. S. M.

Soldiers of Christ, a - rise, And put your ar - mor on, Strong in the strength which God supplies Thro' his e - ter - nal Son. . . . .

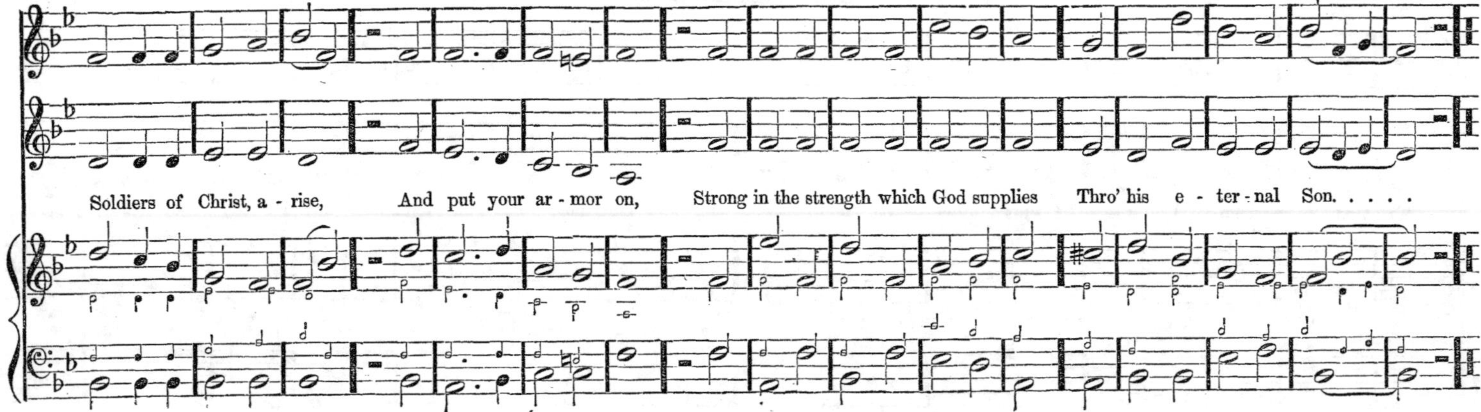

STAPENHILL. S. M.

SHIRLAND. S. M.

SACRIFICE. S. M.

ST. BRIDE'S. S. M.

BRIGHAM. S. M.

LEIGHTON. S. M.

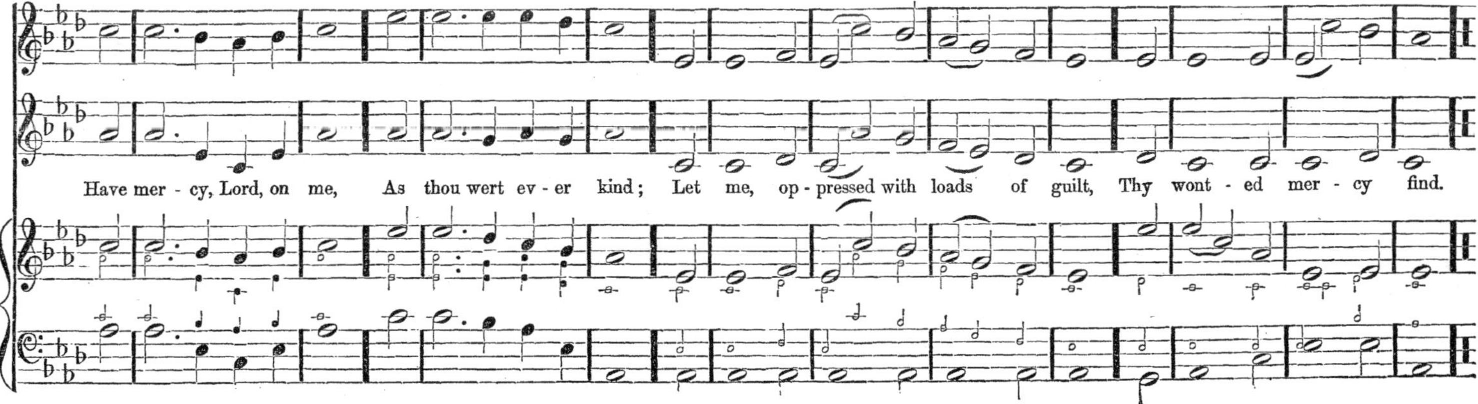

COMBER. S. M.

NEWARK. S. M.

WHITHINGTON. S. M.

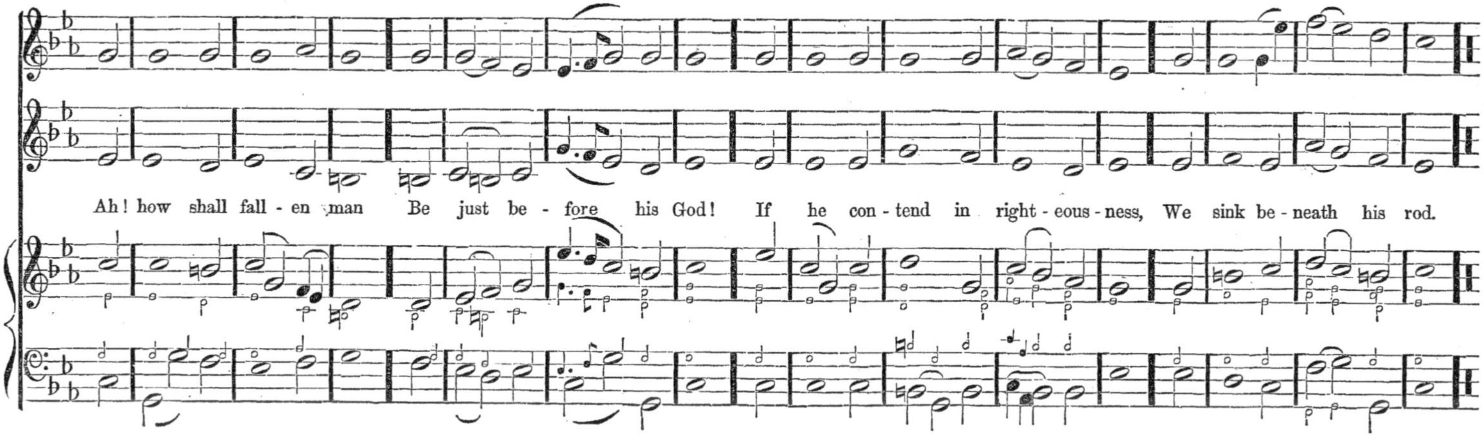

Ah! how shall fall - en man Be just be - fore his God! If he con - tend in right - eous - ness, We sink be - neath his rod.

THORNTON. S. M.

A charge to keep I have, A God to glo - ri - fy; A nev - er - dy - ing soul to save, And fit it for the sky.

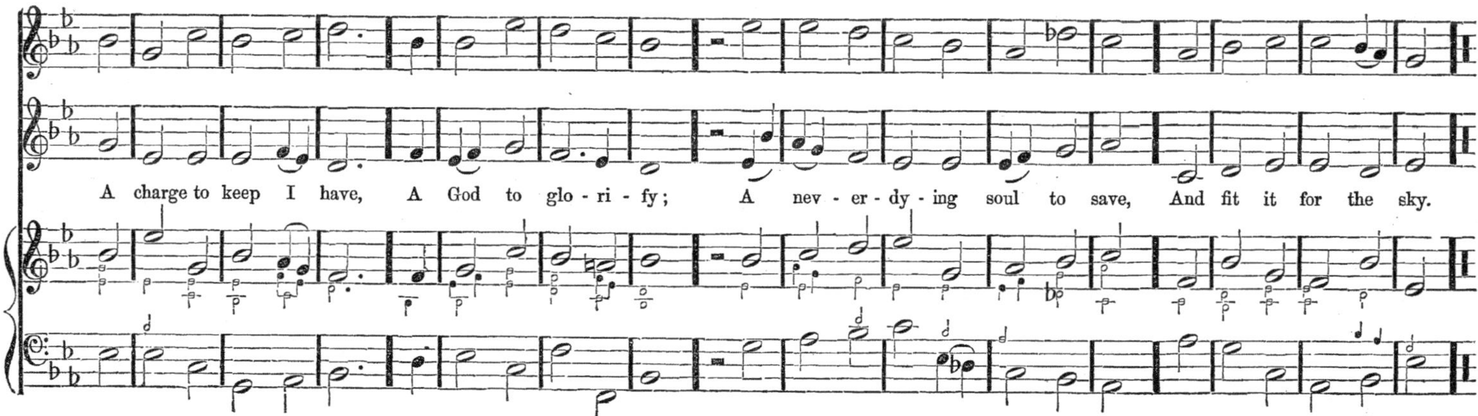

ST. OLAF. S. M.

CARLISLE. S. M.

RIDLEY. S. M.

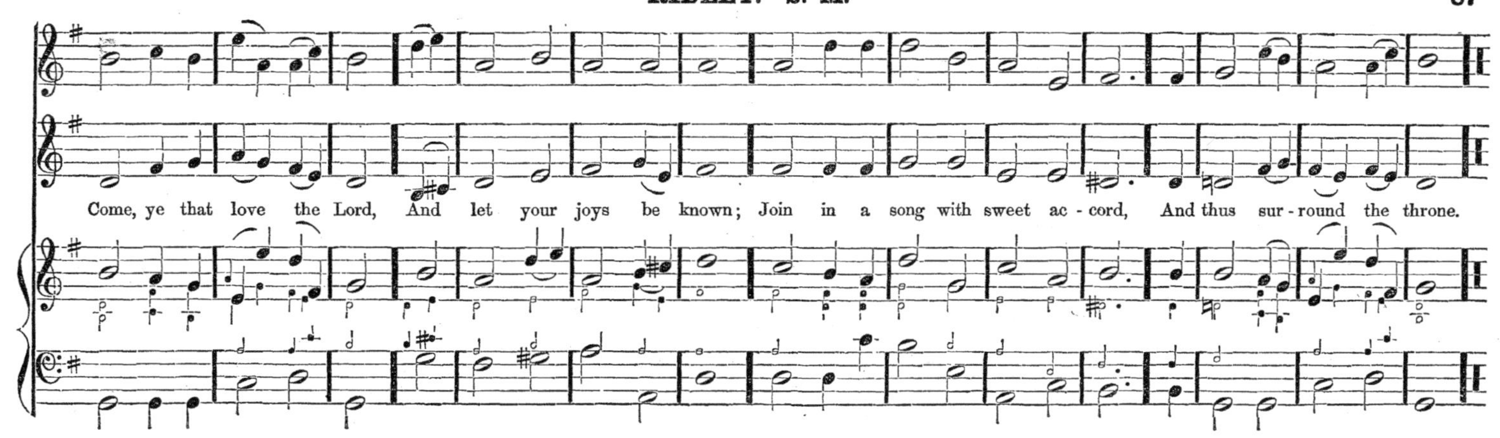

KIDDERMINSTER. S. M.

STANHOPE. II. 1.

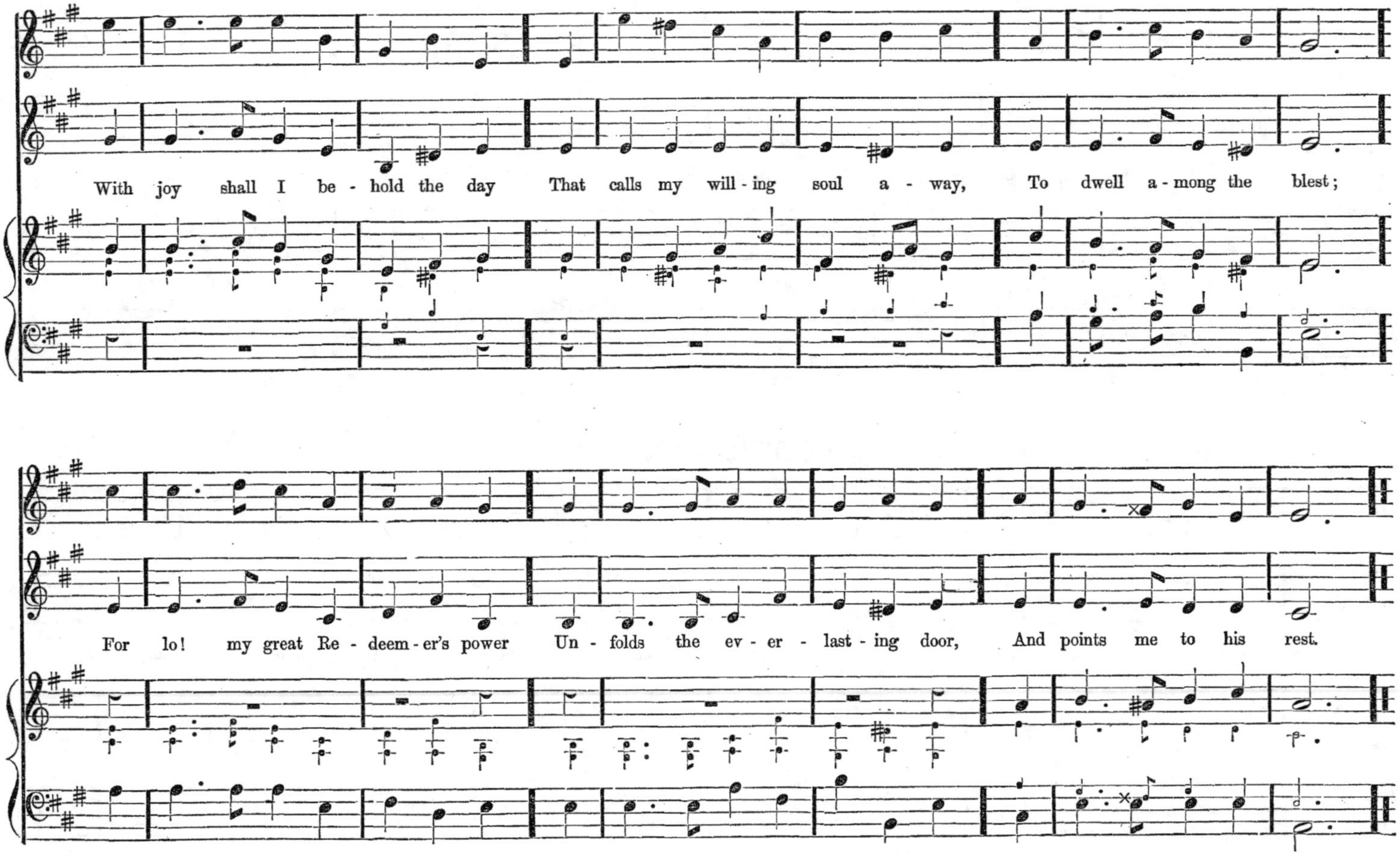

With joy shall I be - hold the day That calls my will - ing soul a - way, To dwell a - mong the blest;
For lo! my great Re - deem - er's power Un - folds the ev - er - last - ing door, And points me to his rest.

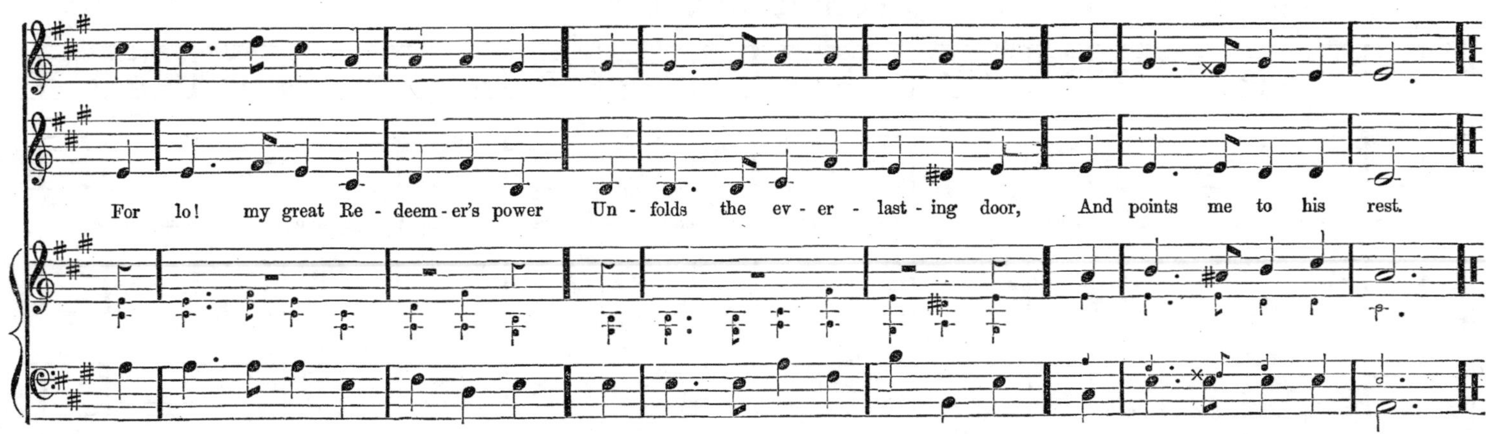

Be - gin, my soul, th' ex - alt - ed lay, Let each en - rap - tured thought o - bey, And praise th' Almighty's name,— And praise th' Almighty's name.
Let heaven and earth, and seas and skies, In one me - lo - dious con - cert rise, To swell th' inspiring theme,— To swell th' inspiring theme.

ILKLEY. II. 1.

Ye fields of light, ce - les - tial plains, Where pure, se - rene ef - fulgence reigns, Ye scenes di - vine - ly fair, Your Maker's wondrous

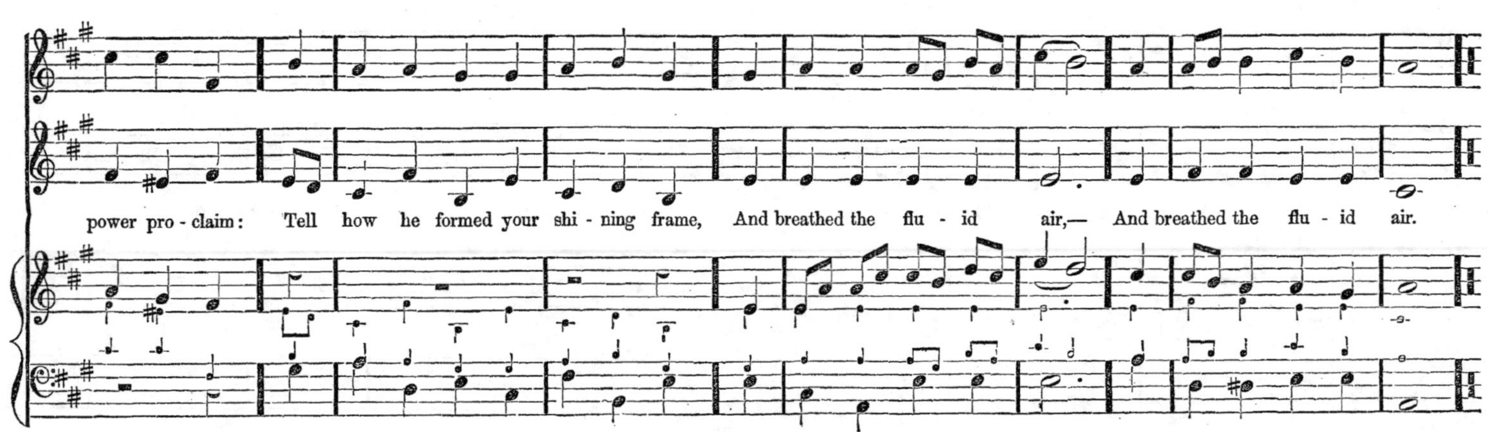
power pro - claim: Tell how he formed your shi - ning frame, And breathed the flu - id air,— And breathed the flu - id air.

The Lord hath spoke, the migh - ty God Hath sent his sum - mons all abroad, From dawn - ing light till day de - clines;
The list - 'ning earth his voice hath heard, And he from Si - on hath appeared, Where beau - ty in per - fec - tion shines.

ASTON. II. 2.

Ye saints and servants of the Lord, The triumphs of his name record, His sacred name for ever bless;
Where-e'er the circling sun displays His rising beams, or setting rays, Due praise to his great name address.

O God! my gra-cious God, to thee My morning prayers, My morning prayers shall of - fered be— For thee, like one who thirsts, I pant;
And still my soul im-plores thy grace, As in a dry and bar - ren place, When I re - fresh - ing, When I re - fresh - ing wa - ters want.

HENWICK. II. 2.

He that has God his guar - dian made, Shall un - der the Al - migh - ty's shade Se - cure and un - dis - turbed a - bide;
Thus, to my soul, of him I'll say, He is my for - tress and my stay, My God, in whom I will con - fide.

When gathering clouds a - round I view, And days are dark, and friends are few, On him I lean, who, not in vain,
Ex - perienced ev - ery hu - man pain; He feels my griefs, he sees my fears, And counts and treasures up my tears.

ARNE. II. 3.

Great God! this sa - cred day of thine De - mands the soul's col - lect - ed powers; Glad - ly we now to thee re - sign

These sol - emn, con - se - cra - ted hours: O, may our souls a - dor - ing own The grace that calls us to thy throne.

As, pant - ing in the sul - try beam, The hart de - sires the cool - ing stream, So to thy pres - ence, Lord, I flee,
So longs my soul, O God, for thee; A - thirst to taste thy liv - ing grace, And see thy glo - ry face to face.

STONEFIELD. II. 3.

The Lord my pas - ture shall pre - pare, And feed me with a shepherd's care; His presence shall my wants sup - ply,
And guard me with a watch - ful eye; My noon - day walks he shall at - tend, And all my mid - night hours de - fend.

PORTSMOUTH. II. 4.

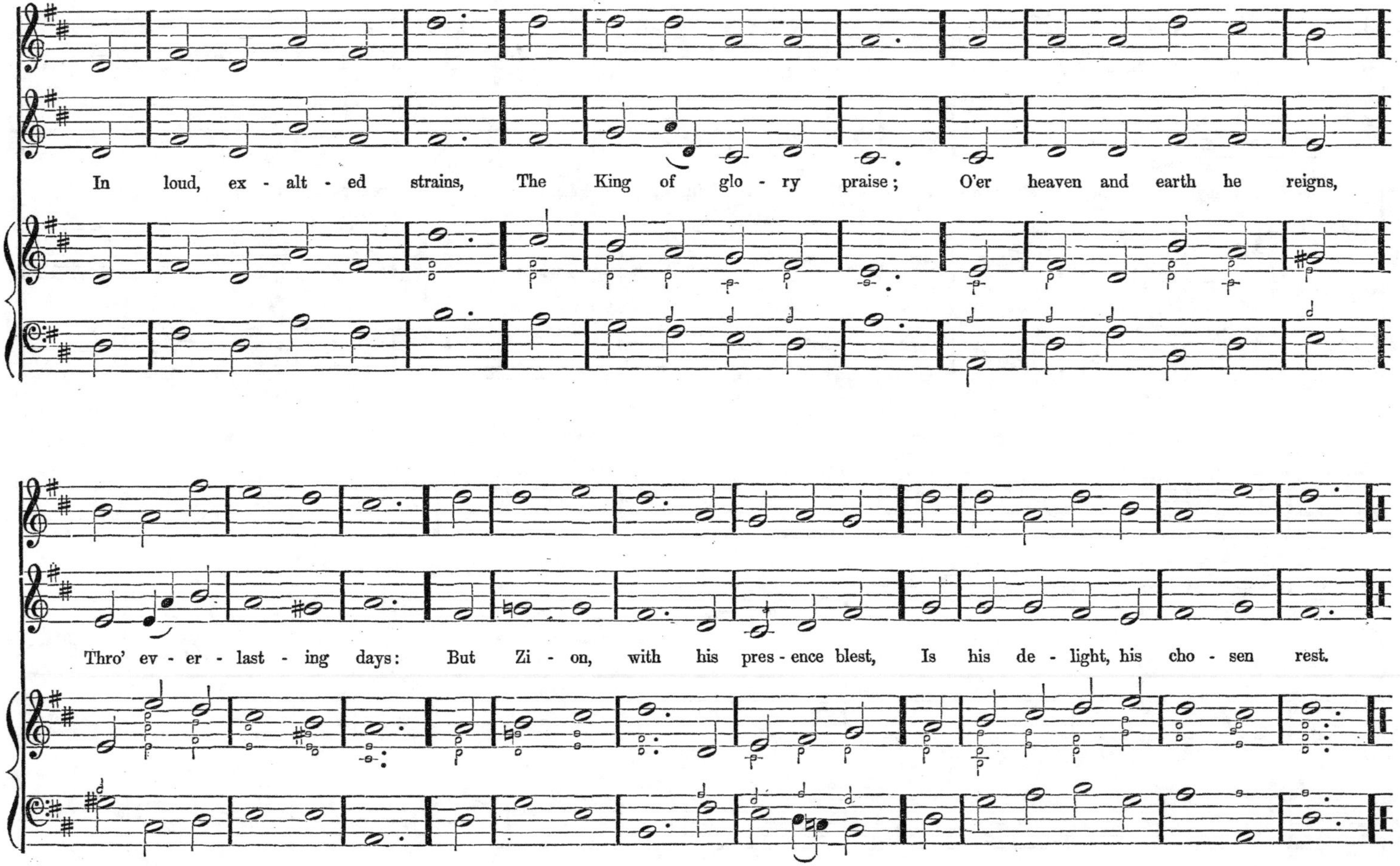

In loud, ex - alt - ed strains, The King of glo - ry praise; O'er heaven and earth he reigns,
Thro' ev - er - last - ing days: But Zi - on, with his pres - ence blest, Is his de - light, his cho - sen rest.

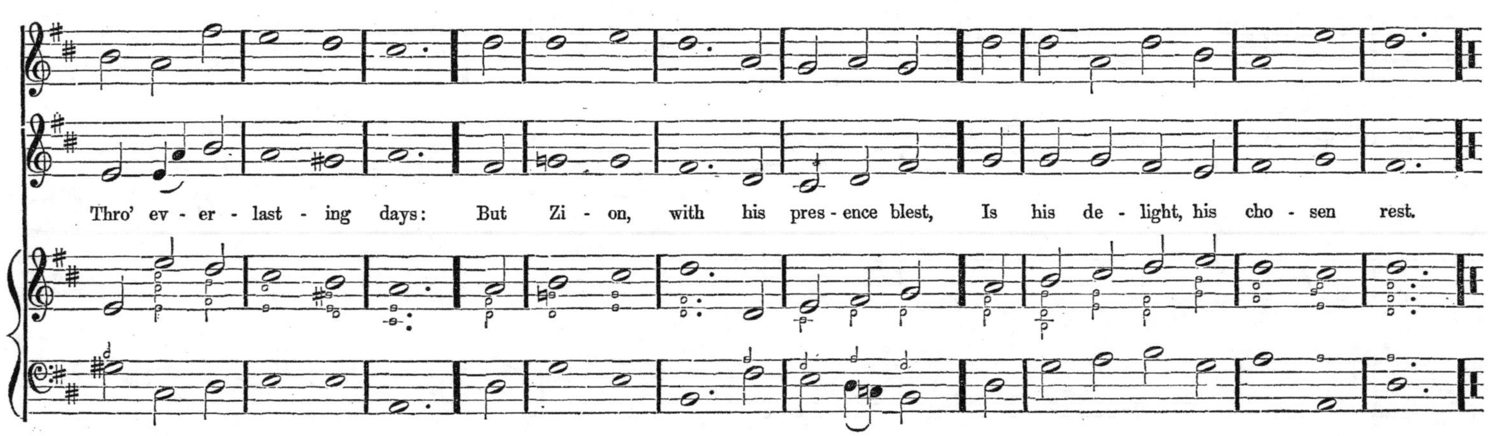

We give im - mor - tal praise, To God the Fa - ther's love, For all our com - forts here,
And all our hopes a - bove; He sent his own E - ter - nal Son To die for sins That man had done.

IRENÆUS. II. 4.

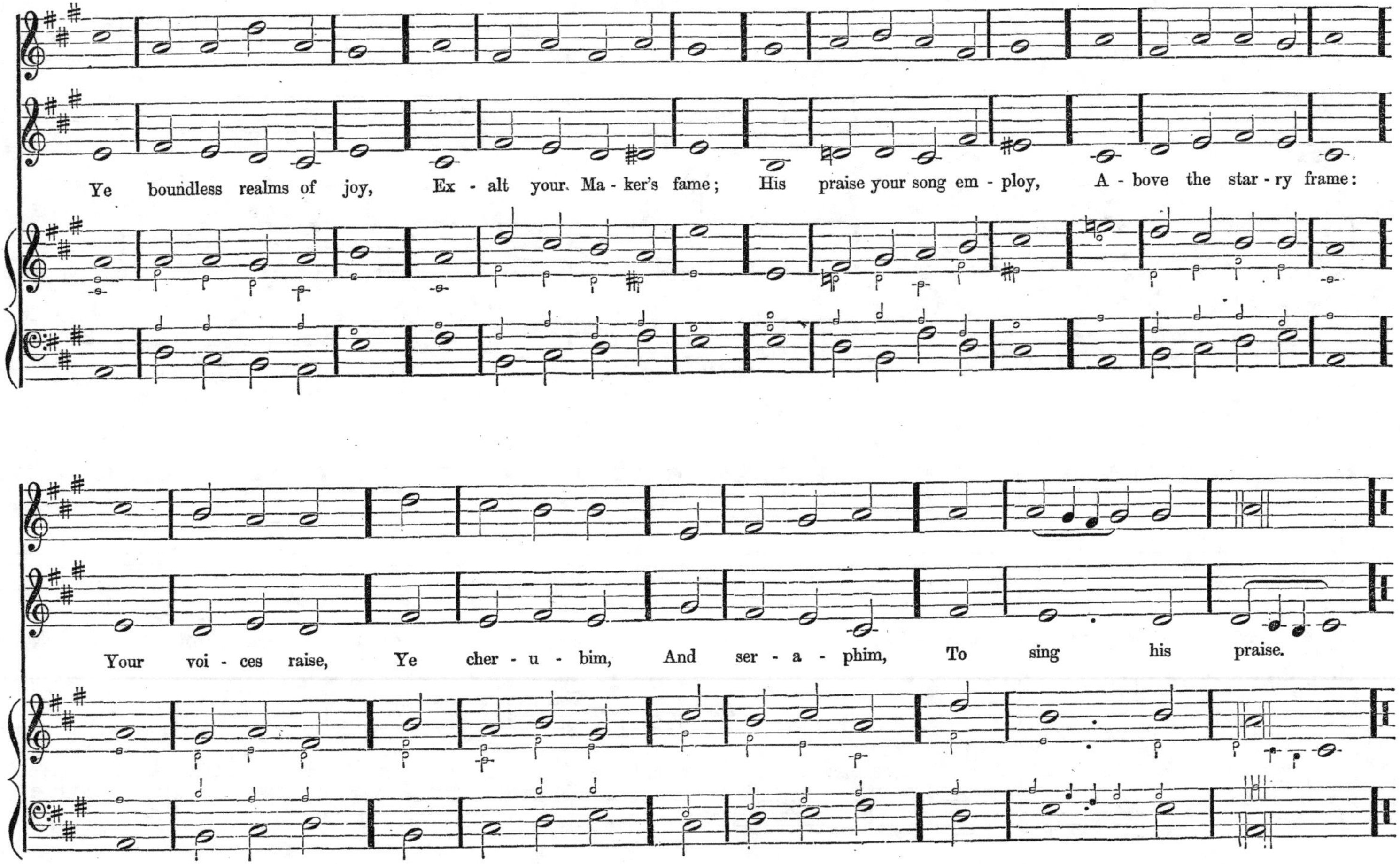

Ye boundless realms of joy, Ex - alt your Ma - ker's fame; His praise your song em - ploy, A - bove the star - ry frame:

Rise, crowned with light, im - pe - rial Sa - lem, rise! Ex - alt thy towering head, and lift thine eyes! See heaven its sparkling
por - tals wide dis - play, And break up - on thee in a flood of day,— And break up - on thee in a flood of day.

HODNET. II. 6.

From Greenland's i - cy mountains, From In - dia's co - ral strand, Where Af - ric's sun - ny fountains Roll down their gold - en sand;
From many an ancient riv - er, From many a palmy plain, They call us to de - liv - er Their land from error's chain.

Great God, what do I see and hear! The end of things cre - a - ted! The Judge of man I see ap - pear, On clouds of glo - ry seat - ed:
The trum - pet sounds— the graves re - store The dead which they con - tained be - fore; Pre - pare, my soul, to meet him.

Sing to the Lord a new-made song; Let earth, in one as - sembled throng, Her common patron's praise resound: Sing to the Lord, and bless his name;
From day to day his praise pro - claim, Who us has with sal - vation crowned; To heathen lands his fame rehearse, His wonders to the u - ni - verse.

CHOLMONDELEY. III. 1.

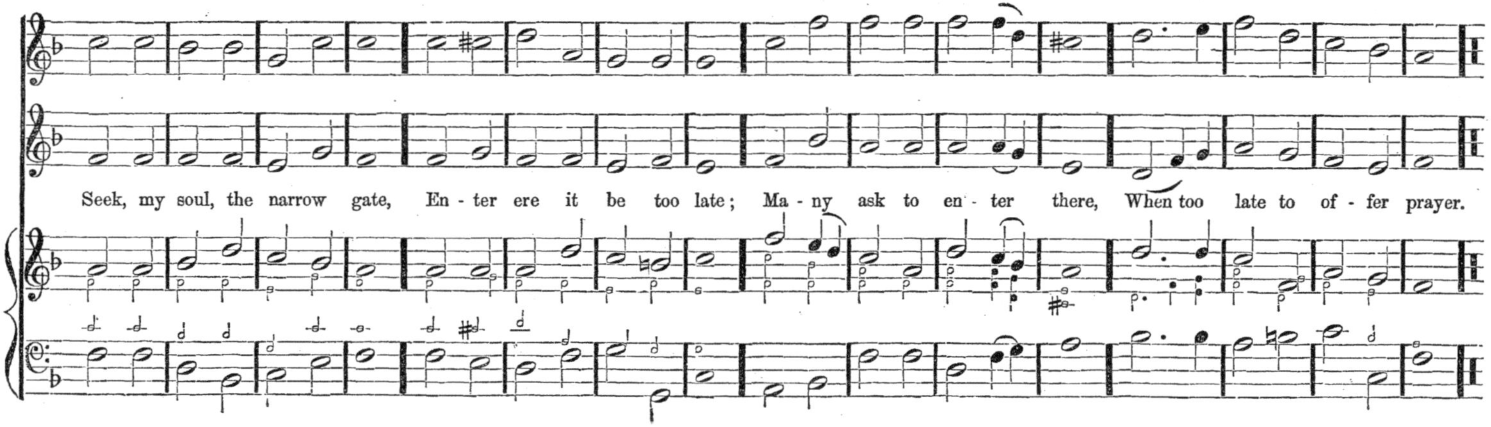
Seek, my soul, the narrow gate, En - ter ere it be too late; Ma - ny ask to en - ter there, When too late to of - fer prayer.

BECKWITZ. III. 1.

Now the shades of night are gone, Now the morning light is come: Lord, may we be thine to - day; Drive the shades of sin a - way.

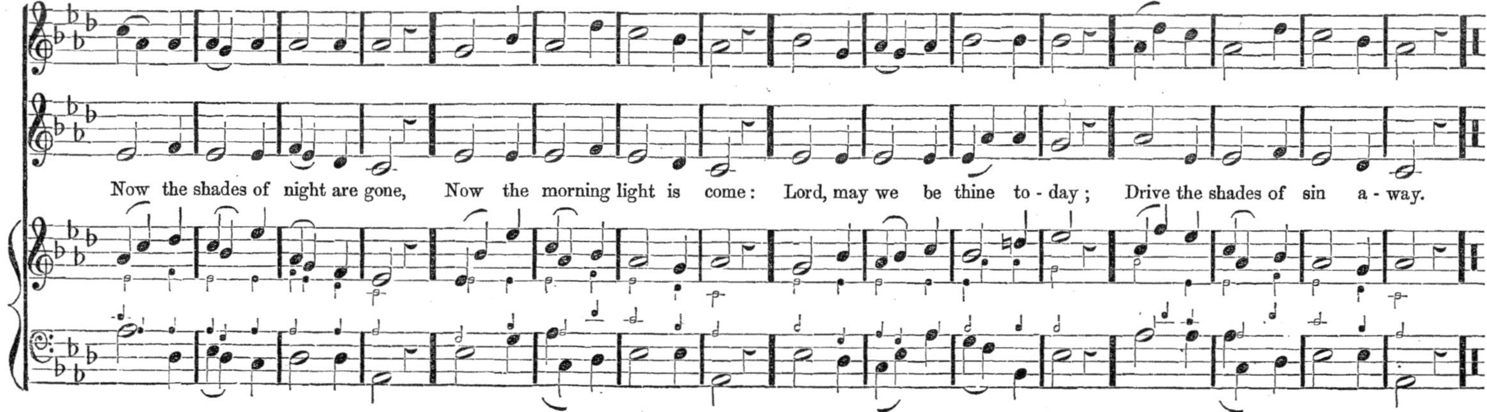

MATLOCK. III. 1. Double.

Hark! the her - - ald an - gels sing, Glo - ry to the new - born King, Peace on earth, and

mer - cy mild, Peace on earth, and mer - cy mild, God and sin - - - ners re - con - ciled.

The Solo may also be sung by the Treble.

GLENELG. III. 1.

TRIUMPH. III. 1.

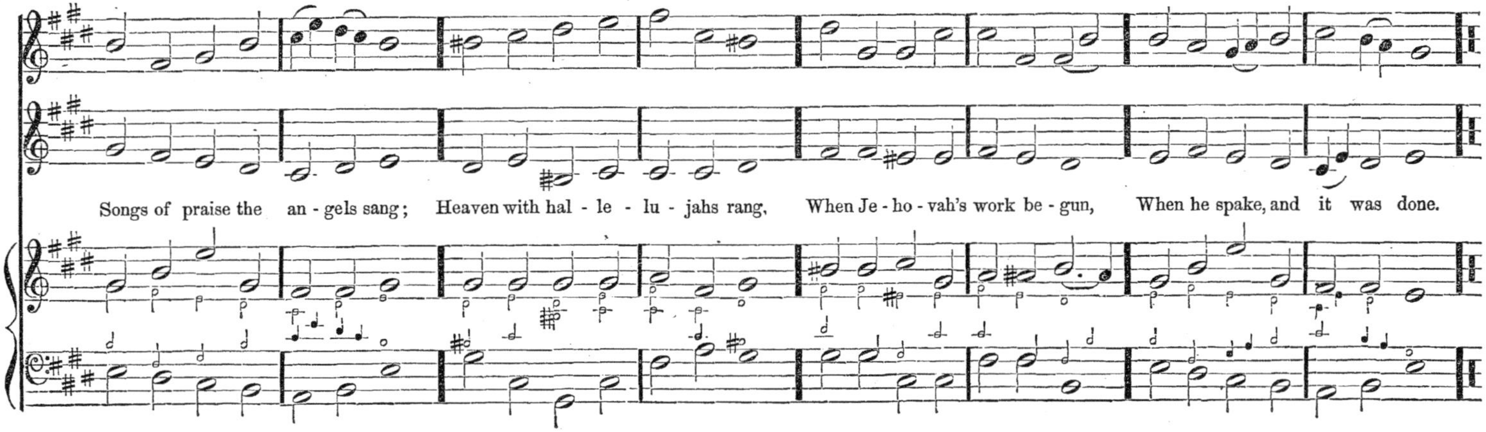
Songs of praise the an - gels sang; Heaven with hal - le - lu - jahs rang, When Je - ho - vah's work be - gun, When he spake, and it was done.

WHEELER. III. 1.

Lord, my God, I long to know, Oft it caus - es anxious thought; Do I love thee, Lord, or no? Am I thine, or am I not?

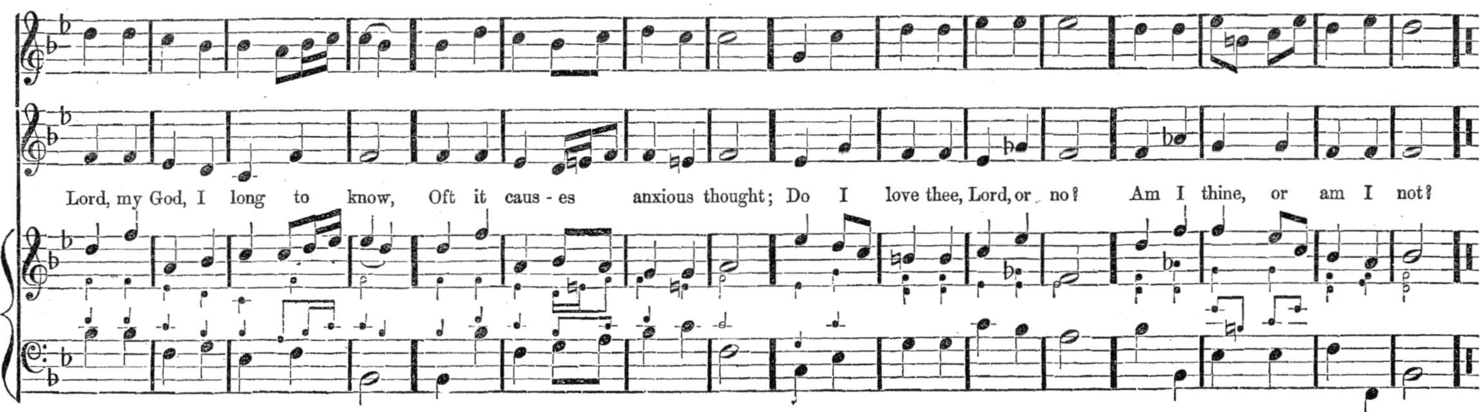

SEYMOUR. III. 1.

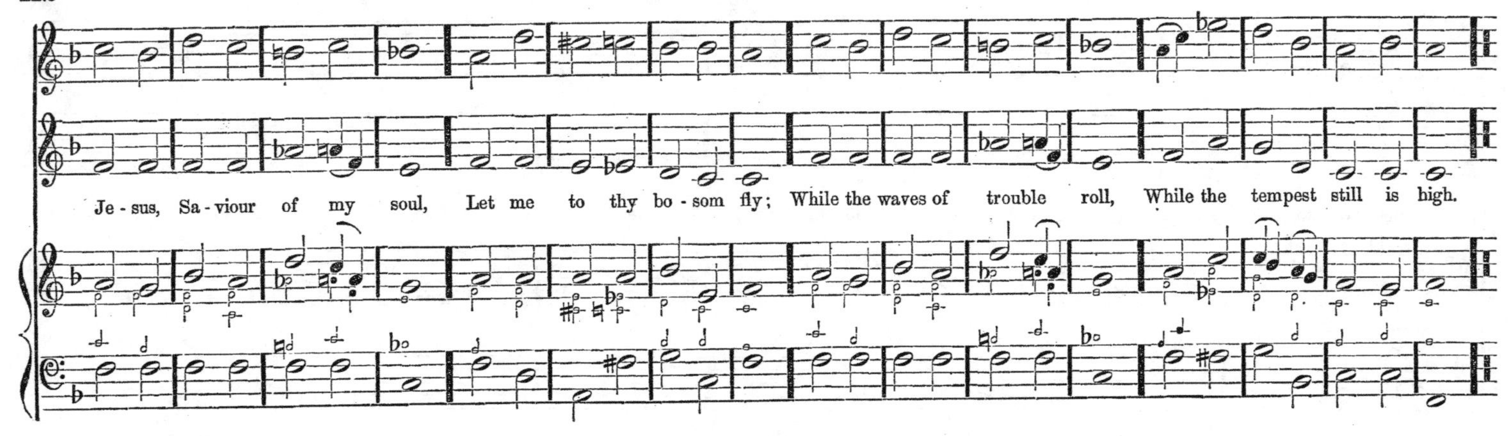

WORTHINGTON. III. 1.

Je - sus, Saviour of my soul, Let me to thy bo - som fly, While the waves of trou - ble roll, While the tempest still is high:
Hide me, O my Saviour, hide, Till the storm of life is past; Safe in - to the ha - ven guide; O, re - ceive my soul at last!

MOIRA. III. 1.

Christ the Lord is risen to-day, Sons of men and angels say: Raise your joys and triumphs high, Sing, ye heavens, and earth reply! Sing, ye heavens, and earth reply!

INCENSE. III. 1.

SOLITUDE. III. 1.

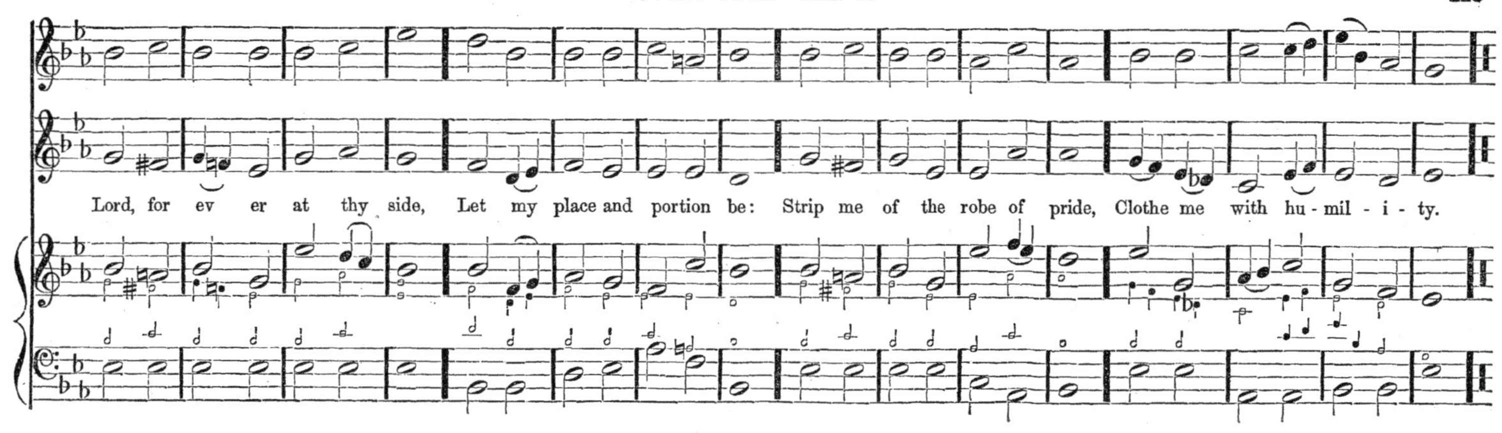

DOWNES. III. 1.

WINGFIELD. III. 1. Double.

Sovereign Ru - ler of the skies, Ev - er gracious, ev - er wise, All our times are in thy hand, All e - vents at thy command.
He that formed us in the womb, He shall guide us to the tomb; All our ways shall ev - er be Ordered by his wise de - cree.

MONSULDALE. III. 1.

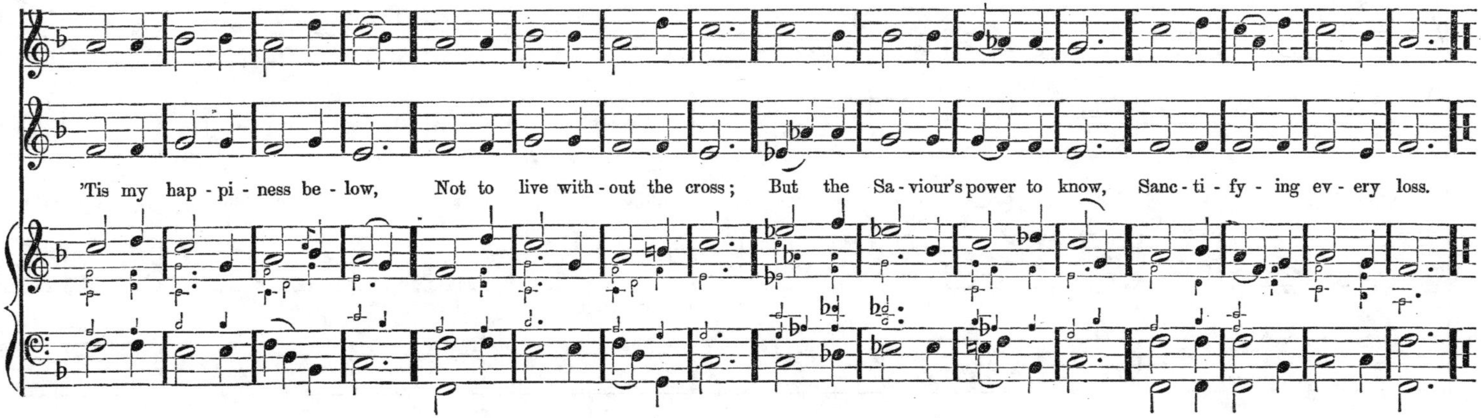
'Tis my hap - pi - ness be - low, Not to live with - out the cross; But the Sa - viour's power to know, Sanc - ti - fy - ing ev - ery loss.

ST. HELEN'S. III. 1.

Sin - ner, rouse thee from thy sleep, Wake, and o'er thy fol - ly weep; Raise thy spi - rit dark and dead, Je - sus waits his light to shed.

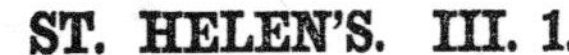

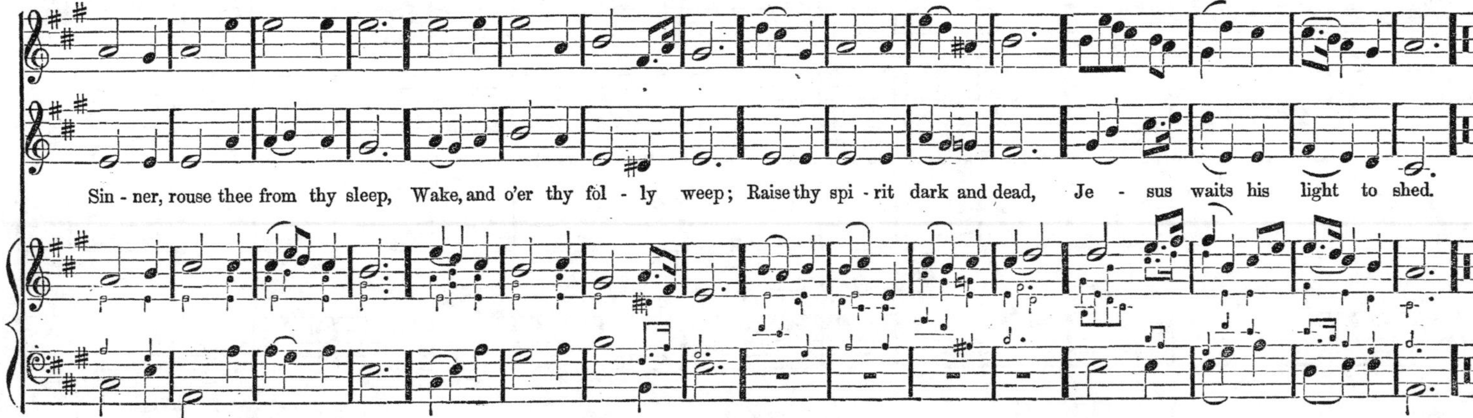

WORSHIP. III. 1.

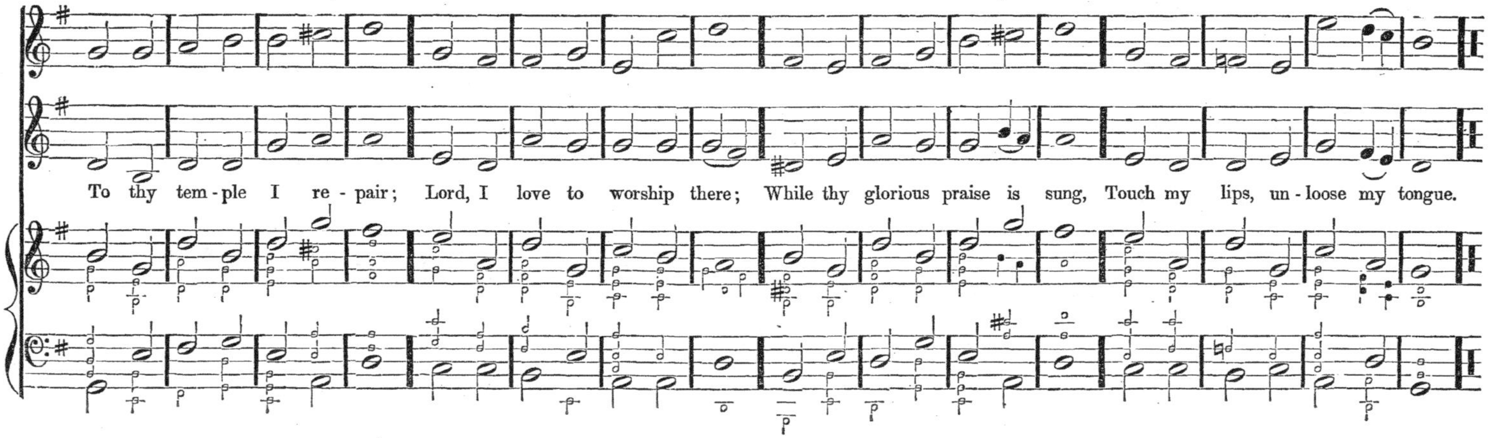

To thy tem - ple I re - pair; Lord, I love to worship there; While thy glorious praise is sung, Touch my lips, un - loose my tongue.

DOVEDALE. III. 1.

Hasten, sin - ner, to be wise; Stay not for the morrow's sun; Wisdom, if you still despise, Harder is it to be won.

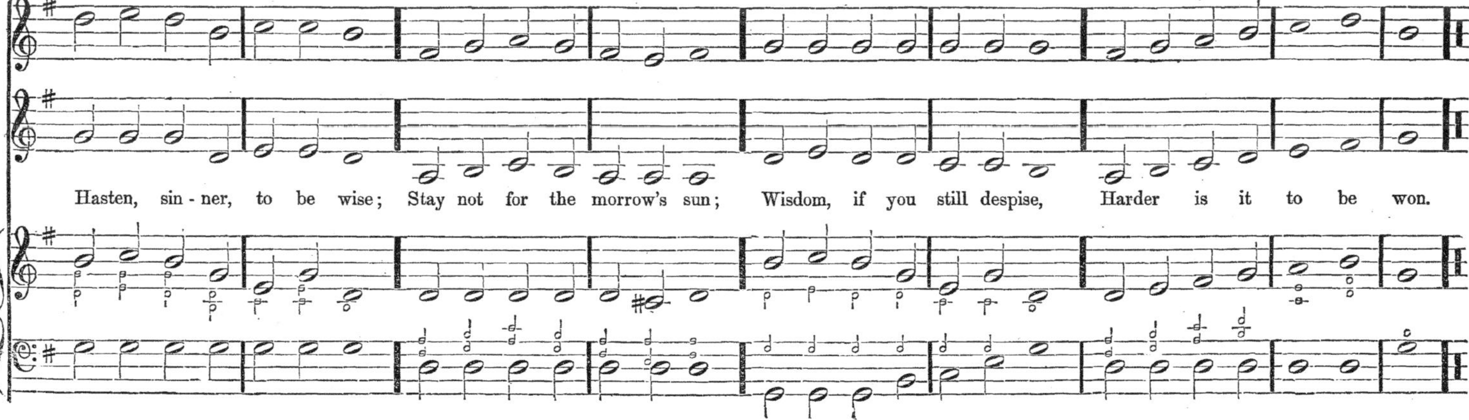

THANKSGIVING HYMN. III. 2.

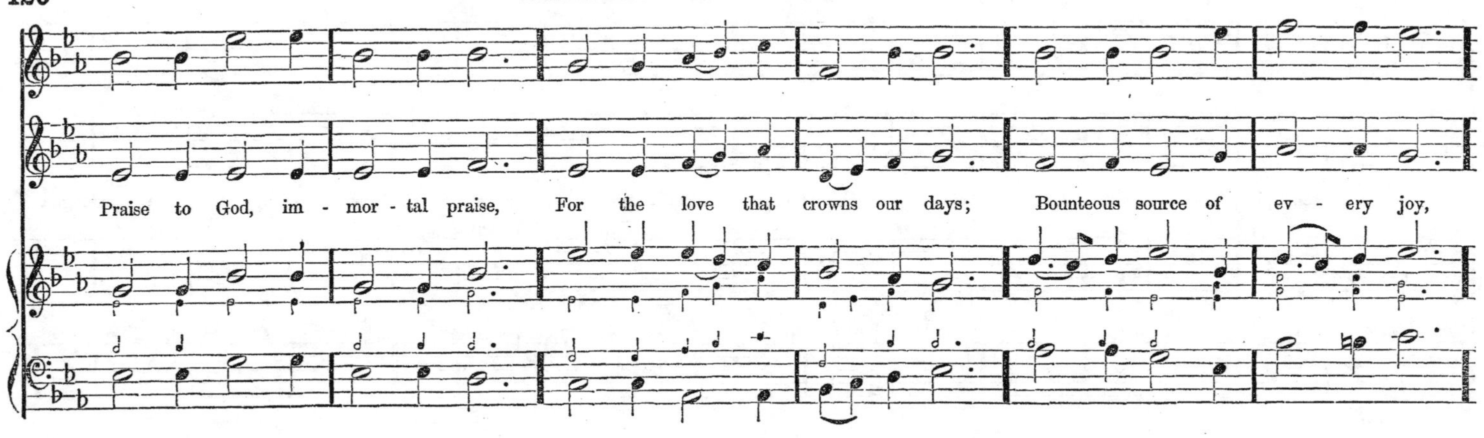

Rock of a - ges! cleft for me, Let me hide my - self in thee; Let the wa - ter and the blood,

From thy side, a heal - ing flood, Be of sin the dou - ble cure, Save from wrath, and make me pure.

MADELEY. III. 3. Double.

RATHBUN. III. 3.

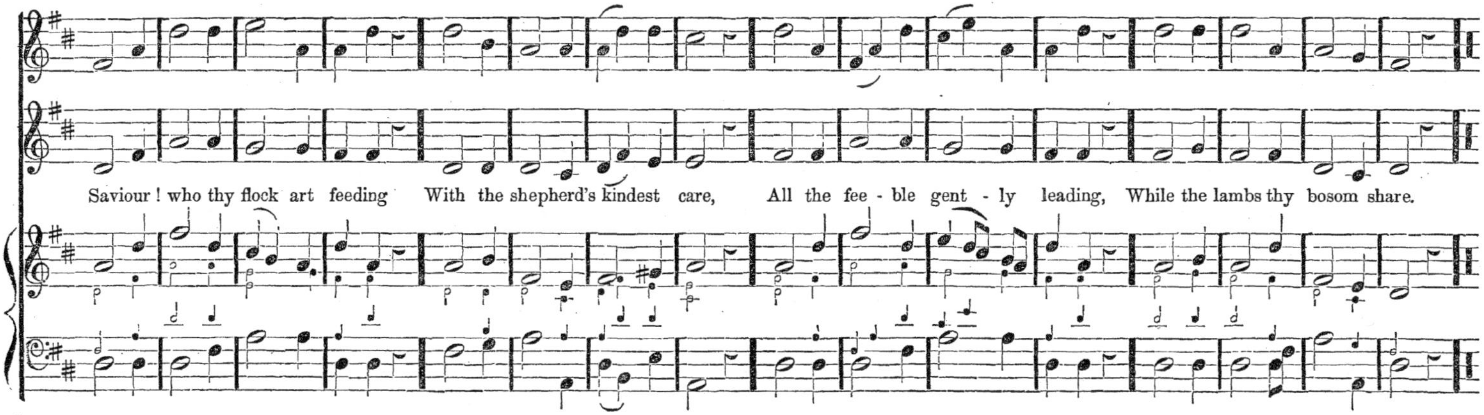
Saviour ! who thy flock art feeding With the shepherd's kindest care, All the fee - ble gent - ly leading, While the lambs thy bosom share.

HOMEWARDS. III. 3.

Hail, thou long ex - pected Jesus, Born to set thy people free! From our sins and fears re - lease us, Let us find our rest in thee.

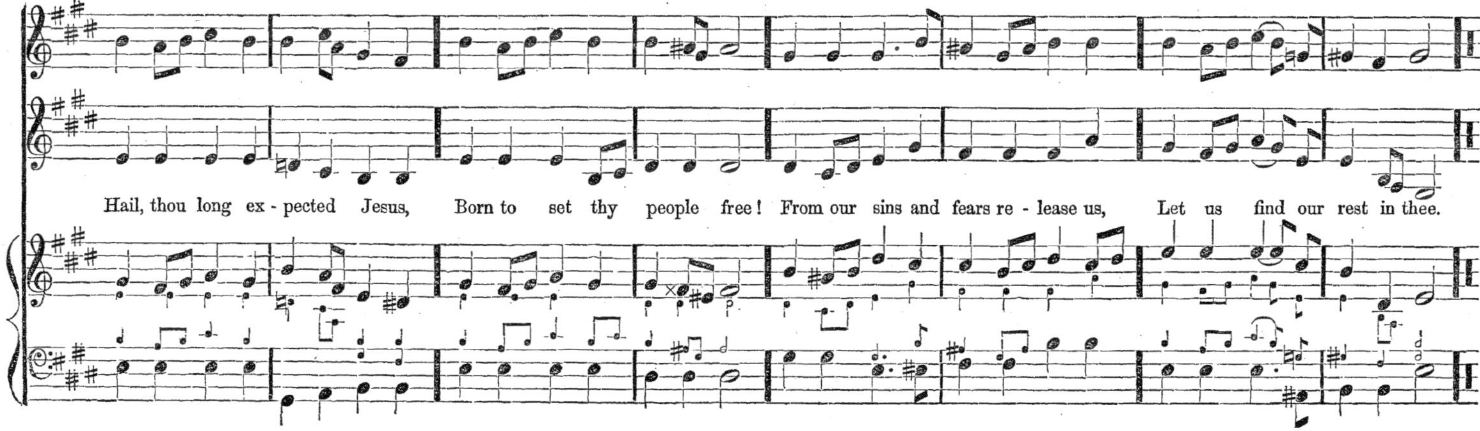

MANT. III. 3. Double.

NELSON. III. 3.

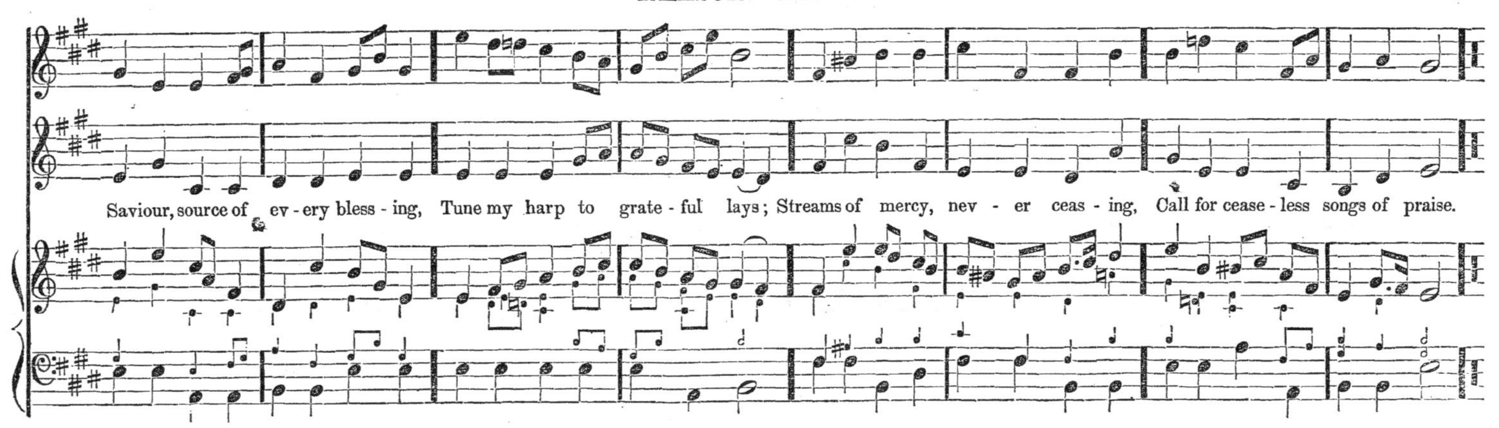

SILESIA. III. 3.

SOLNEY. III. 3.

PORTLAND. III. 3.

Who is he that comes from E - dom, All his gar - ments stained with blood, To the cap - tive speaking free - dom,
Bring - ing and be - stow - ing good; Glo - rious in the garb he wears, Glo - rious in the spoil he bears?

VERNON. III. 5.

Lord! dis - miss us with thy bless - ing, Fill our hearts with joy and peace; Let us each, thy love pos - sess - ing,
Tri - umph in re - deem - ing grace; O re - fresh us, O re - fresh us, Travelling through this wil - der - ness!

O praise ye the Lord, Pre - pare your glad voice His praise in the great As - sem - bly to sing:
In their great Cre - a - tor Let Is - rael re - joice; And chil - dren of Si - on Be glad in their King.

RESIGNATION. IV. 2.

CHIMES. IV. 3.

REFUGE. IV. 4.

How firm a foun - da - tion, ye saints of the Lord, Is laid for your faith in his ex - cel - lent word!

What more can he say, than to you he hath said, You who un - to Je - sus for ref - uge have fled.

I would not live al - way; I ask not to stay
Where storm af - ter storm ri - ses dark o'er the way;

The few lu - cid morn - ings that dawn on us here,
Are e - nough for life's woes, full e - nough for its cheer.

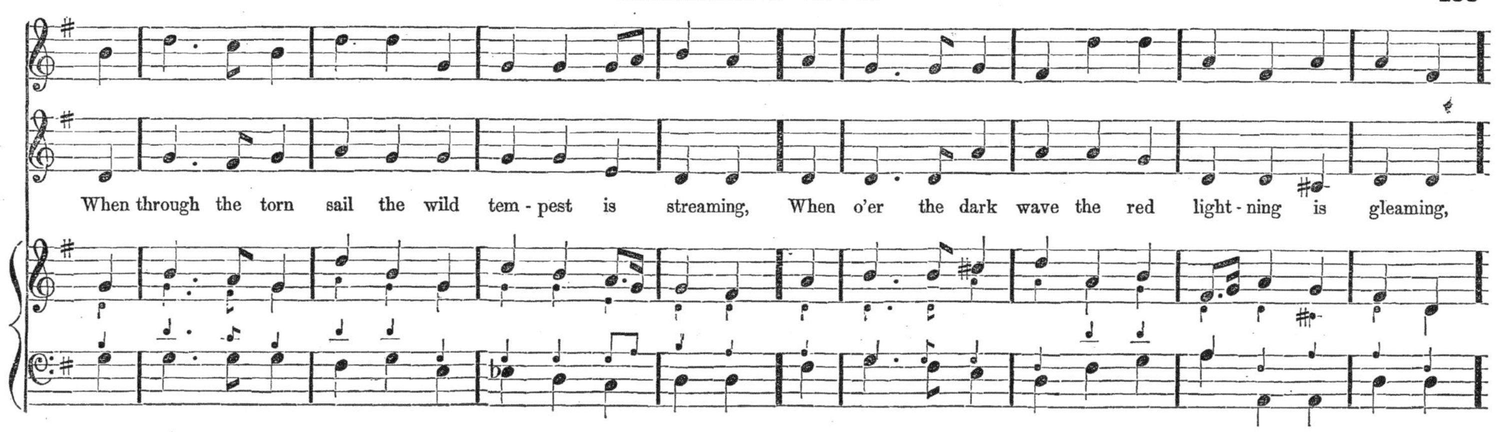
When through the torn sail the wild tem - pest is streaming, When o'er the dark wave the red light - ning is gleaming,

No hope lends a ray the poor sea - man to cher - ish, We fly to our Ma - ker, "Save, Lord! or we per - ish."

"Rise, my soul, and stretch thy wings."

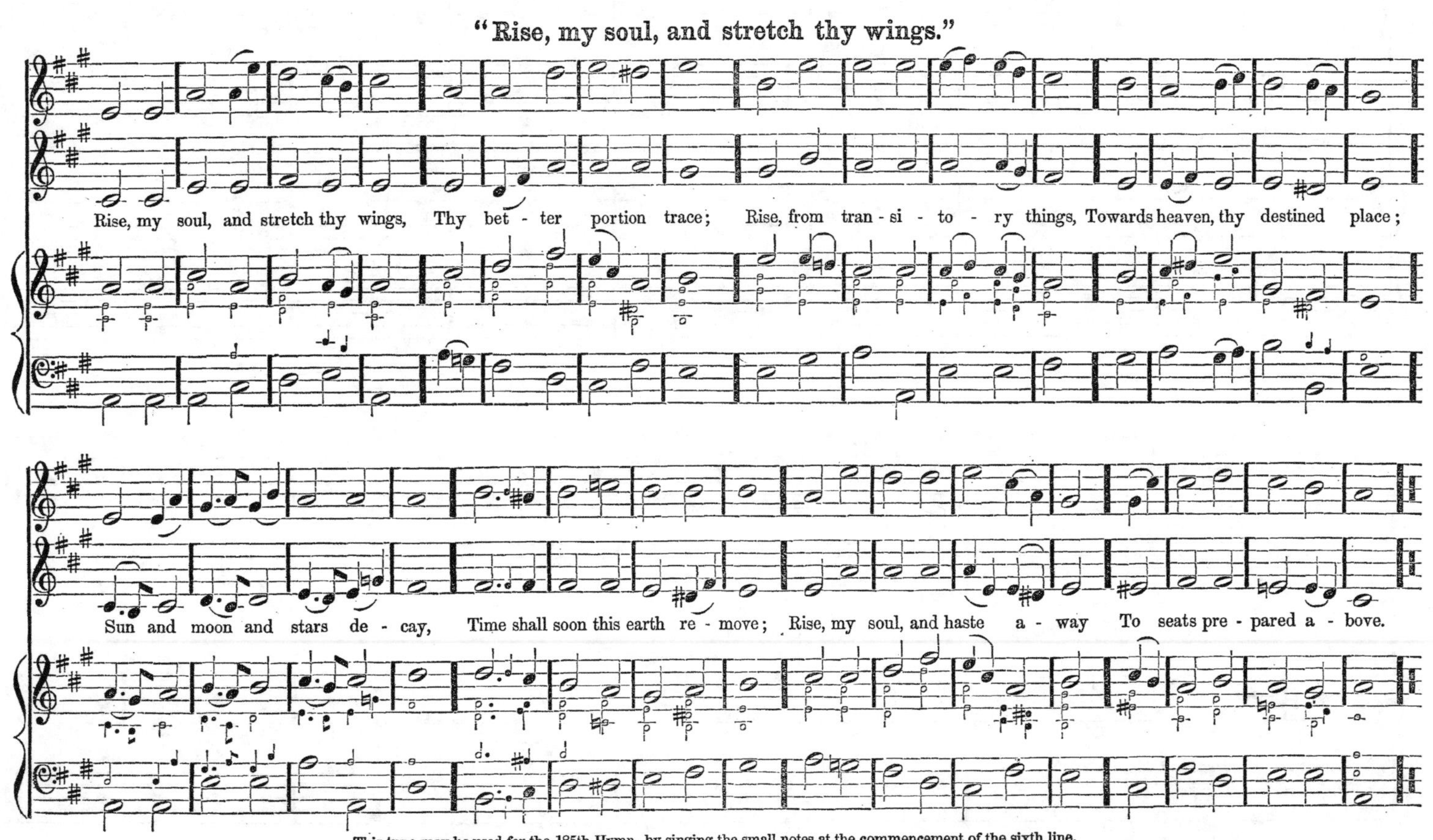

This tune may be used for the 185th Hymn, by singing the small notes at the commencement of the sixth line.

The God of Abraham praise, Who reigns en - throned a - bove; Ancient, of ev - er - last - ing days, And God of love;
Je - ho - vah, great I AM, By earth and heaven con - fessed; I bow and bless the sa - cred name, For ev - er blessed.

"Peace, troubled soul."

Peace, troubled soul, whose plain - tive moan Hath taught each scene the note of wo; Cease thy complaint, sup - press thy groan,

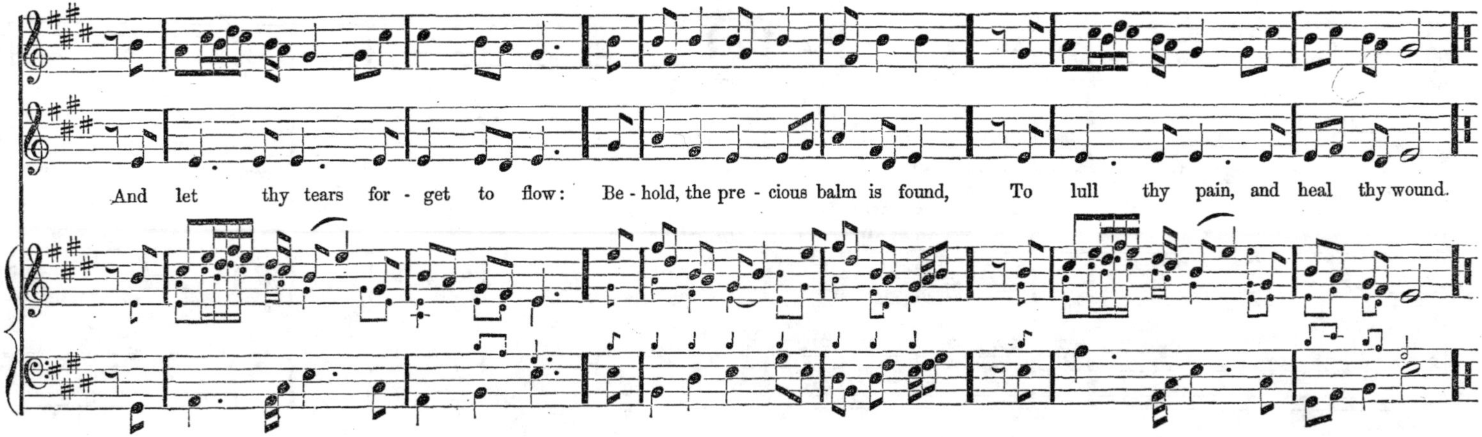

And let thy tears for - get to flow: Be - hold, the pre - cious balm is found, To lull thy pain, and heal thy wound.

Hail to the Lord's A - noint - ed, Great David's greater Son! Hail, in the time ap - point - ed, His reign on earth be - gun!
He comes to break op - pression, To set the captive free, To take away trans - gression, And rule in e - qui - ty.

"Mercy and truth, with sweet accord."

May be sung as a Duett by Treble and Alto.

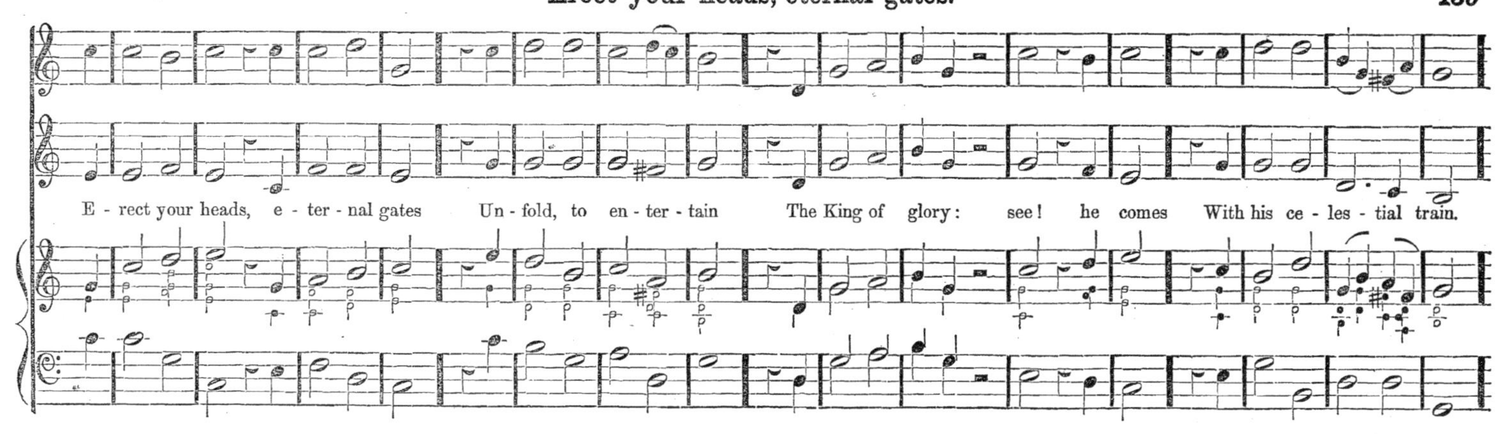
E - rect your heads, e - ter - nal gates Un - fold, to en - ter - tain The King of glory: see! he comes With his ce - les - tial train.

Who is the King of glo - ry? who? The Lord for strength renowned; In battle mighty: o'er his foes E - ter - nal vic - tor crowned.

"Salvation! O, the joyful sound."

Heaven with the echo shall re-
Grace! 'tis a charm-ing sound! Har-mo-nious to the ear; Heaven with the ech-o shall re-sound,
-sound, And all the earth shall hear,
Heaven with the ech-o shall resound, And all the earth shall hear, And all the earth shall hear, And all the earth shall hear.
And all the earth shall hear, And all the earth shall hear.

"The Lord himself, the mighty Lord."

And gent - - ly there re - pose, Then leads me to . . . . . cool
In ten - der grass he makes me feed And gent - ly there re - - pose, Then leads me to . . . . . cool
1st.
2d.
shades, and where . . . . . Re - fresh - ing wa - ter flows, ... Re - freshing wa - - ter flows. Then flows.

VENITE EXULTEMUS DOMINO.

No. 4.
ATTWOOD.
No. 5.
RUSSELL.
No. 6.
NORRIS.
No. 7.
CROTCH.

GLORIA PATRI. No. 1.

Glo - ry be to the Fa - ther, and to the Son, and to the Ho - - - ly Ghost; As it
was in the be - gin - ning, is now, and ev - er shall be, world with - out end. A - men. A - men.

GLORIA PATRI. No. 3.

Glo - ry be to the Fa - ther, and to the Son, and to the Ho - ly Ghost; As it
was in the be - - gin - ning, is now, and ev - er shall be, world with - out end. A - - - men.

GLORIA IN EXCELSIS. No. 1.

5. That takest away the.................. | sins · of the | world,........ | have .... | mer- · cy up - | on us.
6. Thou that takest away the .... | sins · of the | world,........ | have .... | mer- · cy up - | on us.
7. Thou that takest away the .... | sins · of the | world,........ | re-.............................. | ceive · our | prayer.
8. Thou that sittest at the right hand of ... | God · the | Father,....... | have .... | mer- · cy up - | on us.

9. For thou .... | only · art | holy, ... | thou................. | on- · ly | art · the | Lord. | A-............ | men.
10. Thou only, O Christ! with the. | Ho- · ly | Ghost, ... | art most high in the ... | glory · of | God · the | Father.

GLORIA IN EXCELSIS. No. 2.

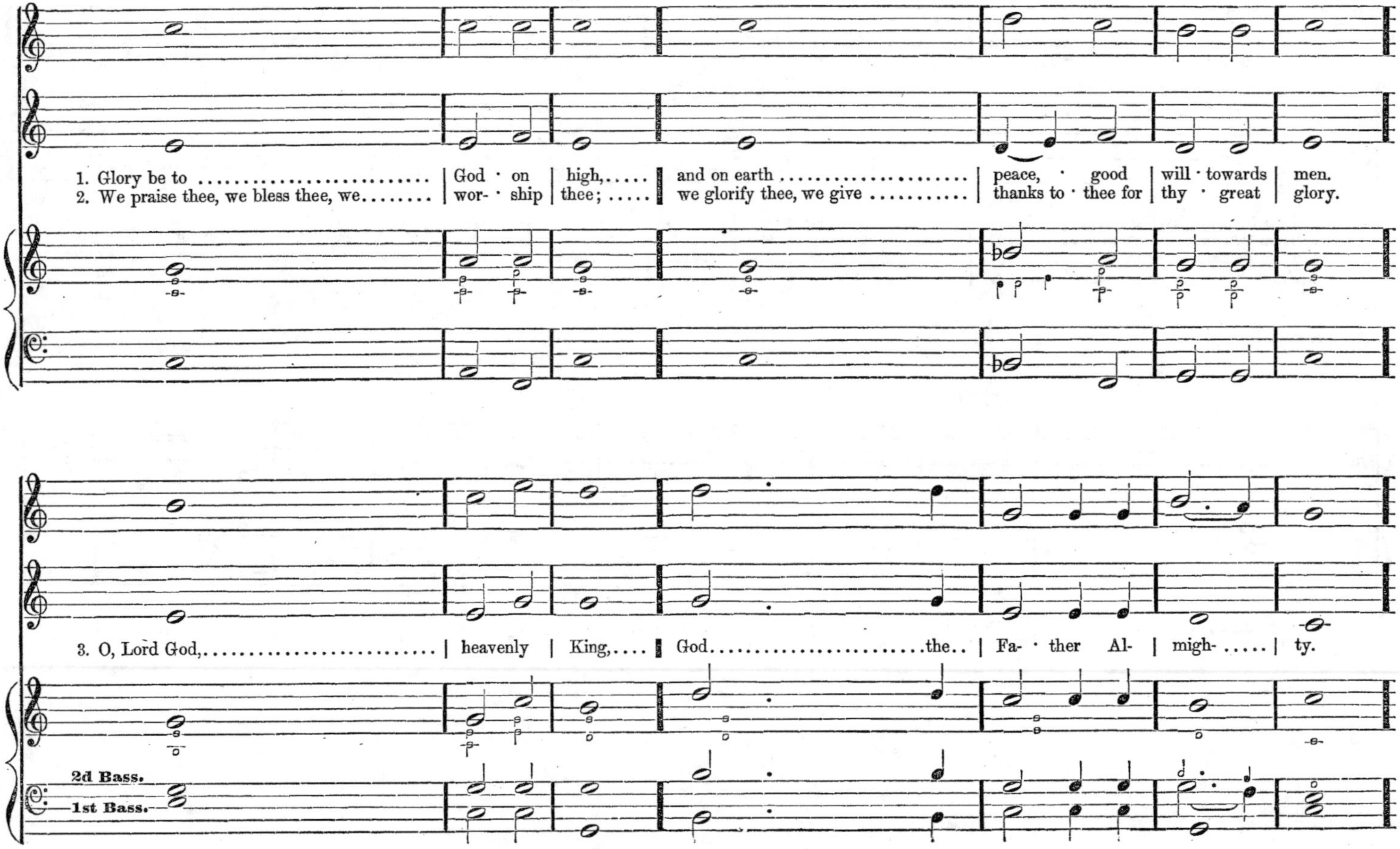

1. Glory be to .... | God · on | high, ... | and on earth .... | peace, · good | will · towards | men.
2. We praise thee, we bless thee, we........ | wor- · ship | thee; ..... | we glorify thee, we give .... | thanks to · thee for | thy · great | glory.

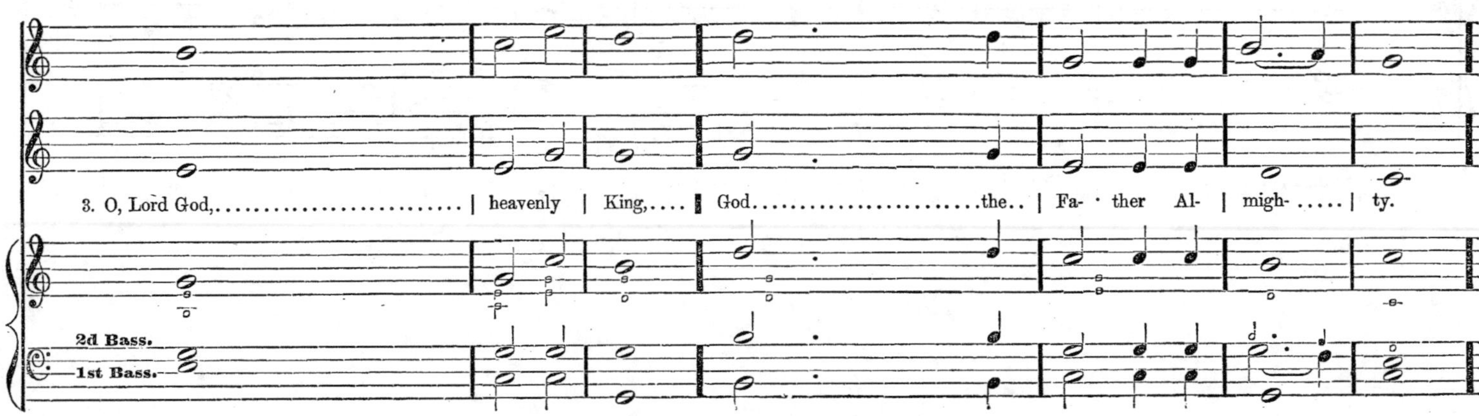

4. O Lord, the only begotten Son, ... | Je- · sus | Christ; ... | O Lord God, ... | Lamb · of God, | Son · of the | Father,
5. That takest away the .... | sins · of the | world,...... | .... have | mer - cy up- | ...... on ...... | ..... us.
SOLO.

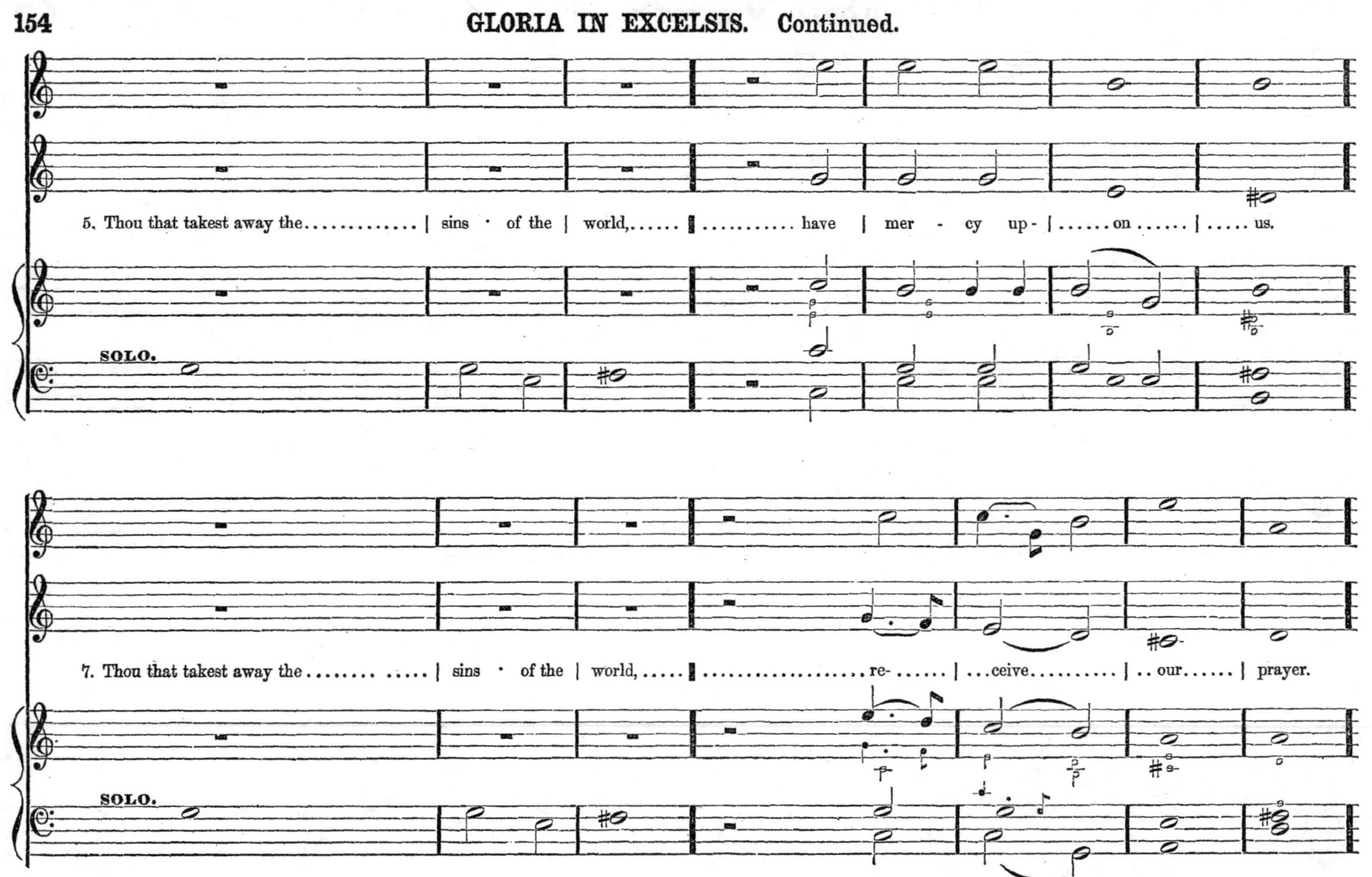
5. Thou that takest away the............ | sins · of the | world,...... .... have | mer - cy up- | ......on...... | ..... us.
SOLO.
7. Thou that takest away the....... ..... | sins · of the | world,..... .... re-...... | ...ceive......... | ..our..... | prayer.
SOLO.

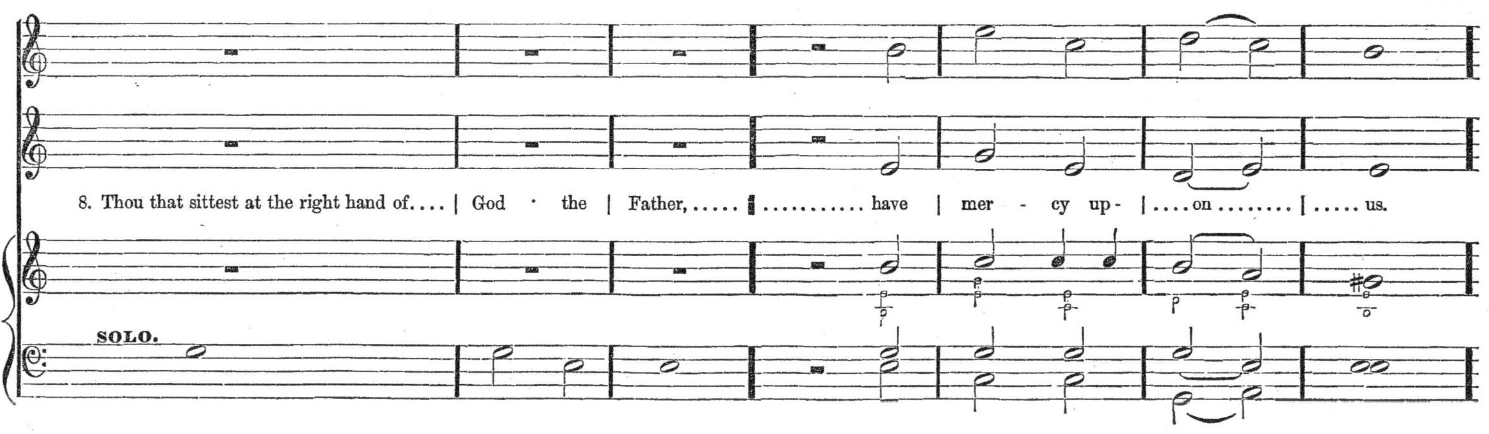
SOLO.
8. Thou that sittest at the right hand of.... | God · the | Father, ... | .... have | mer - cy up- | ....on .... | ..... us.

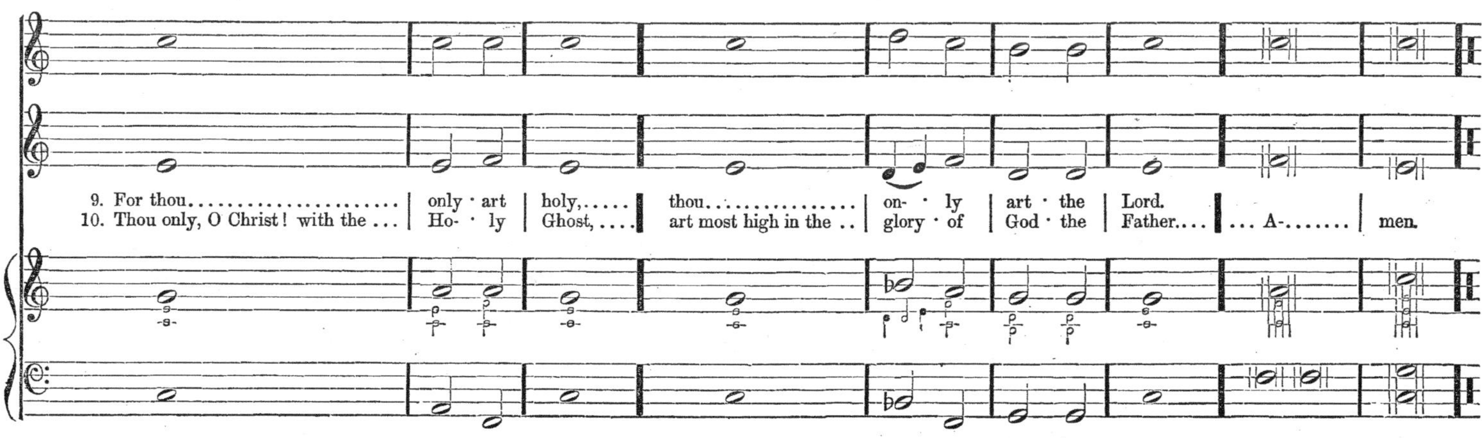
9. For thou...................... | only · art | holy,..... | thou................ | on- · ly | art · the | Lord.
10. Thou only, O Christ! with the ... | Ho- · ly | Ghost, ... | art most high in the .. | glory · of | God · the | Father.... | ... A-....... | men.

TE DEUM LAUDAMUS. No. 1.

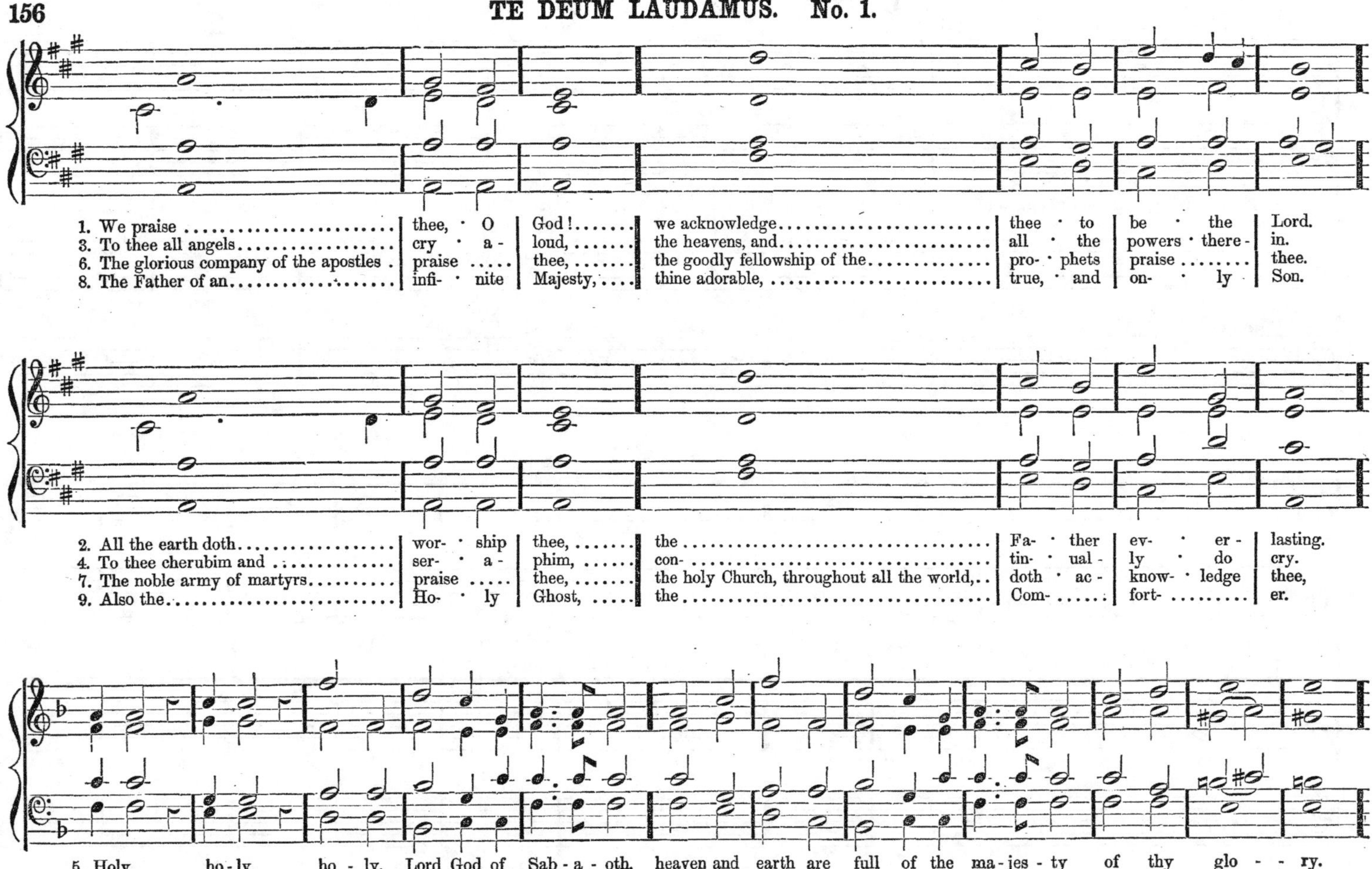

Male Voices.	10. Thou art the King of	glo-ry · O,	Christ!	Thou art the ever-	last- · ing	Son · of the	Father.
Female Voices.	11. When thou tookest upon thee to de-	liv- · er	man, ...	thou didst humble thyself to be.	born	of · a	virgin.
Male.	12. When thou hadst overcome the.....	sharpness · of	death, ...	thou didst open the kingdom of.	heaven · to	all · be-	lievers.
Female.	13. Thou sittest at the right..........	hand · of	God,......	in the	glo- · ry	of · the	Father.
Male.	14. We believe that	thou · shalt	come	shalt	come · to	be · our	Judge.
Female.	15. We therefore pray thee	help · thy	servants, ..	whom thou hast redeemed	with · thy	pre- · cious	blood.
Male.	16. Make them to be numbered	with · thy	saints	in	glo- · ry	ev- · er-	lasting.
Female.	17. O Lord, save thy people, and	bless · thine	heritage, ..	govern them, and	lift · them	up · for	ever.
Male.	18. Day by day we	magni- · fy	thee, ...	and we worship thy name ever,	world · with-	out	end.
Female.	19. Vouch-	safe, · O	Lord, ...	to keep us	this · day	with- · out	sin.
Male.	20. O Lord, have	mercy · up-	on us, ...	have	mer- · cy	up- · on	us.
Female.	21. O Lord, let thy mercy	be · up-	on us, ...	as our	trust	is · in	thee.

To be sung alternately by male and female voices. For the male voices play the Treble an octave lower. For the female voices play and sing the Bass an octave higher. If there are not voices enough to fill all the parts, let the air be sung alternately by Tenor and Soprano.

TE DEUM LAUDAMUS. No. 2.

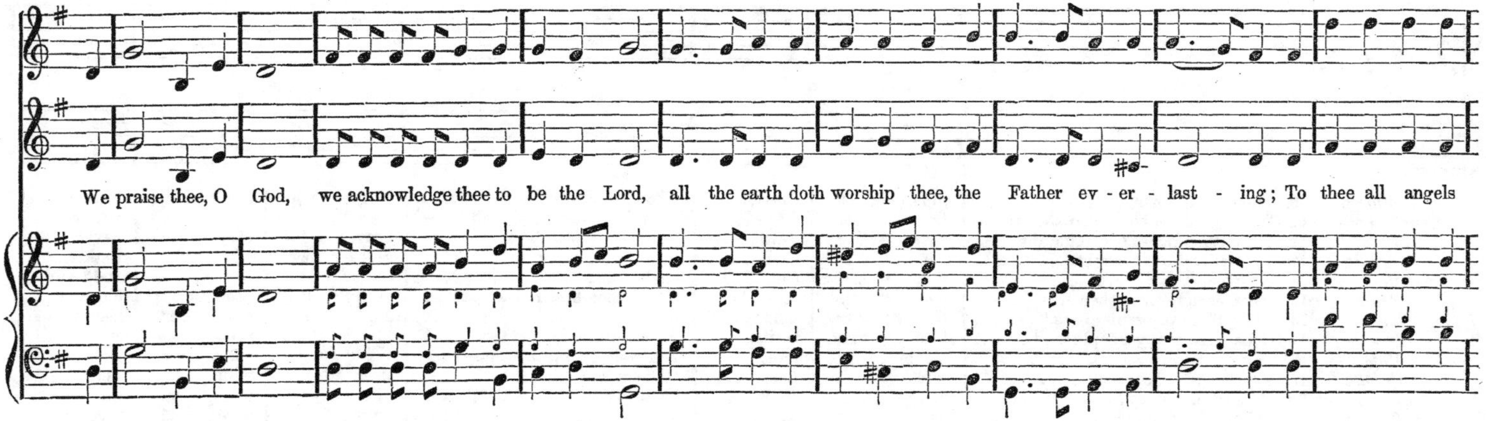

We praise thee, O God, we acknowledge thee to be the Lord, all the earth doth worship thee, the Father ev - er - last - ing; To thee all angels

cry a - loud, the heavens, and all the powers therein; To thee cherubim and ser - aphim contin - ually do cry, Ho - ly, Ho - ly,

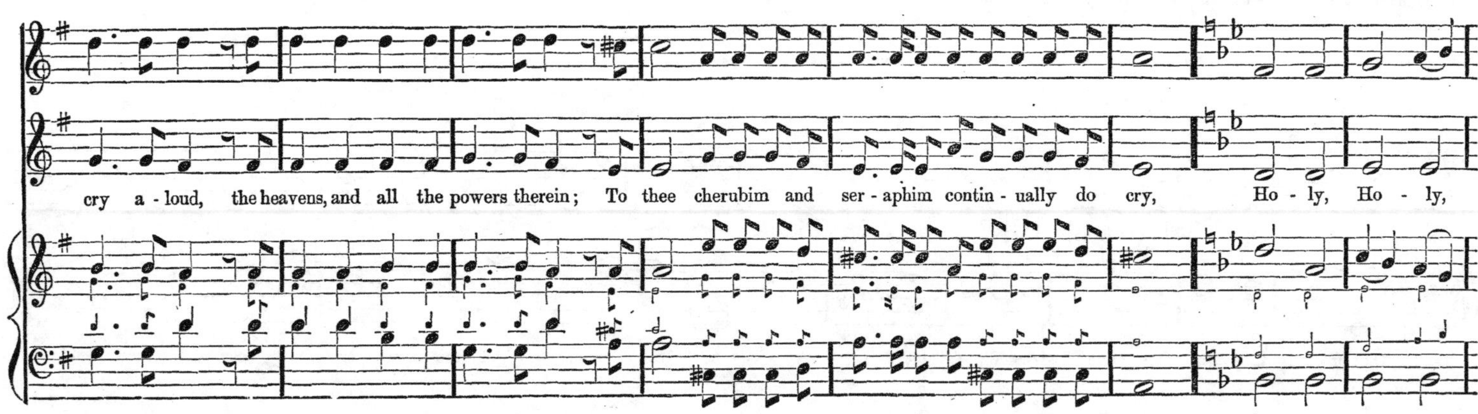

Ho - - - ly Lord God of Sab - a - oth, Heaven and earth are full of the ma-jes-ty of thy great glo - - ry.

The glo - rious com - pa - ny of the a - pos - tles praise thee; the good - ly fel - lowship of the prophets praise thee; the

no - ble ar - my of mar - tyrs praise thee; the ho - ly church throughout all the world doth ac - knowledge thee, the father of an
in - fi - nite ma - jes - ty, thine a - dor - a - ble, true, and on - ly Son; al - so the Ho - ly Ghost, the Com - fort - er.

Thou art the King of glo - ry, O Christ, Thou art the ev - er - last - ing Son of the Fa - ther. When thou tookest up - on thee to de -
liv - - - er man, thou didst hum - ble thy - self, thou didst hum - ble thy - self to be born of a virgin; when thou hadst over - come the sharpness of

death, thou didst o - pen the kingdom of heaven to all be - lievers. Thou sittest at the right hand of God, in the glory of the
Fa - ther. We be - lieve that thou shalt come to be our Judge, we therefore pray thee help thy servants, help thy servants, whom
SOLO.

thou hast re - deemed with thy pre - cious blood, whom thou hast re - deemed with thy pre - cious blood, Make them to be numbered with thy
saints in glo - ry ev - er - last - ing, in glo - ry ev - er - last - ing; O Lord, save thy

people, and bless thine her - i - tage, govern them and lift them up for - ev - er. Day by day we mag - ni - fy thee; and we
worship thy name, ev - er, world without end, ev - er, world with - out end. Vouch - safe, O Lord, to keep us this day, with - out

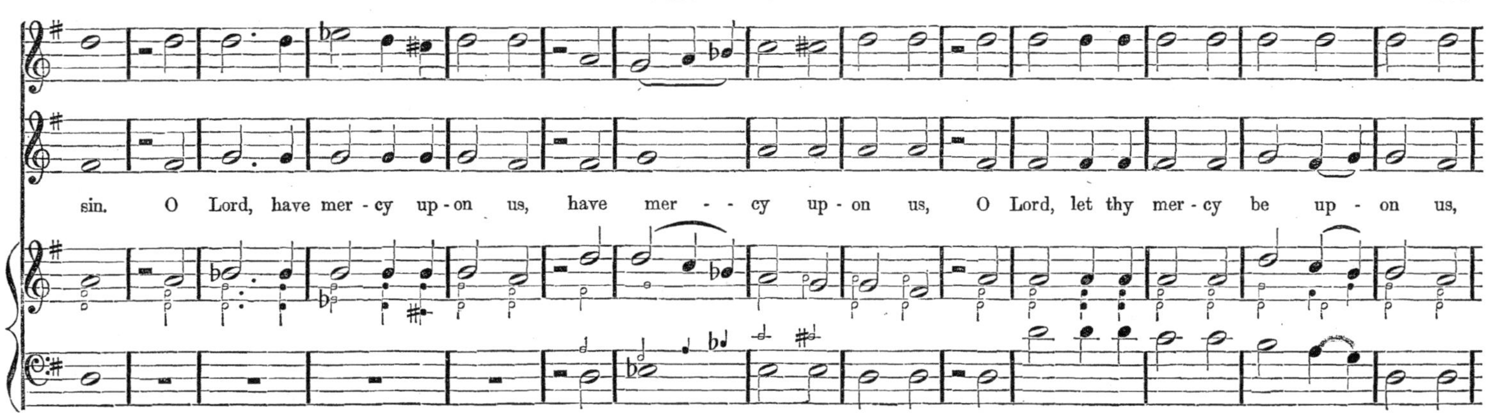
sin. O Lord, have mer - cy up - on us, have mer - - cy up - on us, O Lord, let thy mer - cy be up - on us,

as our trust is in thee. O Lord, in thee, in thee have I trusted, let me nev - er, nev - er be con - found - - - ed.

BENEDICITE, OMNIA OPERA DOMINI.

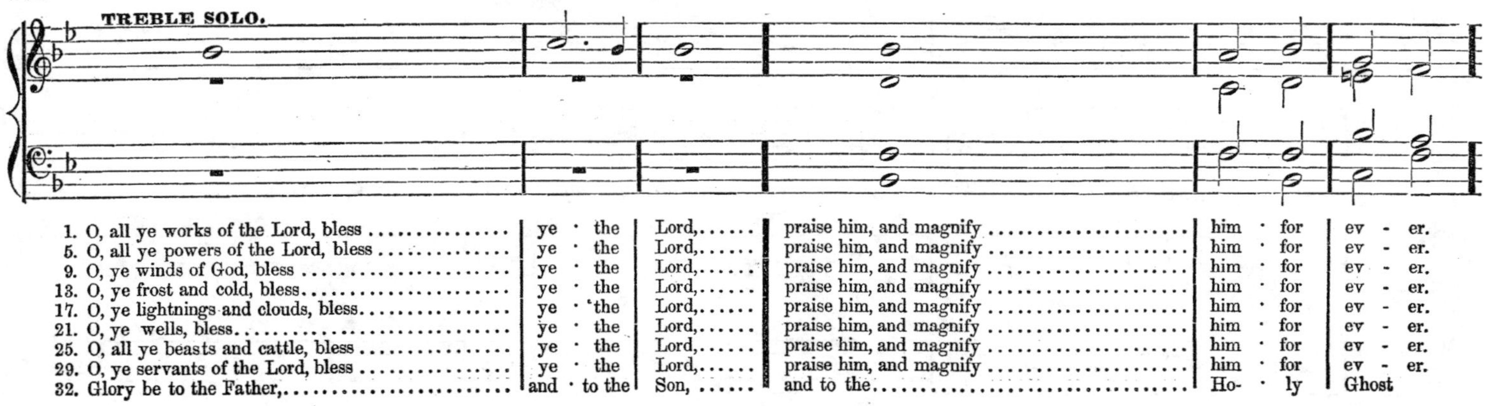

TENOR SOLO.
3. O, ye heavens, bless ye the Lord, praise him, and magnify him for ev - er.
7. O, ye stars of heaven, bless ye the Lord, praise him, and magnify him for ev - er.
11. O, ye winter and summer, bless ye the Lord, praise him, and magnify him for ev - er.
15. O, ye nights and days, bless ye the Lord, praise him, and magnify him for ev - er.
19. O, ye mountains and hills, bless ye the Lord, praise him, and magnify him for ev - er.
23. O, ye whales, and all that move in the waters, bless ye the Lord, praise him, and magnify him for ev - er.
27. O, let Israel bless the Lord, praise him, and magnify him for ev - er.

BASS SOLO.
4. O, ye waters that be above the firmament, bless ye the Lord, praise him, and magnify him for ev - er.
8. O, ye showers and dew, bless ye the Lord, praise him, and magnify him for ev - er.
12. O, ye dews and frost, bless ye the Lord, praise him, and magnify him for ev - er.
16. O, ye light and darkness, bless ye the Lord, praise him, and magnify him for ev - er.
20. O, all ye green things upon the earth, bless ye the Lord, praise him, and magnify him for ev - er.
24. O, all ye fowls of the air, bless ye the Lord, praise him, and magnify him for ev - er.
28. O, ye priests of the Lord, bless ye the Lord, praise him, and magnify him for ev - er.
31. O, ye holy and humble men of heart, bless ye the Lord, praise him, and magnify him for ev - er.
33. As it was in the beginning, is now, and ev- er shall be, world without end. A- men.

JUBILATE DEO.

No. 11.
No. 12.
HENLEY.
No. 13.
RANDAL.
No. 14.
EBDON.

O, be joy - ful in the Lord, all ye lands! Serve the Lord with glad - ness, serve the Lord with glad - ness, and
come be - fore his pres - ence with a song. Be ye sure that the Lord he is God, it is he that has

made us, and not we our - selves; we are his peo - ple, and the sheep, the sheep of his pas ture.
O, go your way in - to his gates with thanks - giv - ing, and in - - to his courts, his courts with

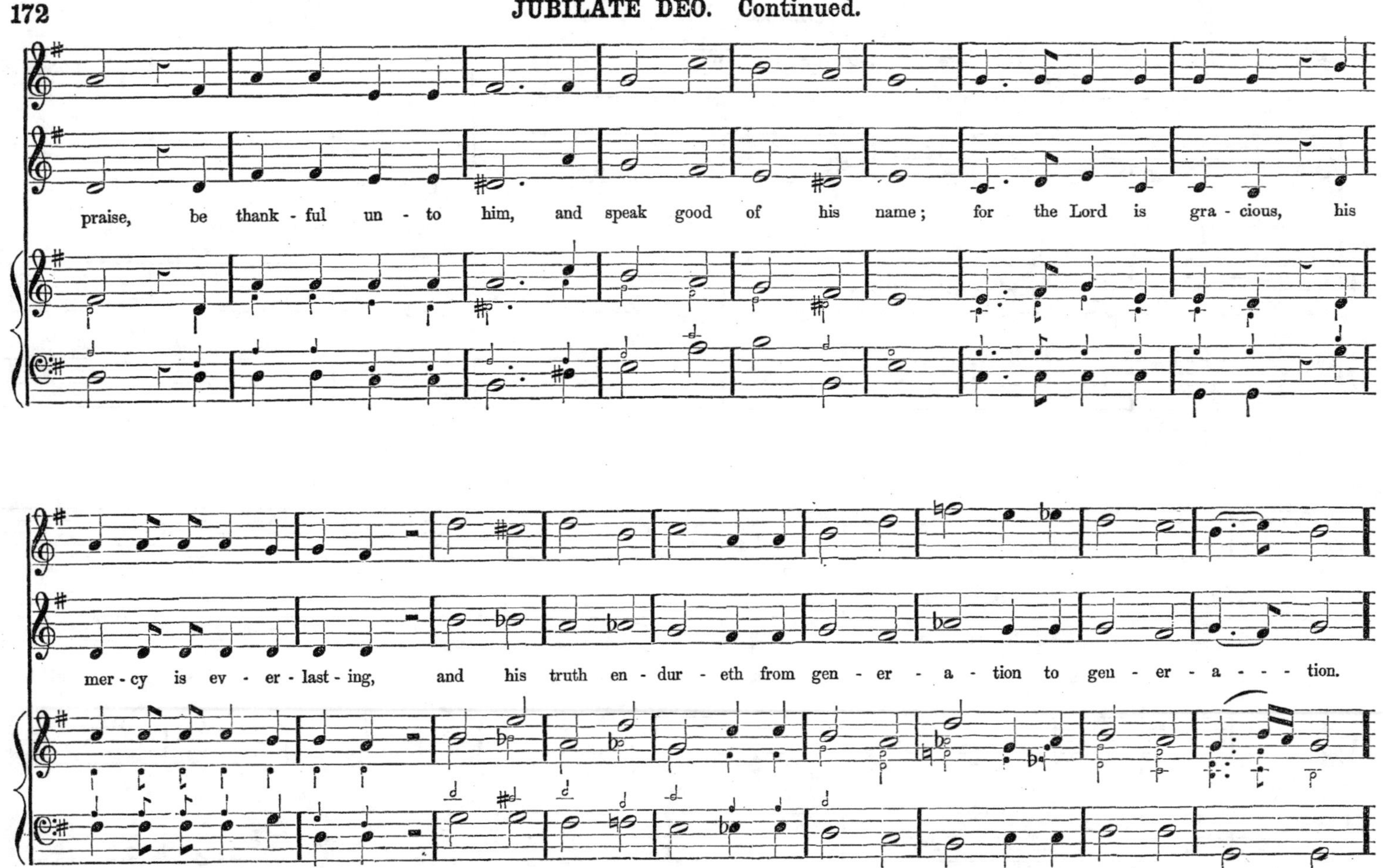
praise, be thank - ful un - to him, and speak good of his name; for the Lord is gra - cious, his
mer - cy is ev - er - last - ing, and his truth en - dur - eth from gen - er - a - tion to gen - er - a - - - tion.

Glo - ry be to the Fa - - ther, and to the Son, and to the Ho - ly Ghost;
as it was in the be - gin - ning, is now, and ev - er shall be, world with - out end. A - men. A - men.

BENEDICTUS.

No. 15.
FARRANT.
1. Blessed be the Lord .... | God · of | Israel, .. | for he hath visited, ... | and · re- | deemed · his | people;
2. And hath raised up a mighty sal- .... | va- · tion | for us, .. | in the house .... | of · his | ser- · vant | David;
3. As he spake by the mouth of his .... | ho · ly | prophets, | which have been .... | since · the | world · be- | gan;
4. That we should be saved .... | from · our | enemies, | and from the .... | hand · of | all · that | hate us.
5. Glory be to the Father, ... | and · to the | Son, ... | and .... | to · the | Ho- · ly | Ghost.
6. As it was in the beginning, is now, and .... | ev- · er | shall be, | world with- .... | out · end. | A- .... | men.
No. 16.
LANGDON.
No. 17.
C. CLARKE.

No. 18.
ARR. BY H. W. G.
No. 19.
H. W. G.
No. 20.
WORGAN.
No. 21.
W. RUSSELL.

KYRIE ELEEISON. No. 1.

The Kyrie Eleeison may be chanted to any single chant, by dividing the words thus:—*Lord, have* | *mer* · *cy up-* | *on us,* ‖ *and in-* | *cline* · *our hearts* · *to* | *keep* · *this* | *law.*
For the Tenth Commandment:—*Lord, have* | *mer* · *cy up-* | *on us,* ‖ *and write all these thy laws in our* | *hearts,* · *we be-* | *seech thee.*

After the Tenth Commandment.

Lord, have mer - cy, have mer - cy up - on us, and in - cline our hearts to keep this law.

After the Tenth Commandment.

and write all these thy laws in our hearts,
Lord, have mer - cy, have mer - cy up - on us, and write all these thy laws in our hearts, we be - seech thee.
[12]

GLORIA TIBI. No. 1.

After the Minister has declared from whence the Gospel for the day is taken.

GLORIA TIBI. No. 2.

Glo - ry be to thee, O Lord.

The Gloria may be sung to the last clause of any Chant, dividing the words thus:—

Glory | be · to | thee, · O | Lord.

TRISAGION.

thee, ev - er - more praising thee, and say - ing, Ho - ly! Ho - ly! Ho - ly! Lord God of Hosts, heaven and
earth are full, are full of thy glo - ry. Glo - ry be to thee, O Lord most high. A - men. A - men.

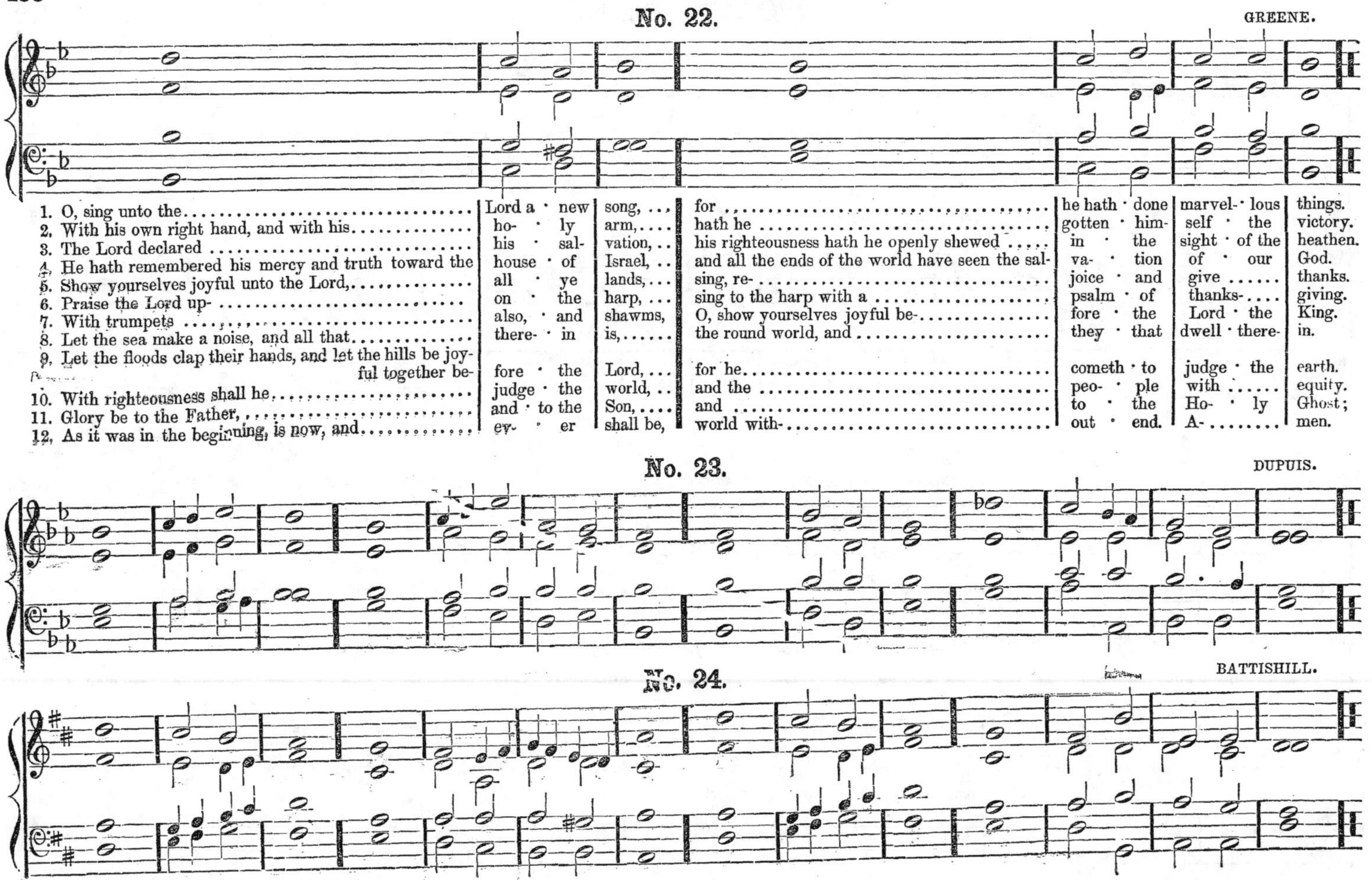
No. 22.
GREENE.
1. O, sing unto the.......... Lord a · new song, .. for .... he hath · done marvel- · lous things.
2. With his own right hand, and with his.......... ho- · ly arm,.... hath he .... gotten · him- self · the victory.
3. The Lord declared .... his · sal- vation, .. his righteousness hath he openly shewed ..... in · the sight · of the heathen.
4. He hath remembered his mercy and truth toward the house · of Israel, .. and all the ends of the world have seen the sal- va- · tion of · our God.
5. Show yourselves joyful unto the Lord,.......... all · ye lands,... sing, re- .... joice · and give ...... thanks.
6. Praise the Lord up- .... on · the harp, ... sing to the harp with a .... psalm · of thanks-.... giving.
7. With trumpets .... also, · and shawms, O, show yourselves joyful be-.......... fore · the Lord · the King.
8. Let the sea make a noise, and all that.......... there- · in is,...... the round world, and .... they · that dwell · there- in.
9. Let the floods clap their hands, and let the hills be joy-ful together be- fore · the Lord, ... for he.......... cometh · to judge · the earth.
10. With righteousness shall he.......... judge · the world, .. and the .... peo- · ple with ...... equity.
11. Glory be to the Father,.......... and · to the Son, ... and .... to · the Ho- · ly Ghost;
12. As it was in the beginning, is now, and.......... ev- · er shall be, world with-.......... out · end. A-........ men.
No. 23.
DUPUIS.
No. 24.
BATTISHILL.

No. 25.
SOAPER.
No. 26.
H. W. G.
No. 27.
DAVY.
No. 28.
S. SMITH.

BONUM EST CONFITERI.

No. 32.
SMYTH.
No. 33.
T. G.
No. 34.
BECKWITH.
No. 35.
RUSSELL.

BONUM EST CONFITERI. No. 2.

and of thy truth, and of thy truth, and of thy truth in the night sea - son.

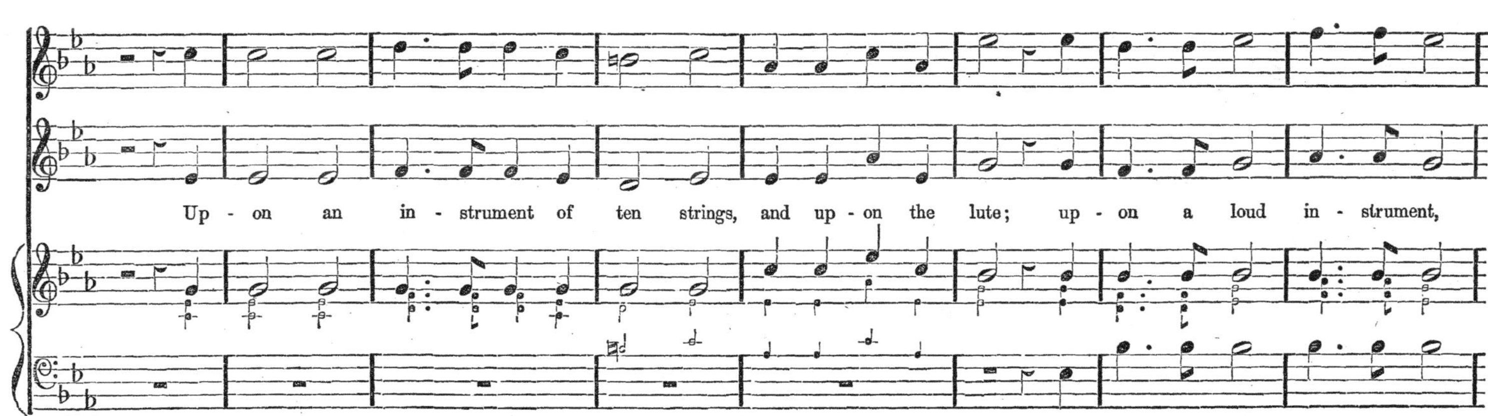
Up - on an in - strument of ten strings, and up - on the lute; up - on a loud in - strument,

and up - on the harp. For thou, Lord, hast made me glad through thy works, and I will re - joice in
giv - ing praise for the op - e - ra - tions of thy hands. Glo - ry be to the

Fa ther, and to the Son, and to the Ho - ly Ghost; as it

was in the be - gin - ning, is now, and ev - er shall be, world with - out end. A - men. A - men.

DEUS MISEREATUR.

No. 39.

BENEDIC ANIMA MEA.

No. 46.
RANDALL.
No. 47.
A. G.
No. 48.
MORNINGTON.
No. 49.
CROTCH.

Praise the Lord, O my soul, and all that is with - in me praise his ho - ly name. Praise the Lord,
O my soul, and for - get not all his ben - e - fits,— who for - giv - eth all thy sins, and heal - eth

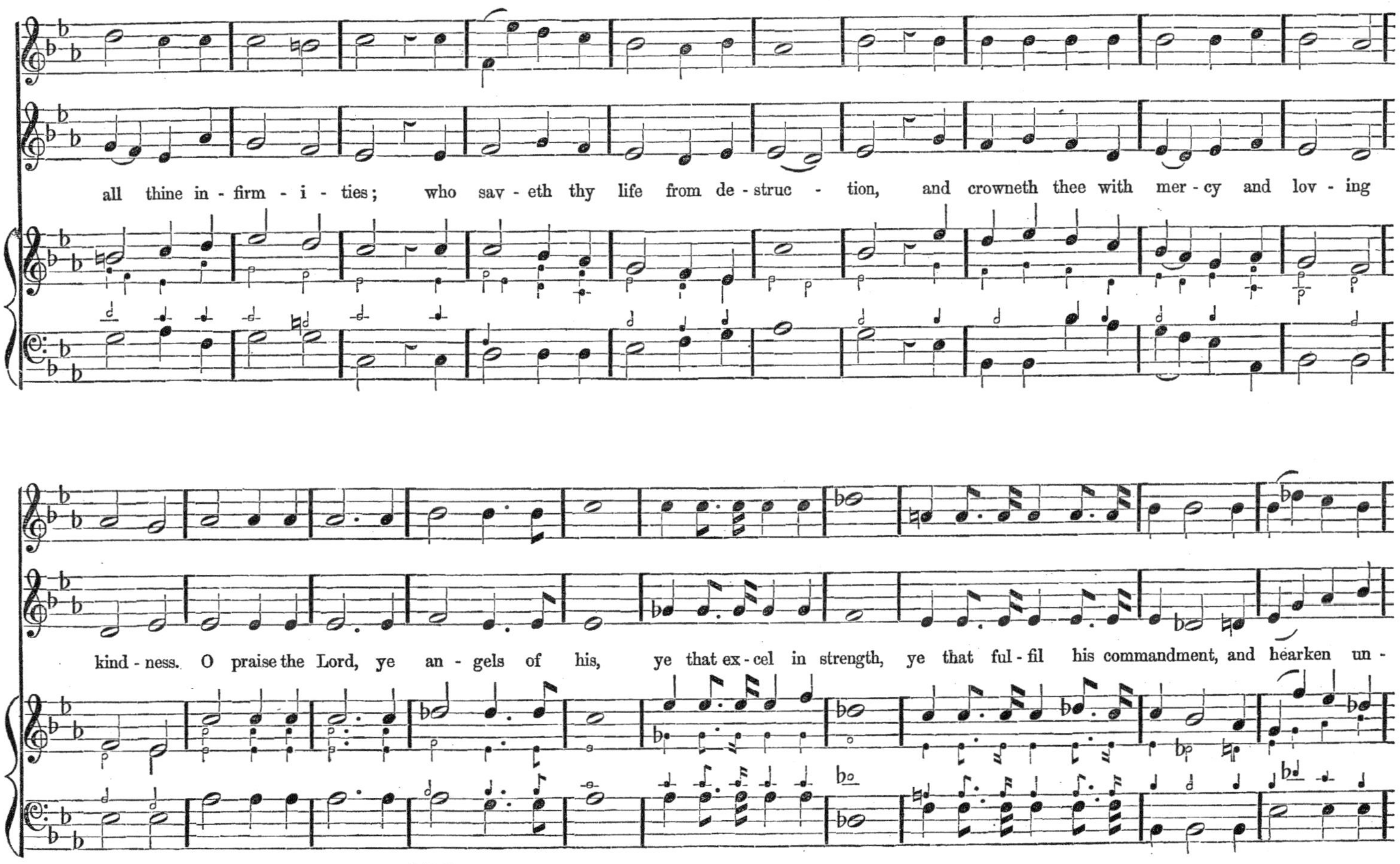

all thine in - firm - i - ties; who sav - eth thy life from de - struc - tion, and crowneth thee with mer - cy and lov - ing
kind - ness. O praise the Lord, ye an - gels of his, ye that ex - cel in strength, ye that ful - fil his commandment, and hearken un -

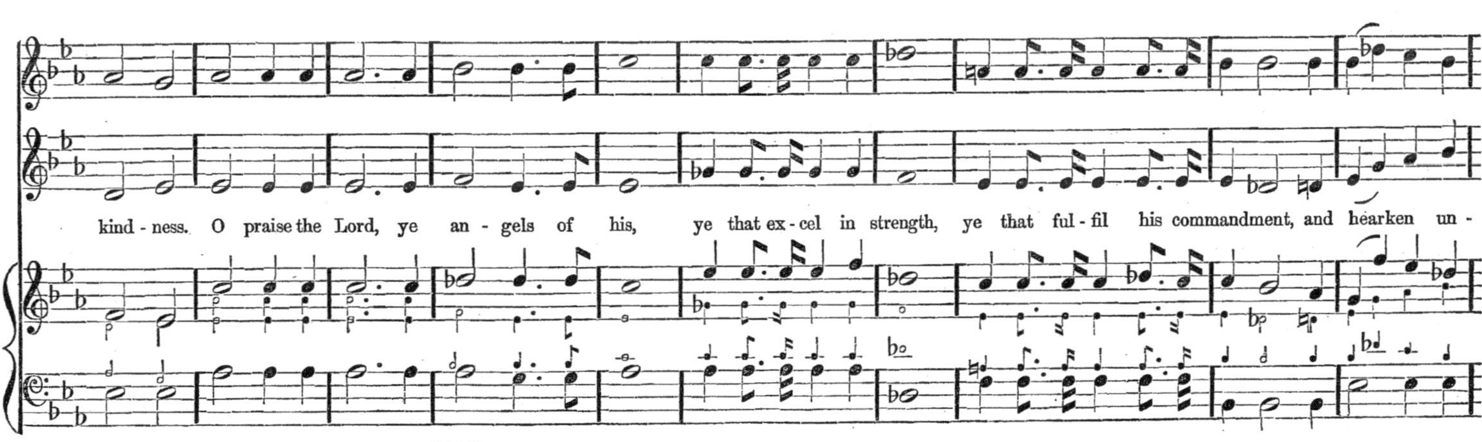

to the voice of his word. O, praise the Lord, all ye his hosts, ye ser - vants of his that do his plea - sure.
O, speak good of the Lord, all ye works of his, in all pla - ces of his do - min - ion; Praise thou the Lord, O my soul.

Glo - ry, Glo - ry be to the Fa - ther, and to the Son, and to the Ho - ly Ghost; as it was in the be - gin - ning, is
now, and ev - er shall be,—is now, and ev - er shall be,—is now, and ev - er shall be, world with - out end. A - men. A - - - men.

EASTER DAY.

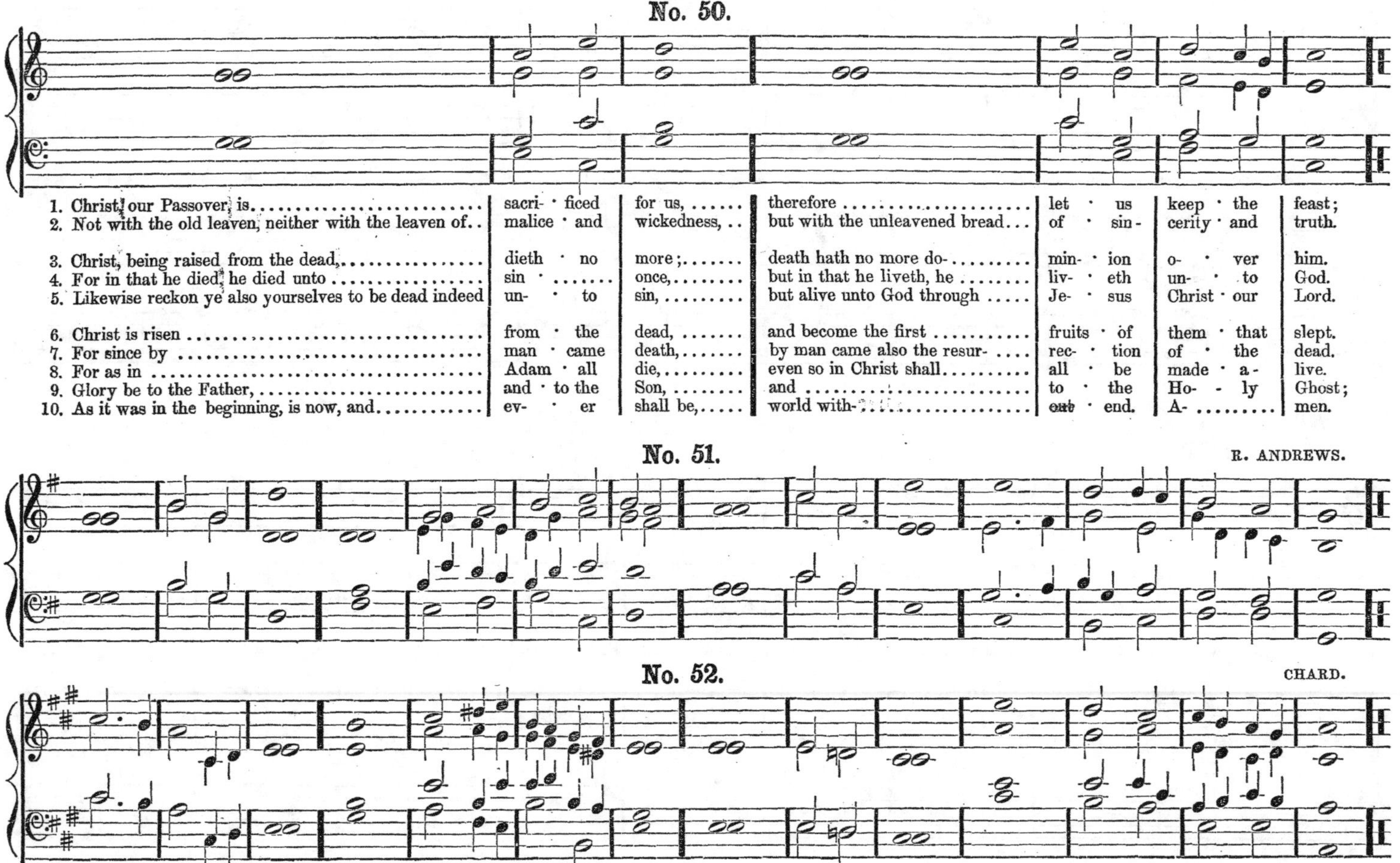
No. 50.
1. Christ our Passover is | sacri- · ficed | for us, | therefore | let · us | keep · the | feast;
2. Not with the old leaven, neither with the leaven of | malice · and | wickedness, | but with the unleavened bread | of · sin- | cerity · and | truth.
3. Christ, being raised from the dead, | dieth · no | more; | death hath no more do- | min- · ion | o- · ver | him.
4. For in that he died, he died unto | sin · | once, | but in that he liveth, he | liv- · eth | un- · to | God.
5. Likewise reckon ye also yourselves to be dead indeed | un- · to | sin, | but alive unto God through | Je- · sus | Christ · our | Lord.
6. Christ is risen | from · the | dead, | and become the first | fruits · of | them · that | slept.
7. For since by | man · came | death, | by man came also the resur- | rec- · tion | of · the | dead.
8. For as in | Adam · all | die, | even so in Christ shall | all · be | made · a- | live.
9. Glory be to the Father, | and · to the | Son, | and | to · the | Ho- - ly | Ghost;
10. As it was in the beginning, is now, and | ev- · er | shall be, | world with- | out · end. | A- | men.
No. 51.
R. ANDREWS.
No. 52.
CHARD.

No. 53.

DEAN.

1. O praise the Lord; laud ye the........	name · of the	Lord;......	praise it, O ye	ser- · vants	of · the	Lord.
2. Ye that stand in the	house · of the	Lord,......	in the courts of the	house · of	our ·	God.
3. O praise the Lord, for the..........	Lord · is	gracious;...	O sing praises unto his	name ·	for it · is	lovely.
4. The Lord is.......................	gracious · and	merciful, ...	long-suffering,......................	and · of	great ·	goodness.
5. The Lord is loving unto	ev- · ery	man, ...	and his mercy is....................	o- · ver	all · his	works.
6. All thy works praise................	thee, · O	Lord,......	and thy	saints · give	thanks · un-	to thee.
7. The Lord doth	build · up Je-	rusalem, ...	and gather together the	out- · casts	of ·	Israel.
8. He healeth those that are..........	broken · in	heart,......	and giveth..........................	medicine · to	heal · their	sickness.
9. The Lord's delight is in............	them · that	fear him, ...	and put their	trust · in	his ·	mercy.
10. Praise the Lord,..................	O · Je-	rusalem, ...	praise	..... · thy	God, · O	Zion.
11. For he hath made fast the	bars · of thy	gates,......	and hath	blessed · thy	children · with-	in thee.
12. He maketh peace..................	in · thy	borders,....	and filleth thee.....................	with · the	flour · of	wheat.
13. He is our God, even the God of whom ..	cometh · sal-	vation;.....	God is the Lord by	whom · we es-	cape ·	death.
14. O God, wonderful art thou in thy	ho- · ly	places,.....	even the God of Israel, he will give strength and power unto his	peo- · ple.	Blessed · be	God.
15. Glory be to the Father, ...	and · to the	Son,.......	and	to · the	Ho- · ly	Ghost;
16. As it was in the beginning, is now, and..	ev- · er	shall be, ...	world with-.........................	out · end.	A-..........	men.

No. 54.

ALCOCK.

No. 55.
KING.
1. Praise ye the Lord; for it is good to sing praises un- | to · our | God, | for it is | pleasant · and | praise · is | comely.
2. The Lord doth | build · up Je- | rusalem, | he gathereth together the | out- · casts | of · | Israel.
3. He healeth those that are | broken · in | heart, | and | bind- · eth | up · their | wounds.
4. He covereth the heaven with clouds, and prepareth | rain · for the | earth, | he maketh the grass to | grow · up- | on · the | mountains.
5. He giveth to the | beast · his | food, | and to the | young · | ravens · which | cry.
6. Praise the Lord, | O · Je- | rusalem, | praise thy | God, · | · O | Zion.
7. For he hath strengthened the | bars of · thy | gates, | he hath | blessed · thy | children · with- | in thee.
8. He maketh | peace · in thy | borders, | and filleth thee with the | fi- · nest | of · the | wheat.
9. Glory be to the Father, | and · to the | Son, | and | to · the | Ho- · ly | Ghost;
10. As it was in the beginning, is now, and | ev- · er | shall be, | world with- | out · end. | A- | men.
No. 56.
TRAVERS.
No. 57.
Z. & H. W. G.

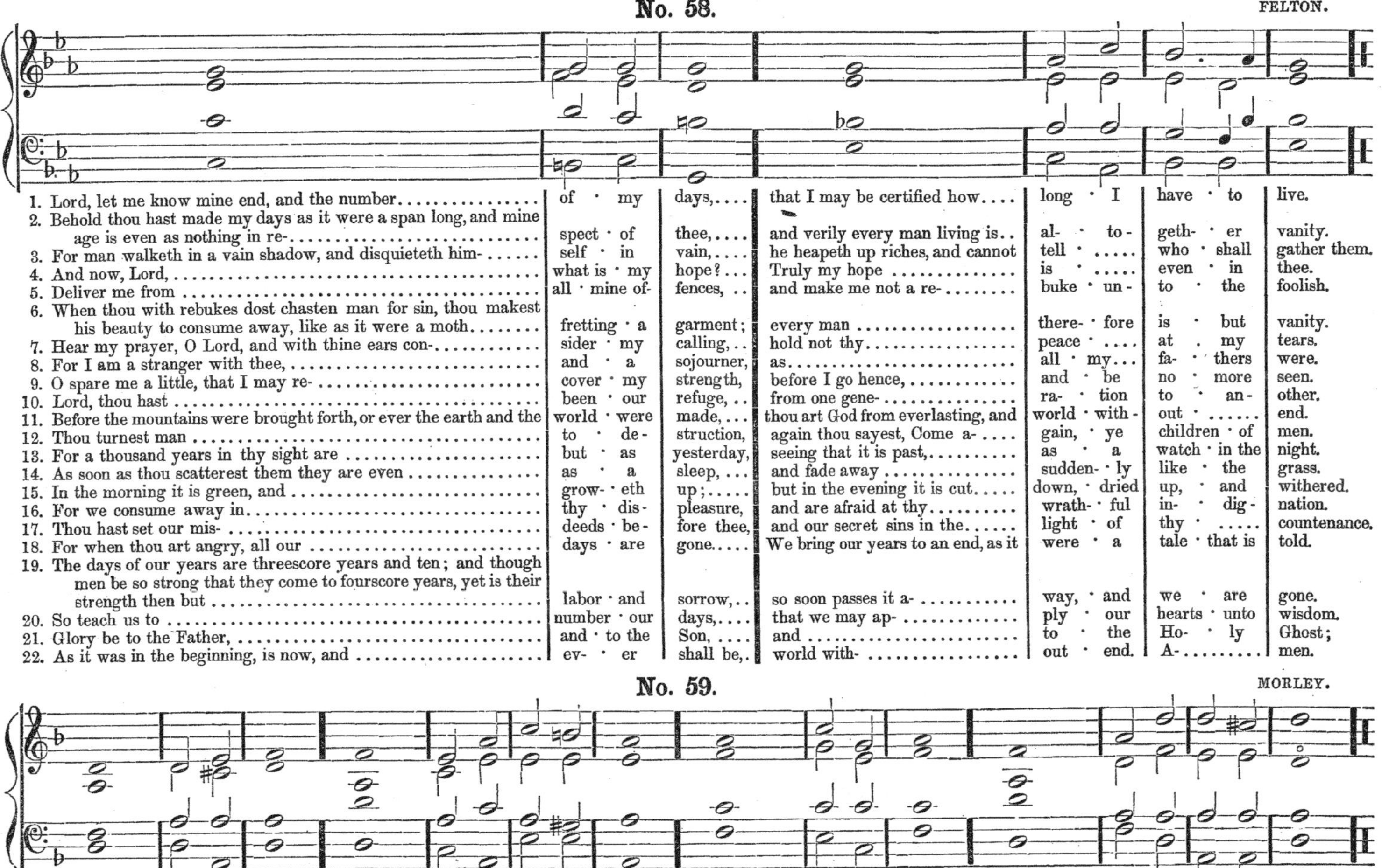
No. 58.
FELTON.
1. Lord, let me know mine end, and the number.............. of · my | days,.... | that I may be certified how.... | long · I | have · to | live.
2. Behold thou hast made my days as it were a span long, and mine age is even as nothing in re-.............. spect · of | thee,.... | and verily every man living is.. | al- · to- | geth- · er | vanity.
3. For man walketh in a vain shadow, and disquieteth him-...... self · in | vain,.... | he heapeth up riches, and cannot | tell · ..... | who · shall | gather them.
4. And now, Lord,.............. what is · my | hope?... | Truly my hope .... | is · ..... | even · in | thee.
5. Deliver me from .... all · mine of- | fences, .. | and make me not a re-........ | buke · un- | to · the | foolish.
6. When thou with rebukes dost chasten man for sin, thou makest his beauty to consume away, like as it were a moth........ fretting · a | garment; | every man .... | there- · fore | is · but | vanity.
7. Hear my prayer, O Lord, and with thine ears con-........ sider · my | calling,.. | hold not thy.............. | peace · .... | at . my | tears.
8. For I am a stranger with thee,.............. and · a | sojourner, | as.............. | all · my... | fa- · thers | were.
9. O spare me a little, that I may re-.............. cover · my | strength, | before I go hence,.......... | and · be | no · more | seen.
10. Lord, thou hast .... been · our | refuge, .. | from one gene-.............. | ra- · tion | to · an- | other.
11. Before the mountains were brought forth, or ever the earth and the world · were | made,... | thou art God from everlasting, and | world · with- | out · ...... | end.
12. Thou turnest man .... to · de- | struction, | again thou sayest, Come a-.... | gain, · ye | children · of | men.
13. For a thousand years in thy sight are .... but · as | yesterday, | seeing that it is past,.......... | as · a | watch · in the | night.
14. As soon as thou scatterest them they are even .... as · a | sleep, ... | and fade away .... | sudden- · ly | like · the | grass.
15. In the morning it is green, and .... grow- · eth | up;..... | but in the evening it is cut..... | down, · dried | up, · and | withered.
16. For we consume away in.............. thy · dis- | pleasure, | and are afraid at thy.......... | wrath- · ful | in- · dig- | nation.
17. Thou hast set our mis-.............. deeds · be- | fore thee, | and our secret sins in the..... | light · of | thy · ..... | countenance.
18. For when thou art angry, all our .... days · are | gone.... | We bring our years to an end, as it | were · a | tale · that is | told.
19. The days of our years are threescore years and ten; and though men be so strong that they come to fourscore years, yet is their strength then but .... labor · and | sorrow,.. | so soon passes it a-.......... | way, · and | we · are | gone.
20. So teach us to .... number · our | days,.... | that we may ap-.............. | ply · our | hearts · unto | wisdom.
21. Glory be to the Father,.............. and · to the | Son, ... | and .... | to · the | Ho- · ly | Ghost;
22. As it was in the beginning, is now, and .... ev- · er | shall be,. | world with-.............. | out · end. | A-......... | men.
No. 59.
MORLEY.

ANTHEM IN BURIAL SERVICE.

No. 60.
TRAVERS.
1. O praise God .... in · his | holiness; ..... | praise him in the .... | firma- · ment | of · his | power.
2. Praise him in his........................ no- · ble | acts; .... | praise him according.......... | to · his | excel- · lent | greatness.
3. Praise him in the sound .... of · the | trumpet; .... | praise him up-.................. | on · the | lute · and | harp.
4. Praise him in the........................ cymbals · and | dances; .... | praise him up-.................. | on · the | strings · and | pipe.
5. Praise him upon the.................... well- · tuned | cymbals; .... | praise him up-.................. | on · the | loud · ..... | cymbals.
6. Let every thing .... that · hath | breath, ... | praise .... | .... | .... · the | Lord.
7. Glory be to the Father, ... and · to the | Son, ... | and .... | to · the | Ho- · ly | Ghost;
8. As it was in the beginning, is now, and ... ev- · er | shall be, ... | world with- .... | out · end. | A-......... | men.
No. 61.
SIMMS.
No. 62.
MORNINGTON.

No. 63.

MORLEY.

TONE.

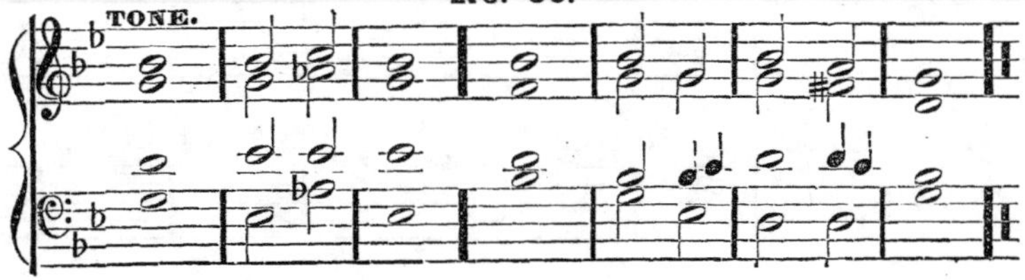

No. 67.

H. W. G.

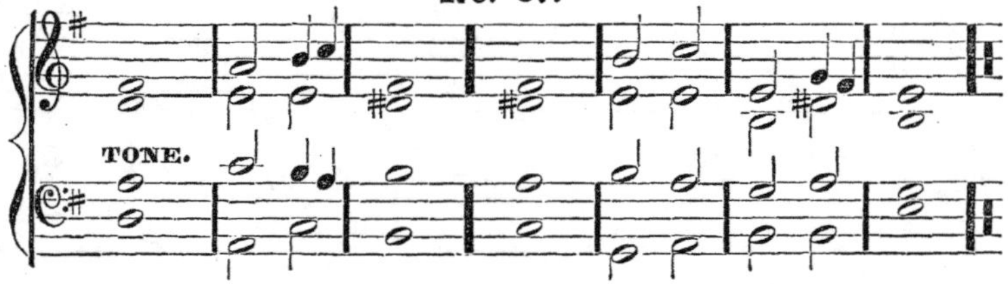

TONE.

No. 64.

TALLIS.

TONE.

No. 68.

DYCE.

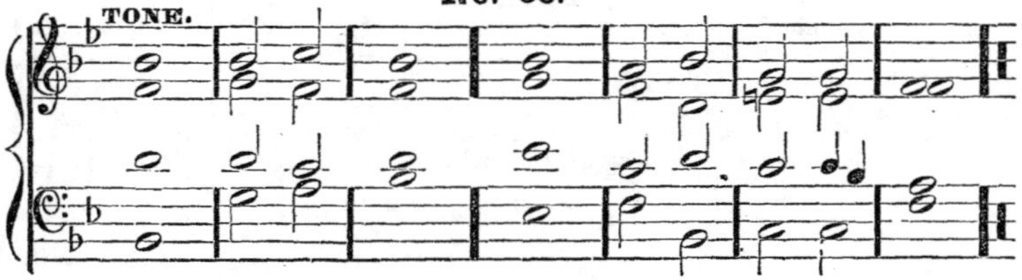

TONE.

No. 65.

MORLEY.

TONE.

No. 69.

DYCE.

TONE.

No. 66.

DYCE.

TONE.

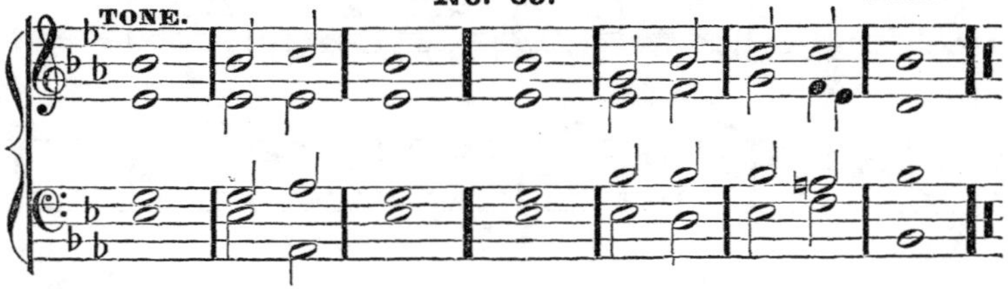

No. 70.

DYCE.

TONE.

No. 71.
DR. W. HAYES.
No. 72.
J. BATTISHILL.
No. 73.
J. KENT.
No. 74.
CORFE.
No. 75.
J. BATTISHILL.
No. 76.
LEE.
No. 77.
A. BENNET.
No. 78.
DUPUIS.

No. 79.
FARRANT.
No. 80.
LEE.
No. 81.
FLINTOFF.
No. 82.
ALCOCK.

No. 83.
R. COOKE.
No. 84.
CROTCH.
No. 85.
SKARRAT.
No. 86.
I. CONKEY.

OCCASIONAL CHANTS.

No. 91.
DUPUIS.
No. 92.
DUPUIS.
No. 93.
SOAPER.
No. 94.
R. COOKE.

No. 95.
No. 96.
WALTER WILSON.
No. 97.
H. W. G.
No. 98.
THOS. BENNETT.

No. 99.
AUNTLETT.
No. 100.
HARRIS.
No. 101.
HACKETT.
No. 102.
CAREY.

No. 103.
No. 104.
A. BENNET.
No. 105.
L. T. D.
No. 106.
H. W. G.

SENTENCE. No. 1. "The Lord is in his holy temple."

The Lord is in his ho - ly tem - ple,— Let all the earth keep si - lence, keep

keep si - lence,

si - lence, keep si - lence be - fore him, keep si - lence be - fore him.

SENTENCE. No. 2. "Let the words of my mouth."

Let the words of my mouth, and the med - i - ta - tions of my heart, be al - way ac - cept - a - ble, be al - way ac - cept - a - ble in thy
O Lord, my strength,
sight, O Lord, my strength, O Lord, my strength and my Re - deem - er, my Re - deem - er.

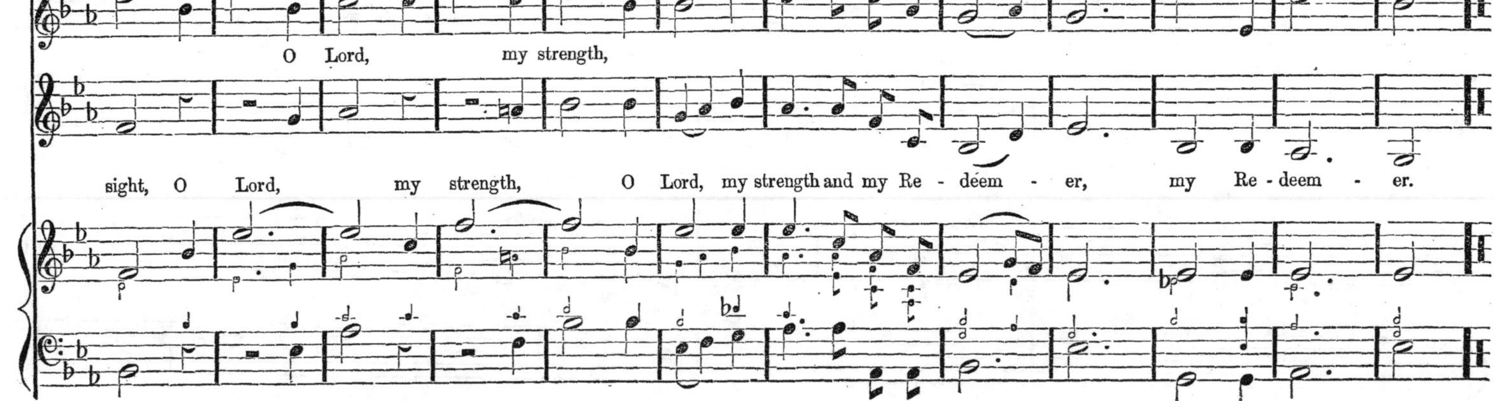

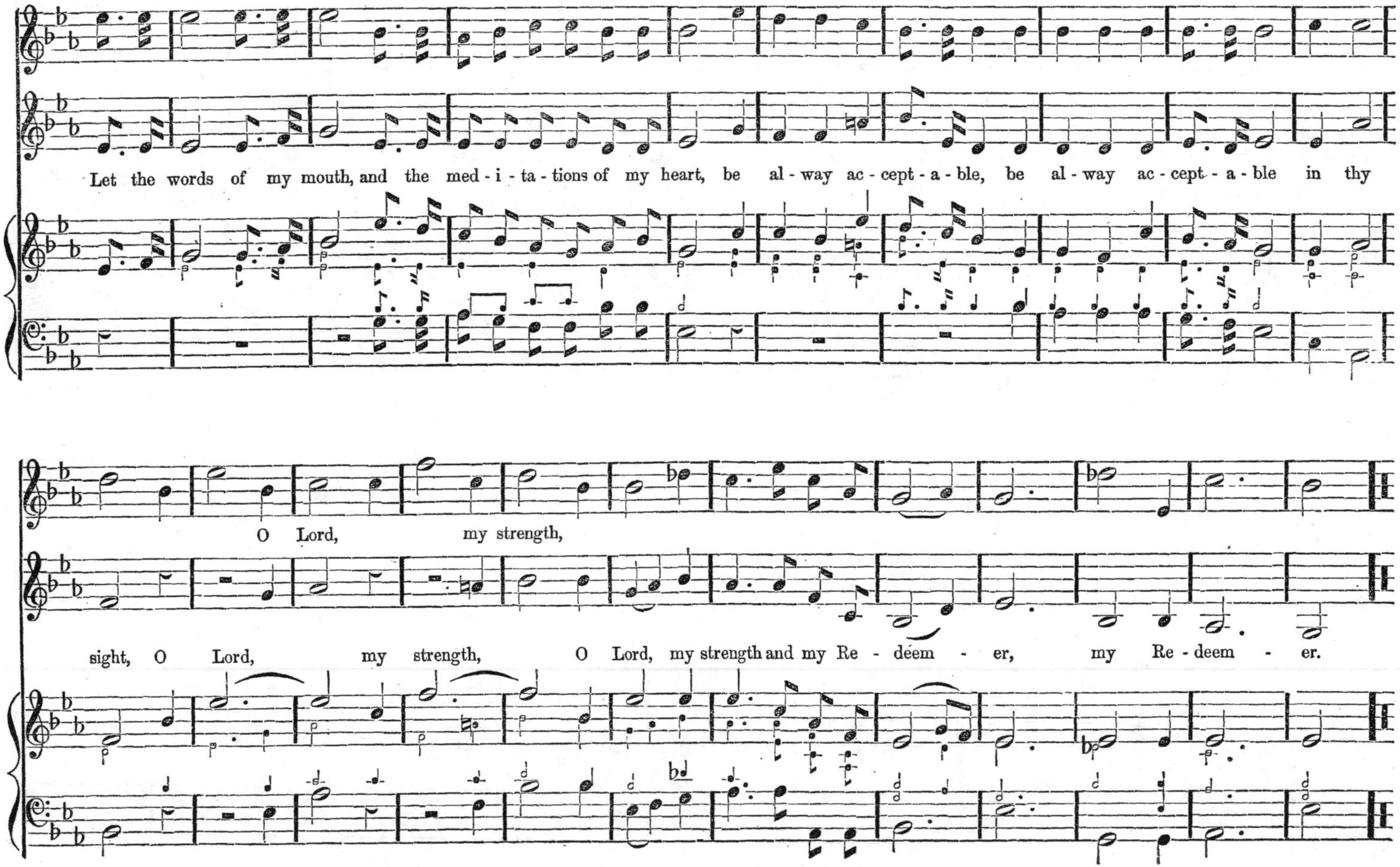

The sac - ri - fi - ces of God are a bro - ken spi - rit: A bro - ken and a con - trite
heart, A bro - ken and a con - trite heart, O God, O God, thou wilt not des - pise.

Rend your heart and not your gar - ments, and turn un - to the Lord your God, for he is gra - cious, is
gra - cious and mer - ci - ful, slow to an - ger, and of great kind - ness, and re - pent - eth him of the e - - - - vil.

SENTENCE. No. 5. "Repent ye."

Re - pent ye, re - pent ye, for the king - dom of heaven is at hand,— Re - pent ye, re-

pent ye, for the king - dom of heaven is at hand,— Re - pent ye, re - pent ye, re - pent ye.

SENTENCE. No. 6. "If we say that we have no sin."

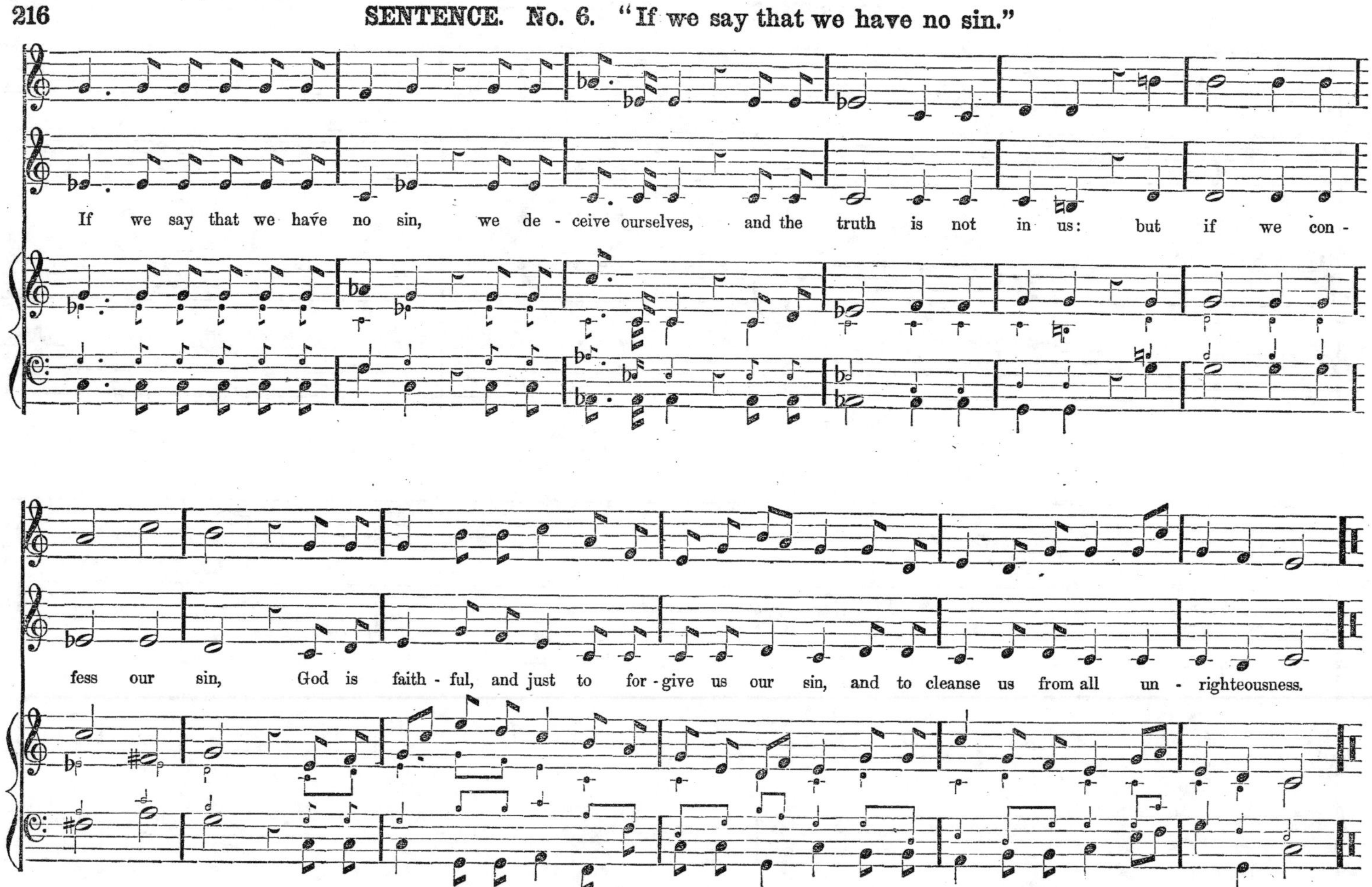

1st TREBLE.
2d TREBLE.
The Lord is my Shepherd, the Lord is my
Shepherd, therefore can I lack nothing, therefore can I lack nothing;
The Lord is my Shepherd, the Lord is my
He is my Shepherd, he is my

Shepherd, therefore can I lack nothing, therefore can I lack nothing. He shall feed me in a green pasture,
He
and lead me, lead me forth, and lead me, lead me, lead me forth beside the
shall con - vert my soul, and bring me, bring me forth, and bring me, bring me, bring me forth,

waters of comfort, in the paths of righteousness, for his name's sake, for his name's sake. Yea, though I walk in the
valley of the shadow of death, I will fear no evil, for thou art with me, thy rod and staff comfort me.
thy rod and

CHORUS.
hal-le - lu-jah, hal-le - lu - jah,
Hal - le - lu - jah, hal - le - lu-jah, hal-le - lu - jah, hal - le - lu-jah, hal - le - lu - jah,
Hal - le - lu - jah, hal - le - lu - jah, hal - le - lu - jah, hal - le - lu - jah, ... hal - le-
Hal - le - lu - jah, hal - le - lu-jah, hal-le - lu - jah, hal - le - lu - jah,
A - men.
hal - le - lu - jah, hal - le - lu - jah, hal - le - lu - jah, A - men. A - men. Hal - le - lu-jah, hal-le - lu - jah,
lu - jah, ... Hal - le - lu - jah, hal - le - lu - jah, A - men.
hal - le - lu - jah, A - men. Hal - le - lu - jah, halle - lu - jah.

ALPHABETICAL INDEX.

www.ingramcontent.com/pod-product-compliance
Lightning Source LLC
LaVergne TN
LVHW050521100826
845148LV00002B/409